Armando Benedetti Villaneda

Pushing LGBTQ Rights in Colombia – Unauthorized

Khadija Patel

ISBN: 9781779696977
Imprint: Telephasic Workshop
Copyright © 2024 Khadija Patel.
All Rights Reserved.

Contents

Embracing the LGBTQ Identity   24

Bibliography   **47**
The Beginnings of Activism   50

Challenging the Status Quo   **73**
Challenging the Status Quo   73
A Vision for Change   76
Armando's Impact on LGBTQ Rights in Colombia   93
Fierce Opposition and Personal Sacrifices   113

Bibliography   **129**

Bibliography   **139**

Armando's Other Advocacies   **141**
Armando's Other Advocacies   141
Intersectionality and Inclusivity   146
Addressing Global LGBTQ Issues   159
Armando's Legacy   173

Armando's Personal Reflections   **185**
Armando's Personal Reflections   185
Looking Back on the Journey   187
Armando's Vision for the Future   201

Bibliography   **213**
The Unauthorized Biography: A Personal Note   215

Bibliography   **223**

Acknowledgments and Resources 229
Acknowledgments and Resources 229
Acknowledging the Contributors 232
Resources and Organizations for LGBTQ Advocacy 236

Bibliography 251
Author's Notes and Disclaimer 251
About the Author 254
About the Publisher 258

Index 263

A Childhood Shaped by Activism

Armando Benedetti Villaneda was born into a world rife with contradictions, where the vibrant culture of Medellín clashed with conservative values. Growing up in this dynamic city, he quickly learned that activism was not just a choice; it was a necessity. His childhood was a tapestry woven with the threads of social justice, resilience, and an unyielding desire to challenge the status quo.

Growing Up in Medellín

Medellín, known for its stunning landscapes and rich history, was also a city grappling with issues of violence and inequality. Armando's early experiences were marked by the stark realities of life in a city that often failed to embrace diversity. The contrast between the beauty of his surroundings and the harshness of societal norms ignited a fire within him. As a child, he often witnessed the struggles of marginalized communities, which left an indelible mark on his psyche.

Armando's Family and Influences

Armando's family played a pivotal role in shaping his worldview. Raised in a household that valued education and empathy, he was encouraged to question societal norms. His parents, although traditional in many respects, instilled in him the importance of standing up for what is right. They often discussed the stories of activists who fought for equality, planting the seeds of activism in Armando's young mind.

First Encounters with Discrimination

As Armando navigated his formative years, he encountered discrimination firsthand. Whether it was subtle remarks from peers or overt hostility, these experiences were painful yet formative. They served as a catalyst for his activism. The theory of Social Identity, as proposed by Henri Tajfel, suggests that individuals derive a sense of self from their group memberships. Armando's realization that he was part of a marginalized group propelled him to advocate for change.

The Spark of Activism Ignites

The spark of activism ignited within Armando during his teenage years, when he participated in a local youth group focused on social justice. Here, he discovered the power of collective action. The group's motto, "United We Stand," resonated deeply with him, and he began to understand that activism was not merely about individual struggles but about community empowerment. This aligns with the theory of Collective Efficacy, which posits that communities with high levels of trust and cooperation can achieve greater outcomes.

Armando's Journey to Self-Discovery

Armando's journey of self-discovery was intertwined with his activism. As he began to explore his identity, he grappled with the complexities of being a young LGBTQ individual in a conservative society. This internal conflict was compounded by societal expectations and familial pressures. However, through activism, he found a sense of belonging and acceptance within the LGBTQ community. This notion is supported by the concept of Affirmative Identity Development, which emphasizes the importance of positive self-identity in marginalized groups.

The Supportive Friends Who Became Family

During this tumultuous time, Armando forged friendships that would become his chosen family. These relationships were vital in providing the emotional support he needed. Together, they created a safe space where they could express their true selves without fear of judgment. The importance of social support networks in the LGBTQ community cannot be overstated, as they often serve as a buffer against discrimination and mental health challenges.

Breaking Free from Gender Stereotypes

Armando's activism also involved breaking free from the rigid gender stereotypes that pervaded his culture. He became increasingly aware of how traditional gender roles limited not only his expression but also the potential of those around him. By challenging these stereotypes, he embraced a more fluid understanding of gender, advocating for a society that celebrates diversity in all its forms. Judith Butler's theory of gender performativity highlights how gender is a social construct, and Armando's journey exemplified this idea.

Discovering a Passion for Politics

As Armando matured, his passion for politics blossomed. He realized that legislative change was essential for achieving LGBTQ rights and social justice in

Colombia. This realization was fueled by his understanding of political theory, particularly the principles of Liberalism, which advocate for individual rights and freedoms. Armando began to engage with local political movements, recognizing that true change required not only grassroots activism but also institutional reform.

Formal Education and its Impact

Formal education played a crucial role in Armando's development as an activist. He pursued studies in sociology and political science, equipping himself with the knowledge and skills necessary to advocate effectively for LGBTQ rights. His academic journey was marked by a commitment to understanding the systemic issues that marginalized communities faced. The integration of theory and practice became a cornerstone of his activism, as he sought to bridge the gap between academia and real-world impact.

Childhood Dreams and Ambitions

Armando's childhood dreams were not limited to personal aspirations; they were intertwined with a vision for a more just society. He envisioned a Colombia where LGBTQ individuals could live freely and openly, without fear of discrimination. This vision became the driving force behind his activism, motivating him to challenge the societal norms that perpetuated inequality. The concept of Visionary Leadership, as articulated by scholars like John Kotter, emphasizes the importance of having a clear vision to inspire others, and Armando embodied this principle throughout his journey.

In summary, Armando Benedetti Villaneda's childhood was a crucible of experiences that shaped his identity as an activist. From the streets of Medellín to the halls of political power, his journey reflects the transformative power of activism in the face of adversity. Through his struggles and triumphs, Armando emerged not only as a champion for LGBTQ rights but also as a beacon of hope for future generations.

A Childhood Shaped by Activism

Armando Benedetti Villaneda's journey toward becoming a pivotal figure in the LGBTQ rights movement in Colombia began long before he took to the streets to advocate for change. His childhood, steeped in the vibrant yet tumultuous atmosphere of Medellín, played a crucial role in shaping his identity and activism.

Growing Up in Medellín

Medellín, known for its rich culture and striking landscapes, was also a city grappling with the shadows of violence and inequality. Armando was born into a family that valued social justice and community engagement. His parents, both educators, often discussed issues of injustice and inequality at the dinner table, instilling a sense of responsibility in Armando from a young age. They taught him that knowledge is power, and with that power comes the duty to fight for those who cannot fight for themselves.

Armando's Family and Influences

Armando's family was a tapestry of diverse influences. His grandmother, a fierce advocate for women's rights, often shared stories of her struggles and triumphs, emphasizing the importance of resilience. This legacy of activism permeated Armando's upbringing, as he absorbed the lessons of courage and tenacity. His parents' involvement in local community initiatives further reinforced the idea that activism is not just a choice but a way of life.

First Encounters with Discrimination

As Armando navigated his early years, he quickly became aware of the discrimination faced by those who did not conform to societal norms. His first encounter with discrimination occurred in school, where he witnessed the bullying of a classmate who was perceived as different. This experience ignited a fire within him, compelling him to stand up for those who were marginalized. He began to understand that discrimination was not just a personal issue; it was a systemic problem that required collective action.

The Spark of Activism Ignites

The spark of activism truly ignited during a school project on human rights. Armando delved into the history of social movements, learning about figures like Martin Luther King Jr. and Harvey Milk. The stories of their struggles resonated deeply with him, and he realized that he, too, could be a voice for change. This newfound awareness propelled him into action, as he began organizing discussions among his peers about equality and justice.

Armando's Journey to Self-Discovery

As he grew older, Armando's journey of self-discovery intertwined with his developing activism. He began to grapple with his own identity as a member of the LGBTQ community. The realization that he was different from his peers was both liberating and terrifying. He sought solace in literature and art, finding expressions of his identity in the works of LGBTQ authors and artists. This exploration of self became a crucial element of his activism, as he understood that embracing one's identity is a powerful act in itself.

The Supportive Friends Who Became Family

Throughout his journey, Armando found a supportive network of friends who became like family. These relationships were vital in helping him navigate the complexities of growing up as a queer individual in a conservative society. Together, they formed a tight-knit community that celebrated individuality and diversity. This camaraderie not only provided emotional support but also fueled their collective activism, as they organized events and discussions to raise awareness about LGBTQ issues in their school and community.

Breaking Free from Gender Stereotypes

Breaking free from gender stereotypes was another significant aspect of Armando's childhood. He often felt constrained by societal expectations of masculinity, which dictated how he should behave and express himself. Through his friendships and exposure to various forms of art, he learned to embrace his authentic self. This defiance against traditional gender norms became a cornerstone of his activism, as he advocated for the acceptance of diverse gender identities and expressions.

Discovering a Passion for Politics

Armando's passion for politics began to blossom during his teenage years. He became increasingly aware of the political landscape in Colombia and the impact of government policies on marginalized communities. Inspired by local activists, he began attending political rallies and discussions, eager to learn how he could contribute to the fight for equality. This engagement with politics not only shaped his understanding of systemic oppression but also solidified his commitment to advocating for LGBTQ rights.

Formal Education and its Impact

Formal education played a pivotal role in Armando's development as an activist. He excelled in his studies, particularly in subjects like history and social studies, where he could explore the narratives of social movements. His teachers recognized his potential and encouraged him to participate in debate clubs and student government, providing him with platforms to voice his opinions and advocate for change. This academic foundation empowered him with the knowledge and skills necessary for effective activism.

Childhood Dreams and Ambitions

Armando's childhood dreams were often intertwined with his aspirations for a more just society. He envisioned a future where LGBTQ individuals could live openly and authentically without fear of discrimination. These dreams fueled his determination to fight for change, propelling him into a lifelong commitment to activism. As he navigated the complexities of adolescence, he held onto the belief that he could make a difference, not just for himself but for countless others who faced similar struggles.

In summary, Armando Benedetti Villaneda's childhood was a rich tapestry of experiences that shaped his identity and fueled his passion for activism. From the lessons learned at home to the friendships forged in the face of adversity, each element contributed to his emergence as a formidable advocate for LGBTQ rights in Colombia. His early encounters with discrimination, coupled with a supportive community and a thirst for knowledge, laid the groundwork for a lifelong journey dedicated to the pursuit of equality and justice.

Armando's Family and Influences

Armando Benedetti Villaneda's formative years were profoundly shaped by the dynamics of his family environment. Born into a middle-class family in Medellín, Colombia, he was surrounded by a rich tapestry of cultural influences and societal expectations. His family, while loving, embodied the complexities of a traditional Colombian household, where gender roles were often rigidly defined. The expectations placed upon Armando as a young boy were reflective of the broader societal norms that dictated masculinity and femininity.

Armando's parents, though well-meaning, often adhered to conventional beliefs about gender. His father, a staunch believer in traditional masculinity, often emphasized traits such as toughness and stoicism. This created a dichotomy for Armando, who found himself more inclined towards the arts and emotional expression—traits that were often dismissed as weaknesses in his father's eyes.

This early tension set the stage for Armando's journey of self-discovery and activism, as he grappled with the expectations placed upon him.

In contrast, Armando's mother played a pivotal role in shaping his understanding of compassion and empathy. A schoolteacher by profession, she often encouraged her children to embrace diversity and to stand up against injustice. Her stories of historical figures who fought for equality and human rights resonated deeply with Armando. She introduced him to literature that celebrated individuality and challenged societal norms, planting the seeds of activism in his young mind. This nurturing environment allowed Armando to explore his identity in a way that was both safe and liberating.

However, the family dynamics were not without their challenges. Armando experienced his first encounters with discrimination within his own home. When he expressed interests that deviated from traditional masculine pursuits—like dance and theater—he faced ridicule from some family members. This early exposure to discrimination was pivotal; it ignited a spark within him that would later fuel his activism. He began to understand that the struggle for acceptance was not just external but also internal, requiring him to reconcile his identity with the expectations of those he loved.

The influences of his extended family also played a significant role in shaping Armando's worldview. Many of his relatives held conservative views, often perpetuating stereotypes about LGBTQ individuals. Family gatherings became battlegrounds of ideology, where Armando found himself defending his identity against the very people who were supposed to love him unconditionally. These experiences were not merely painful; they were transformative. They taught him the importance of resilience and the necessity of advocating for change, even within familial relationships.

Armando's friendships during his formative years also contributed significantly to his development. He found solace in a close-knit group of friends who shared similar struggles. These friendships became a refuge, a place where he could express himself freely without fear of judgment. Together, they explored their identities, challenged societal norms, and celebrated their differences. This supportive network was crucial in helping Armando embrace his LGBTQ identity and in fostering a sense of belonging.

As Armando grew older, the influences of his family began to evolve. His parents, witnessing his passion for activism and the positive impact he had on those around him, gradually shifted their perspectives. They began to understand that love and acceptance were more powerful than societal expectations. This transformation within his family unit became a source of strength for Armando, reinforcing his belief that change was possible, even in the most entrenched environments.

In summary, Armando Benedetti Villaneda's family and influences were a complex interplay of love, expectation, and challenge. His early experiences shaped his understanding of identity and activism, laying the groundwork for his future endeavors in the fight for LGBTQ rights in Colombia. The lessons learned from both the supportive and challenging aspects of his upbringing equipped him with the tools needed to navigate the complexities of societal norms and to advocate for a more inclusive world.

First Encounters with Discrimination

Armando Benedetti Villaneda's journey toward activism did not begin in a vacuum; it was shaped by the harsh realities of discrimination that he faced in his formative years. Growing up in Medellín, a city known for its vibrant culture but also its deep-seated social issues, Armando's first encounters with discrimination were both eye-opening and painful. These experiences acted as catalysts for his later commitment to LGBTQ rights and social justice.

From a young age, Armando was acutely aware of the societal norms that dictated acceptable behavior for boys and girls. The rigid gender roles prevalent in Colombian society created an environment where deviation from the norm was met with hostility. For example, when Armando showed interest in activities deemed "feminine," such as dance and fashion, he encountered ridicule from his peers. This ridicule often manifested as name-calling, ostracism, and even physical bullying. Such experiences are consistent with the findings of social psychologists who argue that children learn to enforce gender norms through peer interactions, often resulting in exclusionary behaviors toward those who do not conform [?].

Armando's family, while loving, was not immune to societal pressures. His parents, influenced by traditional Colombian values, sometimes struggled to understand his identity and interests. This disconnect created an internal conflict for Armando, as he sought acceptance both at home and in his community. According to the minority stress theory, individuals from marginalized groups often experience heightened stress due to societal stigma, discrimination, and internalized homophobia [?]. Armando's initial experiences of discrimination contributed to feelings of isolation and confusion regarding his identity.

One poignant example of discrimination occurred when Armando was in elementary school. During a school play, he was cast as a character that challenged traditional gender roles. While performing, he was met with jeers and derogatory comments from classmates, which not only humiliated him but also reinforced the message that expressing himself authentically was unacceptable. This incident exemplifies the broader societal issue of how educational environments can perpetuate discrimination, often leaving LGBTQ youth feeling unsupported and marginalized [?].

As he navigated his teenage years, Armando began to encounter more systemic forms of discrimination. The media portrayal of LGBTQ individuals in Colombia was often negative, reinforcing stereotypes and stigmatizing those who identified as part of the community. This media representation contributed to a culture of fear and silence, making it difficult for individuals like Armando to find role models or positive representations of themselves in society. The lack of visibility for LGBTQ individuals in mainstream media is a significant barrier to acceptance and understanding, as highlighted by studies on representation in media and its impact on social attitudes [?].

Armando's experiences were not isolated; they reflected a broader societal pattern of discrimination faced by LGBTQ individuals in Colombia. According to a report by the International Lesbian, Gay, Bisexual, Trans and Intersex Association (ILGA), LGBTQ individuals in Colombia frequently experience violence, discrimination in employment, and limited access to healthcare [?]. These systemic issues often stem from deeply ingrained cultural attitudes that view non-heteronormative identities as deviant or unacceptable.

Despite these challenges, Armando's early encounters with discrimination fueled his desire to advocate for change. He began to understand that his experiences were not just personal struggles but part of a larger narrative of LGBTQ oppression. This realization marked the beginning of his journey toward activism, as he sought to transform his pain into purpose.

In conclusion, Armando Benedetti Villaneda's first encounters with discrimination were formative experiences that shaped his identity and activism. By navigating the complexities of societal norms, family expectations, and systemic discrimination, Armando emerged with a profound understanding of the struggles faced by LGBTQ individuals. These early experiences not only ignited his passion for activism but also laid the groundwork for his future endeavors in advocating for LGBTQ rights in Colombia and beyond.

The Spark of Activism Ignites

In the vibrant streets of Medellín, where the rhythm of life pulses through the air like a catchy salsa beat, a young Armando Benedetti Villaneda began to feel the stirring of something profound within him. It was during his early adolescence, a time when the world seemed to explode with colors and possibilities, that the spark of activism ignited in his heart. This awakening was not merely a personal revelation; it was a reaction to the societal injustices that surrounded him.

Armando's initial encounters with discrimination were like the first drops of rain before a storm—small but significant. As he navigated the complexities of his identity in a conservative society, he began to recognize that the laughter and camaraderie he shared with his friends could quickly turn sour in the face of prejudice. For instance, during a school event, Armando witnessed a fellow student being bullied for wearing clothing that defied traditional gender norms. The laughter of the crowd, which had once felt so warm and inviting, turned into a cacophony of mockery and scorn. In that moment, Armando felt a mix of anger and empathy that would later fuel his desire for change.

The turning point came when Armando attended a community meeting organized by local LGBTQ activists. The meeting was held in a modest community center, adorned with rainbow flags and filled with a sense of urgency. As he listened to the stories of resilience and courage shared by the speakers, he felt a fire ignite within him. The words of one speaker, an older activist named Clara, resonated deeply: "To be silent is to be complicit." This statement struck a chord, awakening a sense of responsibility that Armando had never felt before. It was a call to action, a reminder that silence in the face of injustice was not an option.

$$\text{Activism} = \text{Awareness} + \text{Empathy} + \text{Action} \tag{1}$$

This equation symbolizes Armando's journey. Awareness of the injustices faced by the LGBTQ community opened his eyes to the systemic problems that needed addressing. Empathy allowed him to connect with the struggles of others, fueling his passion for advocacy. Finally, action became the necessary step to transform his feelings into tangible change.

Armando began to immerse himself in literature and history, reading about figures like Harvey Milk and Marsha P. Johnson, who had paved the way for LGBTQ rights in the United States. Their stories were not just tales of struggle; they were blueprints for activism. He learned about the Stonewall Riots, the AIDS crisis, and the ongoing fight for marriage equality. Each narrative added fuel to his fire, reinforcing the idea that change was possible and that he could be a part of it.

The challenges faced by the LGBTQ community in Colombia were daunting. Discrimination was rampant, with many individuals facing violence and ostracism for simply being who they were. The legal framework was inadequate, with laws that failed to protect LGBTQ individuals from hate crimes or discrimination in employment and healthcare. Armando understood that these were not just abstract issues; they were realities affecting his friends and family. This realization propelled him into action.

Armando's first act of activism was simple yet profound. He organized a small gathering in his neighborhood, inviting friends and allies to discuss the importance of LGBTQ rights. They shared stories, strategized, and most importantly, supported each other. It was a safe space where they could express their fears and hopes without judgment. This gathering laid the groundwork for what would become a larger movement, as word spread and more individuals joined the cause.

As Armando's involvement deepened, he faced backlash from some community members who viewed his activism as a threat to traditional values. However, he remained undeterred. He learned to navigate the complexities of public perception, understanding that resistance often accompanies progress. The challenges only strengthened his resolve, and he began to realize that every obstacle was an opportunity to educate and advocate.

In essence, the spark of activism that ignited within Armando was not merely a personal journey; it was a collective awakening. It was the realization that change could only occur when individuals came together to challenge the status quo. The camaraderie he found within the LGBTQ community became a source of strength, propelling him forward in his quest for justice and equality.

In conclusion, the spark of activism ignited in Armando Benedetti Villaneda was a pivotal moment not just in his life, but in the broader narrative of LGBTQ rights in Colombia. It served as a reminder that within each individual lies the potential to create change, and that sometimes, all it takes is a single moment of inspiration to set the wheels of progress in motion. As Armando continued on his journey, he would carry this spark with him, lighting the way for others to follow.

Armando's Journey to Self-Discovery

Armando Benedetti Villaneda's journey to self-discovery is a profound narrative that intertwines personal revelations with the broader socio-political landscape of Colombia. Growing up in Medellín, a city marked by its vibrant culture and tumultuous history, Armando's path to understanding his identity was not a straightforward one. The complexities of self-discovery often involve grappling with societal expectations, familial pressures, and the internal conflicts that arise from living authentically in a world that sometimes demands conformity.

The Context of Self-Discovery

Self-discovery is a multifaceted process that can be understood through various psychological theories. One such theory is Erik Erikson's psychosocial development, which posits that individuals go through eight stages of development, each characterized by a specific conflict that must be resolved. For Armando, the stage of identity versus role confusion was particularly salient during his adolescence. This stage typically occurs during the teenage years, when individuals begin to explore their personal identity and the roles they wish to adopt in society.

In Armando's case, he faced the dual challenge of reconciling his emerging LGBTQ identity with the conservative values prevalent in his community. As he navigated the complexities of his identity, he often found himself at a crossroads, grappling with the fear of rejection from his family and peers while yearning for authenticity.

First Encounters with Identity

Armando's journey began with subtle signs of his identity emerging during childhood. The first inklings of self-awareness surfaced through the exploration of interests that diverged from traditional gender norms. For example, while other boys engaged in rough-and-tumble play, Armando found joy in dance and the arts. These passions became a refuge, allowing him to express himself in ways that felt natural, yet they also exposed him to ridicule and discrimination from his peers.

The first significant encounter with discrimination occurred when Armando was just twelve years old. During a school event, he was teased for his flamboyant dance moves, a moment that left a lasting impression on him. This experience was pivotal; it illuminated the harsh realities of societal expectations and the painful consequences of stepping outside the prescribed norms of masculinity.

The Spark of Activism

Despite the challenges, these early experiences ignited a spark within Armando. They propelled him toward activism, as he began to recognize that his struggles were not isolated incidents but part of a larger systemic issue affecting many individuals within the LGBTQ community. This realization marked the beginning of his commitment to advocacy and self-acceptance.

Armando's journey to self-discovery was further enriched by the supportive friendships he cultivated throughout his teenage years. These friendships became a sanctuary, providing him with a sense of belonging and understanding that was often lacking in his familial relationships. Together, they explored their identities, shared their fears, and celebrated their differences, reinforcing the notion that self-discovery is often a collective journey.

Breaking Free from Gender Stereotypes

As Armando continued to grow, he became increasingly aware of the restrictive nature of gender stereotypes. He began to challenge these norms, both within himself and in the world around him. This process of breaking free involved confronting deeply ingrained beliefs about masculinity and femininity, and it required a courageous re-evaluation of what it meant to be true to oneself.

Armando's journey was not without its setbacks. He faced backlash from peers who were uncomfortable with his refusal to conform to traditional gender roles. However, each challenge only solidified his resolve. He began to articulate his experiences through poetry and art, using these mediums as tools for self-expression and as a means to connect with others who shared similar struggles.

The Role of Education

Formal education played a crucial role in Armando's self-discovery. As he pursued higher education, he was exposed to diverse perspectives and theories that challenged his understanding of identity. Courses in sociology and gender studies provided him with the vocabulary and framework to articulate his experiences.

One significant moment occurred during a lecture on intersectionality, a concept coined by Kimberlé Crenshaw that examines how various forms of social stratification, such as race, gender, and class, overlap and impact individuals' experiences. This idea resonated deeply with Armando, as he began to see his own identity as a tapestry woven from multiple threads, each contributing to the complexity of his existence.

Embracing Authenticity

Ultimately, Armando's journey to self-discovery culminated in a profound embrace of his authentic self. He learned that self-acceptance is not a destination but an ongoing process. Each step he took toward embracing his identity—whether through coming out to friends and family or participating in LGBTQ advocacy—was a testament to his resilience.

Armando's story exemplifies the notion that self-discovery is inherently tied to the pursuit of justice and equality. His activism became a natural extension of his journey, as he sought not only to understand himself but also to create a world where others could live authentically without fear of discrimination.

In conclusion, Armando Benedetti Villaneda's journey to self-discovery is a powerful narrative of resilience, courage, and the relentless pursuit of authenticity. It serves as a reminder that the path to self-acceptance is often fraught with challenges, but it is also rich with opportunities for growth, connection, and empowerment. Through his experiences, Armando has not only carved out a space for himself but has also paved the way for future generations to embrace their identities with pride and confidence.

The Supportive Friends Who Became Family

In the vibrant tapestry of Armando Benedetti Villaneda's life, the threads woven by his friendships are as crucial as the fabric of his activism. Growing up in Medellín, a city often characterized by its tumultuous history and complex social dynamics, Armando found solace and strength in the bonds he forged with his friends. These relationships transcended mere companionship; they evolved into a familial support system that played a pivotal role in his journey toward self-acceptance and activism.

The Power of Chosen Family

In LGBTQ communities, the concept of chosen family is a profound one. Many individuals find that their biological families may not fully accept their identities or orientations, leading them to seek out friendships that fulfill the emotional and social needs typically met by family. For Armando, his friends became the pillars of support during his formative years, providing a safe space where he could explore his identity without fear of judgment.

Research indicates that social support is a significant predictor of mental health outcomes in LGBTQ individuals. According to [?], having a supportive network can mitigate the effects of discrimination and internalized stigma. Armando's experiences exemplify this phenomenon; his friends offered not just acceptance but also encouragement, empowering him to embrace his true self.

Navigating Discrimination Together

Armando's early encounters with discrimination were not faced in isolation. His friends, many of whom shared similar experiences, stood by him as he navigated the complexities of growing up in a conservative society. Together, they formed a collective that challenged societal norms, often engaging in discussions about identity, acceptance, and the importance of standing up against prejudice.

For instance, during a particularly challenging period when Armando faced harassment at school, his friends organized a small protest, demonstrating solidarity by wearing rainbow colors and chanting slogans of support. This act of defiance not only bolstered Armando's spirits but also highlighted the collective power of friendship in the face of adversity.

Creating Safe Spaces

The friends Armando surrounded himself with were instrumental in creating safe spaces where he could express himself freely. They held gatherings that celebrated LGBTQ culture, from movie nights featuring queer cinema to discussions about important social issues. These spaces became sanctuaries where Armando could let his guard down, share his struggles, and celebrate his victories.

The concept of safe spaces is vital in LGBTQ advocacy, as highlighted by [?], who argues that such environments foster open dialogue and mutual understanding. Armando's gatherings not only strengthened friendships but also educated participants about the challenges faced by the LGBTQ community, promoting empathy and solidarity.

The Role of Allies

Among Armando's friends were allies who, while not identifying as part of the LGBTQ community, played a crucial role in his life. These allies often took it upon themselves to educate others about LGBTQ issues, advocating for acceptance and understanding in their respective circles. Their willingness to stand up against homophobia and discrimination contributed significantly to the sense of safety that Armando experienced.

For example, one of Armando's closest allies, a straight friend named Laura, frequently challenged derogatory remarks made by peers. Her vocal support not only reinforced Armando's confidence but also encouraged other friends to become advocates for LGBTQ rights. This allyship exemplifies the importance of intersectionality in social justice movements, where individuals from various backgrounds unite for a common cause.

Building Resilience Through Friendship

The emotional resilience that Armando developed can be attributed, in large part, to the unwavering support of his friends. They celebrated his achievements, no matter how small, and provided comfort during times of distress. This network of support helped Armando to view challenges as opportunities for growth rather than insurmountable obstacles.

A poignant example of this resilience occurred when Armando faced a significant setback in his activism efforts. His friends rallied around him, organizing a fundraising event to support his initiatives. This act of solidarity not only provided financial assistance but also reinforced the idea that he was not alone in his fight for equality.

Lasting Bonds

As Armando grew older and transitioned into a prominent activist, the bonds he formed with his friends remained strong. They continued to be his confidants, collaborators, and cheerleaders. The friendships that began in the context of shared struggles evolved into lifelong relationships, illustrating the profound impact of supportive friends who become family.

In summary, the supportive friends who became family for Armando Benedetti Villaneda were instrumental in shaping his identity and activism. Their collective strength, resilience, and unwavering support provided a foundation upon which Armando built his life's work. As he navigated the challenges of growing up LGBTQ in Colombia, these friendships not only offered comfort but also inspired a commitment to advocacy that would resonate throughout his life. The bonds formed during these formative years serve as a testament to the power of friendship in the pursuit of equality and acceptance.

Breaking Free from Gender Stereotypes

In the vibrant streets of Medellín, where the rhythm of life pulsates with both beauty and struggle, Armando Benedetti Villaneda began to recognize the constraints imposed by traditional gender roles. From a young age, he felt the weight of expectations that dictated how boys should behave, what interests they should pursue, and how they should express themselves. These stereotypes, deeply entrenched in Colombian culture, often left little room for individuality or deviation from the norm.

Gender stereotypes are societal constructs that dictate the behaviors, interests, and roles deemed appropriate for individuals based on their gender. According to Judith Butler's theory of gender performativity, gender is not a fixed identity but rather a series of performances shaped by societal expectations. This theory posits that individuals enact their gender identity through repeated behaviors, thus reinforcing the very stereotypes they may wish to escape.

Armando's early experiences in Medellín were marked by the stark contrast between societal expectations and his true self. As a child, he was often drawn to activities and interests that were labeled as "feminine" by his peers and family. Whether it was a passion for dance or a flair for fashion, these interests were met with ridicule and disdain. The message was clear: to be accepted, he had to conform to the rigid standards of masculinity that dictated strength, stoicism, and a lack of emotional expression.

The first pivotal moment in Armando's journey toward breaking free from these stereotypes occurred during his teenage years. He discovered a supportive community of friends who encouraged him to embrace his authentic self. This camaraderie provided a safe space where he could express his interests without fear of judgment. It was within this nurturing environment that Armando began to challenge the conventional notions of masculinity and femininity, realizing that true strength lies in vulnerability and self-acceptance.

One of the most significant challenges Armando faced was the internalized stigma associated with deviating from gender norms. The societal pressure to conform often led to self-doubt and confusion. Armando grappled with feelings of inadequacy, questioning whether he would ever be accepted for who he truly was. This internal conflict is not uncommon among individuals who challenge gender stereotypes, as highlighted in the work of sociologist Raewyn Connell, who discusses the concept of hegemonic masculinity—the dominant form of masculinity that marginalizes those who do not conform.

Armando's journey took a transformative turn when he began to engage with LGBTQ advocacy groups that emphasized the importance of breaking free from gender stereotypes. These organizations provided him with resources and support, fostering a sense of belonging that was previously absent in his life. Through workshops and discussions, he learned about the impact of gender norms on mental health and well-being, reinforcing his resolve to advocate for a more inclusive society.

As Armando embraced his identity, he became increasingly aware of the intersectionality of gender and sexuality. He realized that breaking free from gender stereotypes was not only about personal liberation but also about challenging systemic oppression. He began to advocate for the recognition of diverse gender identities and expressions, emphasizing that everyone should have the right to define their own identity without fear of discrimination.

Armando's activism took shape as he organized community events aimed at raising awareness about gender diversity. These events served as platforms for individuals to share their stories and experiences, fostering a sense of solidarity among those who had faced similar struggles. Through art, music, and dialogue, Armando and his peers created an atmosphere that celebrated individuality and challenged the status quo.

One particularly impactful event was a fashion show that showcased the talents of LGBTQ designers and models. The event not only highlighted the creativity within the community but also served as a powerful statement against rigid gender norms. Attendees were encouraged to express themselves freely, regardless of societal expectations. This celebration of diversity resonated deeply within the community, inspiring many to embrace their true selves.

In conclusion, Armando Benedetti Villaneda's journey to breaking free from gender stereotypes serves as a testament to the power of self-acceptance and community support. By challenging societal norms and advocating for inclusivity, he has paved the way for future generations to live authentically. His story exemplifies the importance of recognizing and dismantling the barriers imposed by gender stereotypes, ultimately fostering a society that celebrates diversity in all its forms. As Armando continues to advocate for LGBTQ rights in Colombia, his commitment to breaking free from gender stereotypes remains a cornerstone of his activism, inspiring others to embrace their true identities without fear or hesitation.

Discovering a Passion for Politics

As Armando Benedetti Villaneda navigated the vibrant streets of Medellín, he found himself increasingly drawn to the world of politics. It was not merely a fascination with the power dynamics at play, but a deep-seated desire to effect change in a society that had often marginalized voices like his own. His early experiences with discrimination and the injustices faced by the LGBTQ community ignited a fire within him, compelling him to explore the political landscape of Colombia.

The Influence of Political Climate

Growing up in a country marked by political turmoil, Armando was acutely aware of how governance could either uplift or oppress. The civil conflict that gripped Colombia for decades had left scars on its populace, and the marginalized communities often bore the brunt of these struggles. This environment fostered in Armando a critical understanding of the interconnectedness of social justice and political action. He realized that to advocate for LGBTQ rights, one must engage with the political system that dictated the rights and freedoms of citizens.

Key Theoretical Frameworks

Armando's passion for politics can be examined through various theoretical frameworks that elucidate the relationship between social movements and political change. One such theory is the **Resource Mobilization Theory**, which posits that the success of social movements depends on their ability to gather resources—be it financial support, human capital, or organizational infrastructure. In Armando's case, he recognized the importance of forming alliances with established political entities to amplify the LGBTQ cause.

Another relevant framework is **Framing Theory**, which focuses on how social movements construct meaning around their struggles. Armando learned the art of framing LGBTQ rights as a fundamental human rights issue, thereby appealing to a broader audience beyond the community itself. This strategic framing was crucial in garnering support from allies and shifting public perception.

Challenges Faced

However, Armando's journey into politics was not without its challenges. The societal stigma attached to LGBTQ individuals in Colombia often translated into political resistance. Armando faced numerous obstacles, including skepticism from traditional political actors and backlash from conservative factions. The prevailing notion that LGBTQ issues were secondary to more pressing national concerns posed a significant hurdle.

Moreover, the lack of representation in political spaces meant that LGBTQ voices were often silenced or ignored. This systemic exclusion fueled Armando's determination to not only advocate for his community but also to carve out a space for LGBTQ individuals within the political discourse. He understood that representation was not merely about visibility; it was about having the power to influence policy and effect tangible change.

Early Political Engagement

Armando's first foray into politics came during his university years when he joined a student-led organization advocating for LGBTQ rights. This platform allowed him to hone his skills in public speaking, grassroots organizing, and coalition-building. He quickly learned the importance of mobilizing students and engaging them in political discussions. Through rallies, workshops, and awareness campaigns, Armando and his peers began to challenge the status quo, demanding recognition and rights for LGBTQ individuals.

His involvement in student politics also exposed him to the intricacies of legislative processes. He began to understand how laws were formulated, debated, and enacted. This knowledge proved invaluable as he sought to push for legal reforms that would protect LGBTQ rights in Colombia. Armando's passion for politics evolved into a commitment to advocacy, as he recognized that true change required not just passion but also strategic political engagement.

Influential Figures and Moments

Throughout this journey, Armando encountered several influential figures who shaped his political ideology. Mentors within the LGBTQ rights movement provided guidance and encouragement, helping him navigate the complexities of political activism. Additionally, historical moments, such as landmark rulings in favor of LGBTQ rights in other countries, inspired him to envision a similar future for Colombia.

One pivotal moment was the global response to the legalization of same-sex marriage in various nations. Armando saw how these victories galvanized activists and reshaped public discourse. He was determined to bring that momentum to Colombia, believing that with the right strategies, change was possible.

Conclusion

Armando's discovery of his passion for politics marked a significant turning point in his life. It was a realization that politics was not just a distant realm but a powerful tool for change. His early experiences, coupled with a theoretical understanding of social movements, equipped him with the knowledge and determination needed to challenge the political landscape in Colombia. As he continued to navigate this path, Armando understood that the fight for LGBTQ rights was inextricably linked to the broader struggle for justice and equality in society.

Through his journey, he would not only advocate for LGBTQ rights but also inspire a new generation of activists to harness the power of politics in their quest for equality. The road ahead would be fraught with challenges, but Armando was ready to take on the political establishment, armed with passion, knowledge, and an unwavering commitment to justice.

Formal Education and its Impact

Formal education plays a crucial role in shaping an individual's worldview, skills, and capabilities, particularly for someone like Armando Benedetti Villaneda, who emerged as a pivotal figure in the LGBTQ rights movement in Colombia. Education does not merely impart knowledge; it also fosters critical thinking, social awareness, and the ability to advocate for oneself and others. This section delves into the various ways formal education influenced Armando's journey as an activist.

The Role of Education in Activism

Education serves as a foundation for activism by equipping individuals with the tools necessary to challenge societal norms and injustices. Armando's formal education began in Medellín, where he attended local schools that, while traditional, offered him a glimpse into the world beyond his immediate environment. The curriculum often reflected the conservative values prevalent in Colombian society, yet it also introduced him to subjects such as history, sociology, and political science, which would later inform his understanding of social justice.

Critical Thinking and Awareness

One of the key benefits of formal education is the development of critical thinking skills. Through engaging with diverse perspectives and analyzing historical events, Armando learned to question the status quo. For instance, when studying the civil rights movements in various parts of the world, he recognized parallels with the struggles faced by the LGBTQ community in Colombia. This awareness ignited a passion for activism, prompting him to seek out ways to advocate for change.

Social Networks and Support Systems

Moreover, formal education provided Armando with access to a network of like-minded individuals. Universities and educational institutions often serve as incubators for social movements, bringing together students who share similar values and goals. Armando's involvement in student organizations and LGBTQ groups at his university allowed him to connect with peers who were equally passionate about advocating for LGBTQ rights. These relationships became instrumental in forming a support system that bolstered his confidence and commitment to activism.

Challenges in the Educational Environment

However, the path of education was not without its challenges. Armando faced discrimination and prejudice within academic settings, which mirrored the societal attitudes he encountered outside the classroom. Instances of bullying and exclusion based on his sexual orientation served as painful reminders of the work that lay ahead. Yet, these experiences also strengthened his resolve to fight against injustice, as he recognized the importance of creating inclusive spaces for all individuals, regardless of their identity.

The Impact of Higher Education

As Armando progressed to higher education, his exposure to more progressive ideologies further shaped his understanding of LGBTQ rights. Courses on human rights, gender studies, and international relations provided him with a broader context for his activism. He learned about the legal frameworks that protect marginalized communities and the ongoing struggles for equality in various countries. This knowledge empowered him to articulate the need for legal recognition and protections for LGBTQ individuals in Colombia, transforming his personal experiences into a broader advocacy agenda.

Practical Applications of Education

In addition to theoretical knowledge, formal education offered Armando practical skills that would prove invaluable in his activism. Public speaking, research methodologies, and advocacy strategies became essential tools in his arsenal. For example, his experience in debate clubs honed his ability to articulate arguments effectively, enabling him to engage with policymakers and the public. The ability to present compelling narratives around LGBTQ issues helped garner support and raise awareness about the challenges faced by the community.

Conclusion

In conclusion, formal education significantly impacted Armando Benedetti Villaneda's journey as an LGBTQ activist in Colombia. It provided him with critical thinking skills, a supportive network, and practical tools for advocacy. Despite facing challenges within the educational system, Armando's experiences fueled his commitment to creating a more equitable society. As he continued to navigate the complexities of activism, the lessons learned in the classroom remained at the forefront of his mission to champion LGBTQ rights and promote social justice for all.

Childhood Dreams and Ambitions

As a young boy growing up in the vibrant city of Medellín, Armando Benedetti Villaneda was not only shaped by his surroundings but also by the dreams that danced in his imagination. These dreams were not mere fantasies; they were reflections of the aspirations he held deep within his heart, often influenced by the socio-political climate of Colombia and the rich tapestry of its culture. Armando's childhood ambitions were intricately tied to his burgeoning identity, as he navigated the complexities of being a queer child in a conservative society.

From an early age, Armando exhibited a fascination with storytelling and performance, often putting on shows for his family and friends. This inclination towards the arts was more than just a hobby; it was a means of expression and a way to explore his identity. Armando would often say, "If you can make people laugh, you can make them listen." This belief became a cornerstone of his activism later in life, as he recognized the power of humor and performance in challenging societal norms.

Armando's dreams extended beyond the stage. Inspired by the activists he saw on television and in the news, he envisioned himself as a champion for social justice. He often daydreamed about leading rallies, speaking out against injustice, and advocating for the rights of those who, like him, felt marginalized. These ambitions were fueled by the stories of historical figures such as Harvey Milk and Marsha P. Johnson, whose legacies ignited a fire within him. He learned that activism was not just about fighting for one's rights but also about uplifting the voices of the oppressed.

However, the journey to realizing these dreams was fraught with challenges. Armando faced societal pressures that dictated what a young boy should aspire to be. Traditional gender roles were deeply ingrained in Colombian culture, and any deviation from the norm was often met with ridicule or hostility. This societal pressure created a conflict within him, as he grappled with the expectations placed upon him versus his authentic self.

In the face of these challenges, Armando found solace in education. He immersed himself in books, often losing himself in stories of resilience and courage. Literature became a refuge, allowing him to explore different perspectives and understand the struggles faced by LGBTQ individuals around the world. It was during these formative years that he developed a profound understanding of intersectionality, recognizing that the fight for LGBTQ rights was intertwined with other social justice movements, including those advocating for racial and gender equality.

Armando's childhood dreams were also influenced by his relationships with his family and friends. He was fortunate to have a supportive network that encouraged him to pursue his passions. His mother, in particular, played a pivotal role in nurturing his ambitions. She often reminded him, "You can be anything you want to be, as long as you believe in yourself." This unwavering support instilled in him a sense of confidence and determination.

Despite the obstacles, Armando's ambitions continued to flourish. He began to envision a future where he could combine his love for performance with his passion for activism. He dreamed of creating a platform where stories of LGBTQ individuals could be shared, celebrated, and amplified. This dream would later manifest in various forms, including community events, workshops, and advocacy campaigns that aimed to educate and empower others.

In conclusion, Armando Benedetti Villaneda's childhood dreams and ambitions were characterized by a unique blend of creativity, resilience, and a deep commitment to social justice. These dreams laid the foundation for his future endeavors as an LGBTQ activist, shaping his identity and fueling his drive to challenge the status quo. As he navigated the complexities of his youth, Armando learned that dreams are not just visions of the future; they are powerful motivators that can inspire change and ignite a movement.

Embracing the LGBTQ Identity

Coming Out to Friends and Family

Coming out is often described as a personal journey, a rite of passage that many LGBTQ individuals must navigate. For Armando Benedetti Villaneda, coming out to friends and family was both a moment of liberation and a source of anxiety. The act of coming out can be understood through various psychological and sociocultural lenses, highlighting the complexities involved in revealing one's sexual orientation or gender identity.

Theories of identity development, such as Cass's Model of Sexual Identity Formation, provide a framework for understanding the stages individuals often go through when coming out. According to Cass, the process includes stages such as identity confusion, identity comparison, identity tolerance, identity acceptance, identity pride, and identity synthesis. Armando's experience can be mapped onto this model, illustrating both the emotional turmoil and the eventual acceptance that many face.

$$\text{Identity Development} = f(\text{Personal Experience, Social Context, Support Systems}) \tag{2}$$

In Armando's case, the social context of Medellín played a significant role. Growing up in a conservative society where traditional gender roles were strictly enforced, the fear of rejection loomed large. He often grappled with the question:

"What will they think of me?" The societal stigma attached to being LGBTQ in Colombia posed a considerable barrier, leading to internalized homophobia that many individuals face.

Armando's first step in coming out was to confide in his closest friends. He chose a casual setting—a local café where they often gathered. The atmosphere was relaxed, but his heart raced as he prepared to share his truth. "I have something important to tell you guys," he began, his voice shaking slightly. The response from his friends was overwhelmingly supportive, with one friend exclaiming, "We love you for who you are!" This moment marked a pivotal shift in Armando's journey, reinforcing the importance of having a supportive network.

However, the experience was not universally positive. When Armando finally gathered the courage to tell his family, the reaction was mixed. His mother, a traditionalist at heart, struggled to understand. "You're still my son, but this is so... unexpected," she said, her voice filled with concern. This reaction exemplifies the common challenges faced during the coming-out process, where familial acceptance can be fraught with tension.

The psychological implications of coming out are profound. Research indicates that individuals who receive support during their coming-out process report lower levels of depression and anxiety. Armando's story reflects this, as he found solace in the LGBTQ community, which provided him with a sense of belonging that he had longed for. He began attending local LGBTQ events, where he met others who had similar experiences, fostering a sense of camaraderie and shared identity.

$$\text{Mental Health} = \frac{\text{Support}}{\text{Rejection}} \tag{3}$$

The balance of support and rejection plays a crucial role in mental health outcomes for LGBTQ individuals. Armando's ability to navigate the complexities of coming out was significantly influenced by the presence of supportive friends and allies. He learned that while coming out is a deeply personal journey, it is also a communal experience that can empower others.

In conclusion, Armando's coming-out journey was marked by both triumphs and challenges. His experiences underscore the importance of understanding the sociocultural dynamics at play in the coming-out process. By sharing his story, Armando not only embraced his identity but also paved the way for others in Colombia to find their voices. Coming out is not merely an individual act; it is a collective movement toward acceptance and understanding, one that continues to evolve within the broader context of LGBTQ rights in Colombia and beyond.

The Struggles of Acceptance

Acceptance is a multifaceted journey that often presents significant challenges for LGBTQ individuals. For Armando, this journey was no exception. Growing up in a conservative society like Colombia, where traditional values often overshadowed personal identity, the path to self-acceptance was fraught with obstacles that tested his resilience and determination.

Societal Pressures and Expectations

In Colombia, societal norms dictate rigid expectations regarding gender roles and sexual orientation. The pressure to conform can be overwhelming, leading many individuals to suppress their true selves. For Armando, the fear of rejection from family and friends was a significant barrier. The pervasive stigma surrounding LGBTQ identities often manifests in various forms of discrimination, which can severely affect mental health. According to the *American Psychological Association*, LGBTQ youth are at a higher risk for depression and anxiety, often stemming from societal rejection and internalized homophobia.

Internal Conflicts

Armando experienced profound internal conflicts as he grappled with his identity. He often found himself caught between the desire to be true to himself and the fear of societal backlash. This internal struggle is not uncommon among LGBTQ individuals and can lead to a phenomenon known as *internalized homophobia*, where one internalizes negative societal attitudes towards homosexuality. The psychological impact of this can be debilitating, leading to feelings of shame and self-hatred.

$$\text{Internalized Homophobia} = \frac{\text{Societal Stigma} \times \text{Personal Identity Crisis}}{\text{Support System}} \quad (4)$$

In this equation, the lack of a supportive environment can exacerbate the internalized homophobia experienced by individuals like Armando. The more significant the societal stigma and the more profound the personal identity crisis, the greater the internalized homophobia, especially when support systems are weak or absent.

Family Dynamics

One of the most challenging aspects of Armando's struggle for acceptance was his relationship with his family. Coming out to his parents was a pivotal moment that highlighted the complexities of familial acceptance. Many LGBTQ individuals face rejection from their families, which can lead to emotional distress and a sense of isolation. Armando's experience was no different; he faced mixed reactions from his family, ranging from confusion to outright denial.

Research indicates that familial acceptance is crucial for the well-being of LGBTQ youth. According to a study published in the *Journal of Family Psychology*, youth who reported high levels of family acceptance experienced significantly lower levels of depression and suicidal ideation. Armando's journey toward acceptance was marked by moments of hope and despair, as he navigated the delicate balance of seeking acceptance while remaining true to himself.

Finding Community

Despite the struggles he faced, Armando discovered that the LGBTQ community could provide the acceptance he yearned for. The sense of belonging he found among fellow activists and allies played a crucial role in his journey. Community support can serve as a powerful antidote to the isolation often felt by LGBTQ individuals. In Armando's case, connecting with others who shared similar experiences allowed him to embrace his identity more fully.

$$\text{Community Support} = \text{Acceptance} + \text{Shared Experiences} + \text{Empowerment} \quad (5)$$

This equation illustrates how community support can facilitate acceptance through shared experiences and empowerment, enabling individuals like Armando to overcome the struggles of acceptance.

The Road to Self-Acceptance

Ultimately, Armando's journey toward self-acceptance involved a combination of personal reflection and external support. He learned to challenge societal norms and redefine what acceptance meant for him. This process was not linear; it involved setbacks and moments of doubt. However, through activism and engagement with the LGBTQ community, Armando began to embrace his identity fully.

In conclusion, the struggles of acceptance are a profound aspect of the LGBTQ experience, particularly for individuals like Armando. These struggles highlight the need for greater societal understanding and acceptance, emphasizing the importance of supportive environments that foster self-acceptance. As Armando continued to advocate for LGBTQ rights, he not only sought acceptance for himself but also worked tirelessly to create a world where others could find the same.

Finding Pride and Support in the LGBTQ Community

In the vibrant tapestry of LGBTQ life, finding pride and support within the community is a transformative experience that shapes the identities and lives of individuals like Armando Benedetti Villaneda. This section explores the profound impact of community support on personal identity, resilience, and activism.

The Importance of Community

The LGBTQ community serves as a vital support network for individuals navigating their identities in a world that can often be hostile. The sense of belonging that emerges from shared experiences fosters pride, courage, and a collective voice. According to [2], community support is essential for psychological well-being among LGBTQ individuals, as it helps mitigate feelings of isolation and alienation.

$$P = \frac{S}{C} \qquad (6)$$

Where:

- P = Pride
- S = Support from the community
- C = Challenges faced

This equation illustrates that as support from the community increases, so does the individual's sense of pride, particularly in the face of challenges.

Finding Role Models and Mentors

For Armando, the journey to self-acceptance was significantly influenced by the presence of role models within the LGBTQ community. Figures such as Marsha P. Johnson and Harvey Milk served as beacons of hope, demonstrating that it is possible to live authentically and advocate for change. These role models not only provided inspiration but also a framework for understanding the importance of visibility and representation.

Research by [?] highlights that mentorship within the LGBTQ community can lead to increased engagement in activism and advocacy. Armando's connection with mentors allowed him to navigate the complexities of his identity while fostering a commitment to social justice.

Creating Safe Spaces

Safe spaces are essential for fostering pride and support within the LGBTQ community. These environments allow individuals to express themselves freely without fear of judgment or discrimination. Armando found solace in local LGBTQ centers, which provided not only resources but also a sense of belonging.

The concept of safe spaces aligns with the theory of *intersectionality*, as described by [3]. This theory emphasizes the importance of recognizing how various social identities intersect and impact experiences of discrimination and privilege. Safe spaces serve as a refuge where individuals can explore their identities in a supportive environment.

Participating in LGBTQ Events and Activism

Engagement in LGBTQ events, such as pride parades and community forums, played a pivotal role in Armando's journey. These events not only celebrate identity but also serve as platforms for advocacy and visibility. Armando recalls the exhilaration of participating in Medellín's pride parade, where the streets were filled with vibrant colors, music, and a palpable sense of unity.

$$E = \sum_{i=1}^{n}(C_i \times V_i) \tag{7}$$

Where:

- E = Energy and enthusiasm generated
- C_i = Community participants
- V_i = Visibility of LGBTQ identities

This equation suggests that the collective energy of community participants significantly enhances the visibility and impact of LGBTQ events, fostering pride and solidarity.

Building Alliances and Solidarity

Armando's activism also emphasized the importance of building alliances within and beyond the LGBTQ community. Collaborating with other marginalized groups, such as women and racial minorities, highlights the interconnectedness of social justice movements. This approach aligns with the principles of *solidarity* and *intersectionality*, promoting a more inclusive advocacy strategy.

Through these alliances, Armando and his peers were able to amplify their voices and address broader societal issues, such as poverty and discrimination. This intersectional approach not only strengthened the LGBTQ movement but also created a more cohesive community.

The Role of Social Media in Fostering Pride

In the digital age, social media has emerged as a powerful tool for fostering pride and support within the LGBTQ community. Platforms like Instagram and Twitter allow individuals to share their stories, connect with others, and mobilize for change. Armando utilized social media to raise awareness about LGBTQ rights in Colombia, creating a virtual community that transcended geographical boundaries.

Research by [?] indicates that social media can significantly enhance community engagement and support, particularly for those in conservative environments where traditional support systems may be lacking.

Conclusion

Finding pride and support in the LGBTQ community is a multifaceted journey that encompasses personal growth, collective action, and the celebration of identity. For Armando Benedetti Villaneda, this journey was marked by the powerful influences of role models, safe spaces, and community engagement. As he navigated the complexities of his identity, the support of the LGBTQ community not only fueled his activism but also instilled a deep sense of pride that continues to inspire others.

By fostering an environment of acceptance and solidarity, the LGBTQ community plays a crucial role in empowering individuals to embrace their identities and advocate for change, ensuring that future generations can continue the fight for equality and justice.

Exploring Different Facets of his Identity

Armando Benedetti Villaneda's journey of self-exploration is a rich tapestry woven with the threads of culture, sexuality, and identity politics. Growing up in Medellín, a city known for its vibrant culture yet marred by conservative values, Armando found himself at the intersection of multiple identities—each facet contributing to his understanding of self and the world around him.

Theoretical Framework

To understand Armando's exploration of identity, we can employ the concept of *intersectionality*, introduced by Kimberlé Crenshaw. Intersectionality posits that individuals experience overlapping social identities that interact with systems of oppression, discrimination, and privilege. For Armando, this meant navigating the complexities of being a gay man in a predominantly heterosexual society, while also being influenced by his socio-economic background and cultural heritage.

$$I = \sum_{n=1}^{N} \text{Identity}_n \qquad (8)$$

Where I represents the overall identity, and Identity_n represents each individual facet of identity, such as sexual orientation, gender identity, ethnicity, and socio-economic status.

Cultural Influences

In Medellín, traditional values often clash with modern perspectives on sexuality. Armando's cultural background played a significant role in shaping his understanding of masculinity and femininity. The Colombian cultural narrative often emphasizes hyper-masculinity, which posed challenges for Armando as he began to embrace his LGBTQ identity. He faced societal expectations that dictated how men should behave, often leading to internal conflicts and feelings of inadequacy.

For instance, the pressure to conform to traditional gender roles often left him feeling alienated. He recalls moments in school where he was teased for not fitting the mold, which only fueled his desire to understand and embrace the different aspects of his identity. This experience aligns with Judith Butler's theory of gender performativity, which suggests that gender is not an inherent quality but rather a performance shaped by societal norms.

Self-Discovery and Acceptance

As Armando began to explore his identity, he encountered various facets that were often in conflict with each other. He found solace in literature and the arts, which provided him a platform to express his thoughts and feelings. Influential figures in LGBTQ literature, such as James Baldwin and Audre Lorde, inspired him to embrace his identity boldly. Their works emphasized the importance of self-acceptance and the power of storytelling as a means of understanding one's place in the world.

Armando's exploration also led him to engage with different LGBTQ communities. He discovered that each subgroup within the community had its own unique experiences and challenges. For example, the experiences of transgender individuals differ significantly from those of gay men, yet both groups face systemic discrimination. This realization deepened his understanding of the spectrum of identities within the LGBTQ community, prompting him to advocate for inclusivity and representation.

Challenges in Embracing Identity

Despite his growing awareness and acceptance, Armando faced significant challenges in fully embracing his identity. The societal stigma attached to homosexuality in Colombia often manifested in overt discrimination and violence. He recalls an incident where a close friend was attacked for being openly gay, which served as a stark reminder of the dangers that accompany visibility.

This experience highlighted the pervasive issues of homophobia and transphobia that still exist in Colombian society. Armando's journey underscores the importance of allyship and solidarity within the LGBTQ community. He began to realize that exploring one's identity is not just a personal journey but a collective struggle against societal norms that seek to marginalize individuals based on their sexual orientation.

Finding Community and Support

Through his exploration, Armando found a supportive network of friends who shared similar experiences. These friendships became a lifeline, providing him with a sense of belonging and acceptance. They engaged in discussions about identity, politics, and the future of LGBTQ rights in Colombia. This community fostered an environment where he could express his fears, dreams, and aspirations without judgment.

Armando also became involved in LGBTQ organizations that focused on advocacy and education. These platforms allowed him to connect with others who were navigating their own journeys of self-discovery. The collective experiences shared within these spaces reinforced the idea that identity is multifaceted and continually evolving.

Conclusion

Exploring different facets of his identity was a transformative process for Armando Benedetti Villaneda. It involved grappling with societal expectations, embracing intersectionality, and finding community amidst adversity. His journey reflects the broader struggles faced by LGBTQ individuals in Colombia and emphasizes the importance of understanding identity as a complex interplay of various factors. As Armando continued to evolve, he became an advocate not only for himself but for others who sought to navigate the intricate landscape of identity in a world that often demands conformity.

The Impact of LGBTQ Rights Movements on Armando

The LGBTQ rights movements have played a pivotal role in shaping Armando Benedetti Villaneda's identity and activism. From a young age, Armando was influenced by the stories of resilience and courage exhibited by activists who fought for equality and justice. These movements not only provided a framework for understanding his own experiences but also ignited a passion for advocacy within him.

Theoretical Framework

To understand the impact of LGBTQ rights movements on Armando, it is essential to consider the theoretical frameworks that underpin these movements. Social movement theory, particularly the resource mobilization theory, posits that successful movements require adequate resources, organization, and collective action. According to [1], social movements are characterized by their ability to mobilize individuals around shared grievances and collective identities. For Armando, these movements provided a sense of belonging and a platform to express his identity.

The concept of intersectionality, introduced by [3], further enriches this discussion. Intersectionality emphasizes that individuals experience oppression in varying degrees based on their intersecting identities, such as race, gender, and sexual orientation. Armando's activism was informed by this understanding, as he recognized the need to address not only LGBTQ rights but also the broader spectrum of social justice issues affecting marginalized communities in Colombia.

Personal Experiences and Examples

Armando's journey into activism began when he first encountered the LGBTQ rights movements in Medellín. He attended local rallies and events where he met individuals who shared their stories of struggle and triumph. For instance, at a pride parade, he met a transgender woman who recounted her experiences of violence and discrimination. This encounter profoundly impacted Armando, as he realized that the fight for LGBTQ rights was not just about legal recognition but also about the dignity and safety of individuals.

One significant moment in Armando's life was when he participated in a campaign advocating for same-sex marriage in Colombia. This movement, which gained momentum in the early 2010s, was a defining moment for many LGBTQ individuals. Armando recalls standing alongside other activists, holding signs that read "Love is Love." This experience solidified his commitment to the cause and demonstrated the power of collective action. The campaign eventually led to the historic ruling by the Colombian Constitutional Court in 2016, which legalized same-sex marriage, marking a significant victory for LGBTQ rights in the country.

Challenges Faced

Despite the progress made by LGBTQ rights movements, Armando faced numerous challenges. The backlash against these movements often manifested in the form of violence, discrimination, and political opposition. For instance, during a protest advocating for LGBTQ rights, Armando and his fellow activists were met with hostility from counter-protesters. This confrontation highlighted the ongoing struggle for acceptance and the need for continued advocacy.

Moreover, Armando grappled with the internalized stigma that many LGBTQ individuals face. The societal pressures and expectations often made him question his worth and place within both the LGBTQ community and society at large. However, the resilience of the LGBTQ rights movements provided him with the tools to combat these feelings. Through workshops and support groups, he learned about self-acceptance and the importance of mental health in the fight for equality.

The Broader Impact on Society

The influence of LGBTQ rights movements extends beyond individual activists like Armando; they have catalyzed broader societal changes. Armando witnessed shifts in public perception regarding LGBTQ issues, particularly among younger generations. Educational initiatives aimed at promoting LGBTQ-inclusive curricula have begun to reshape how society views sexual orientation and gender identity.

For example, Armando collaborated with local schools to implement programs that educate students about diversity and inclusion. This initiative not only empowered LGBTQ youth but also fostered empathy and understanding among their peers. As a result, he observed a decline in bullying and discrimination within schools, demonstrating the positive ripple effects of advocacy work.

Conclusion

In conclusion, the impact of LGBTQ rights movements on Armando Benedetti Villaneda has been profound and transformative. These movements provided him with a sense of identity, purpose, and community, fueling his passion for activism. Through personal experiences, challenges, and triumphs, Armando has become a vital voice in the ongoing struggle for LGBTQ rights in Colombia. His journey exemplifies the power of collective action and the importance of intersectionality in the fight for social justice. As Armando continues to advocate for equality, he remains committed to uplifting the voices of those who have been marginalized, ensuring that the fight for LGBTQ rights is inclusive and intersectional.

Role Models and Inspirations

In the journey of self-discovery and activism, having role models and inspirations can serve as powerful catalysts for change. For Armando Benedetti Villaneda, the influences that shaped his identity and activism were both diverse and profound. These role models not only provided guidance but also illuminated pathways to self-acceptance and advocacy for LGBTQ rights in Colombia.

Historical Figures

One of Armando's earliest inspirations was the legendary figure of Marsha P. Johnson, a prominent activist in the LGBTQ rights movement in the United States. Johnson's role in the Stonewall Riots of 1969 marked a pivotal moment in the fight for LGBTQ rights, demonstrating the power of grassroots activism. Armando admired Johnson's fearless spirit and her ability to mobilize marginalized communities. He often reflected on her famous quote: "No pride for some of us without liberation for all of us," which resonated deeply with his vision of inclusivity in activism.

Similarly, the influence of Sylvia Rivera, another key figure in the Stonewall movement, was significant for Armando. Rivera's dedication to the rights of transgender individuals and her work with the Street Transvestite Action Revolutionaries (STAR) showcased the importance of intersectionality within the LGBTQ movement. Armando recognized that Rivera's struggles against discrimination and her advocacy for the most vulnerable within the community were lessons he needed to internalize as he navigated his own path.

Local Activists

In Colombia, Armando found inspiration in local activists who were making strides in the fight for LGBTQ rights. Figures such as María José Pizarro, a Colombian politician and human rights advocate, served as a beacon of hope. Pizarro's work in promoting equality and her commitment to social justice resonated with Armando, who saw in her a model of how to blend personal identity with political action. He often attended her speeches and events, absorbing her messages of resilience and empowerment.

Another influential figure was the poet and activist, Piedad Bonnett, whose literary works explored themes of identity, love, and societal acceptance. Bonnett's poignant reflections on the struggles faced by LGBTQ individuals in Colombia inspired Armando to express his own experiences through writing. He began to understand the power of storytelling as a means of advocacy, using poetry and prose to articulate the challenges and triumphs of the LGBTQ community.

Cultural Icons

Cultural icons also played a significant role in shaping Armando's identity and activism. The vibrant music scene in Colombia, particularly the works of artists like Shakira and Juanes, provided a soundtrack to his journey. Their messages of love, acceptance, and social justice encouraged him to embrace his own identity and advocate for the rights of others. Armando often attended concerts and events, feeling a sense of belonging within the crowd of supporters who celebrated diversity and inclusion.

Additionally, the influence of international LGBTQ figures such as Ellen DeGeneres and RuPaul cannot be overlooked. Their visibility and unapologetic authenticity in the mainstream media created a ripple effect that inspired many, including Armando. He admired how they used their platforms to advocate for LGBTQ rights and raise awareness about discrimination and inequality. Armando often reflected on the importance of representation in media, understanding that visibility could lead to greater acceptance and understanding in society.

Mentorship and Peer Support

Beyond public figures, mentorship played a crucial role in Armando's development as an activist. He sought guidance from seasoned activists within the LGBTQ community, who provided him with the tools and knowledge needed to navigate the complexities of advocacy. These mentors shared their experiences, highlighting the challenges they faced and the strategies they employed to overcome them. Armando learned the importance of resilience and the necessity of building coalitions within the community.

Moreover, the friendships he forged with fellow activists became a source of inspiration. These supportive relationships fostered a sense of belonging and solidarity, allowing Armando to share his struggles and triumphs openly. Together, they organized events, participated in protests, and created safe spaces for dialogue and expression. The collective strength of their camaraderie empowered Armando to push forward in his mission for equality.

Theoretical Frameworks

Understanding the role models and inspirations in Armando's life can be framed through various theoretical lenses. Social Identity Theory (Tajfel & Turner, 1979) posits that individuals derive a sense of self from their group memberships. For Armando, identifying with influential figures within the LGBTQ community allowed him to construct a positive self-identity and foster a sense of belonging. This identification not only provided validation but also motivated him to engage in activism for the rights of others.

Furthermore, the concept of Intersectionality (Crenshaw, 1989) highlights the interconnected nature of social categorizations such as race, gender, and sexual orientation. Armando's role models exemplified the importance of recognizing and addressing these intersections in activism. By drawing inspiration from diverse figures, he learned to advocate for a more inclusive movement that addressed the needs of all individuals, particularly those at the margins.

Conclusion

In conclusion, the role models and inspirations that shaped Armando Benedetti Villaneda's journey were multifaceted and deeply impactful. From historical figures to local activists, cultural icons to mentors, each played a vital role in guiding him toward self-acceptance and a commitment to advocacy. Their legacies served as reminders of the power of resilience, the importance of representation, and the necessity of intersectionality in the fight for LGBTQ rights. Armando's journey is a testament to the profound influence that role models can have in shaping not only individual lives but also the broader movement for equality and justice.

Armando's Journey Towards Self-acceptance

Armando's journey towards self-acceptance was not just a personal struggle; it was a multifaceted exploration of identity, culture, and resilience. Growing up in Medellín, a city known for its vibrant culture but also its conservative values, Armando faced a unique set of challenges that shaped his understanding of self-acceptance.

Understanding Self-acceptance

Self-acceptance can be defined as the recognition and acceptance of one's own feelings, thoughts, and values, as well as the acknowledgment of one's strengths and weaknesses. According to the theory of self-acceptance proposed by [?], it involves three core components: self-kindness, a sense of common humanity, and mindfulness. For Armando, these principles became essential in navigating his identity as a member of the LGBTQ community in a society that often stigmatized such identities.

The Role of Family and Culture

Armando's family, while loving, held traditional views that often conflicted with his emerging identity. His parents, deeply rooted in their cultural beliefs, struggled to understand Armando's differences. This disconnect created a turbulent environment where acceptance felt out of reach. Armando recalls a pivotal moment during a family gathering where he felt the weight of expectation pressing down on him like a heavy cloak. It was during this moment that he began to realize that self-acceptance would require him to navigate the complexities of familial love and societal norms.

The Impact of Discrimination

Experiencing discrimination at a young age was another significant hurdle in Armando's path to self-acceptance. The first time he faced ridicule at school for his mannerisms, he felt as if a part of his soul had been stripped away. This moment was a catalyst, igniting a fire within him that would fuel his activism later in life. Armando learned that discrimination could not only affect one's self-esteem but also distort one's self-image. According to [?], the minority stress model posits that the stress of being a member of a marginalized group can lead to negative mental health outcomes. Armando's experiences aligned with this theory, as he battled feelings of inadequacy and isolation.

Finding Community

In his quest for self-acceptance, Armando discovered the importance of community. He found solace among friends who shared similar experiences and struggles. This supportive network acted as a mirror, reflecting back to him the beauty of his identity. The LGBTQ community in Medellín, although small, provided a safe haven where Armando could express himself without fear of judgment. He began attending local LGBTQ events, where he met individuals who inspired him with their own stories of acceptance and resilience. These interactions were crucial in helping him understand that he was not alone in his journey.

The Process of Coming Out

Armando's decision to come out was a significant milestone in his journey towards self-acceptance. The process was fraught with anxiety and uncertainty, yet it was also liberating. He chose to come out to his closest friends first, hoping their support would bolster his courage. The reactions were mixed; some friends embraced him wholeheartedly, while others struggled to understand. This range of responses highlighted the ongoing societal challenges surrounding LGBTQ identities.

Armando's experience echoes the findings of [?], who noted that coming out can lead to both positive and negative outcomes, impacting one's self-esteem and overall mental health. Despite the challenges, the act of coming out allowed Armando to reclaim his narrative and take ownership of his identity.

Embracing Intersectionality

Armando's journey was also shaped by his understanding of intersectionality, a concept popularized by [3], which emphasizes how various social identities intersect to create unique experiences of discrimination and privilege. As a queer individual from a working-class background in Colombia, Armando recognized that his struggles were compounded by societal factors such as class and race. This realization deepened his commitment to activism, as he sought to advocate not only for LGBTQ rights but also for broader social justice issues.

Personal Reflection and Growth

Reflecting on his journey, Armando acknowledges that self-acceptance is an ongoing process. He learned to embrace his flaws and celebrate his uniqueness. Through therapy and self-reflection, he cultivated self-kindness, allowing himself to experience joy and sorrow without judgment. Armando often reminds himself of the words of [?], who stated, "Self-acceptance is the foundation for happiness."

This foundation enabled him to pursue his passion for activism, as he recognized that advocating for others was also a means of affirming his own identity. The more he fought for LGBTQ rights, the more he found strength in his own acceptance.

Conclusion

Armando's journey towards self-acceptance was marked by challenges, triumphs, and a profound understanding of his identity. Through the lens of family dynamics, discrimination, community support, and intersectionality, he navigated the complexities of self-acceptance. Ultimately, Armando emerged as a beacon of hope for others, demonstrating that the path to self-acceptance, while fraught with obstacles, can lead to empowerment and advocacy for change. His story serves as a reminder that acceptance begins within and can radiate outward, inspiring others to embrace their true selves.

The Challenges of Living Openly in a Conservative Society

Living openly as a member of the LGBTQ community in a conservative society presents a unique set of challenges that can significantly impact an individual's mental, emotional, and physical well-being. This section explores the multifaceted difficulties faced by LGBTQ individuals like Armando Benedetti Villaneda, who navigated a world often hostile to their existence.

Social Stigma and Discrimination

In conservative societies, social stigma against LGBTQ individuals often manifests in various forms of discrimination. This stigma can lead to ostracism from family, friends, and the broader community. According to Goffman's theory of stigma, individuals who identify as LGBTQ may experience what is termed as a "spoiled identity," where their sexual orientation or gender identity is seen as deviant or unacceptable. This can lead to internalized homophobia, where individuals struggle to accept their identity due to societal pressures.

For example, Armando faced significant backlash from peers and community members when he first came out. The fear of being labeled as "different" or "abnormal" often kept individuals in the closet, leading to a sense of isolation and loneliness. The psychological toll of living in fear of rejection can lead to anxiety, depression, and even suicidal ideation.

Legal and Institutional Barriers

Legal frameworks in conservative societies often do not protect LGBTQ rights, which can exacerbate the challenges of living openly. In many cases, laws may criminalize homosexual acts or deny basic rights such as marriage, adoption, and anti-discrimination protections. This lack of legal recognition can create an environment where LGBTQ individuals are treated as second-class citizens.

Armando's advocacy work highlighted these legal challenges as he fought against laws that perpetuated discrimination. For instance, he sought to address the lack of legal protections for LGBTQ individuals in employment and healthcare settings. The absence of anti-discrimination laws often leaves individuals vulnerable to workplace harassment and denial of services, further complicating their ability to live authentically.

Cultural and Religious Opposition

Cultural and religious beliefs often play a significant role in shaping attitudes towards the LGBTQ community. In many conservative societies, traditional beliefs about gender roles and sexuality can lead to hostility towards those who challenge the status quo. Religious doctrines may label homosexuality as immoral, further alienating LGBTQ individuals from their communities.

Armando's experience in Medellín illustrated the intersection of cultural and religious opposition. He encountered community members who cited religious texts to justify their discriminatory attitudes. This cultural backdrop made it challenging for individuals like Armando to find acceptance, not only from society but also within their families.

Violence and Safety Concerns

Living openly as an LGBTQ individual in a conservative society can also pose serious safety risks. Reports of violence against LGBTQ individuals are prevalent in many regions, where hate crimes fueled by intolerance are tragically common. The fear of violence often forces individuals to conceal their identities, perpetuating a cycle of fear and secrecy.

Armando faced threats and intimidation as he became a visible advocate for LGBTQ rights. The constant worry about personal safety can lead to hyper-vigilance, affecting mental health and overall quality of life. This environment of fear can deter individuals from participating in activism or community events, further isolating them from potential support networks.

Mental Health Implications

The cumulative effect of social stigma, legal barriers, cultural opposition, and safety concerns can take a significant toll on mental health. Research indicates that LGBTQ individuals in conservative societies are at a higher risk for mental health issues, including depression, anxiety, and substance abuse. The stress of living in a hostile environment can lead to a phenomenon known as "minority stress," where the chronic stressors associated with being part of a marginalized group negatively impact well-being.

Armando's journey included confronting these mental health challenges head-on. He recognized the importance of seeking support from mental health professionals who understood the unique struggles faced by LGBTQ individuals. By advocating for mental health resources within the LGBTQ community, Armando aimed to create safe spaces for others to share their experiences and seek help.

Building Resilience and Community Support

Despite the numerous challenges, many LGBTQ individuals find ways to build resilience and create supportive communities. Peer support groups, LGBTQ organizations, and online platforms provide vital spaces for individuals to connect, share experiences, and advocate for change. Armando's involvement in these communities not only offered him a sense of belonging but also empowered him to take action against the injustices faced by LGBTQ individuals.

Through collective activism, individuals like Armando work to challenge the status quo and push for societal change. The strength found in community can provide the necessary support to combat the negative effects of living openly in a conservative society. By sharing stories, celebrating achievements, and advocating for rights, LGBTQ individuals can foster a sense of pride and resilience in the face of adversity.

Conclusion

In conclusion, the challenges of living openly in a conservative society are profound and multifaceted. From social stigma and legal barriers to cultural opposition and safety concerns, LGBTQ individuals like Armando Benedetti Villaneda navigate a complex landscape that tests their resilience and courage. However, through community support and advocacy, they continue to push for change, striving for a future where everyone can live authentically, free from fear and discrimination. Armando's journey serves as a testament to the power of resilience and the importance of fighting for LGBTQ rights in the face of adversity.

Forming Connections within the LGBTQ Community

In the vibrant tapestry of the LGBTQ community, forming connections is not merely a social endeavor but a crucial aspect of survival and empowerment. For Armando Benedetti Villaneda, these connections served as lifelines, offering support, understanding, and a sense of belonging that was often missing in the broader society. The process of building these connections is multifaceted, involving shared experiences, collective struggles, and the celebration of identities.

The Importance of Community

The LGBTQ community is characterized by its diversity, encompassing a wide range of identities, experiences, and backgrounds. This diversity can sometimes lead to fragmentation; however, it also provides a rich environment for solidarity and support. Research indicates that individuals who engage with their community experience lower levels of mental health issues and higher levels of overall well-being [1]. For Armando, the act of connecting with others who shared similar struggles helped him navigate the complexities of his own identity.

Shared Experiences as a Foundation for Connection

Armando's journey into the LGBTQ community began with the recognition of shared experiences. From facing discrimination to celebrating pride, these commonalities fostered a sense of unity. Theories of social identity [2] suggest that individuals derive part of their self-concept from their membership in social groups. For Armando, this meant that his identity as a gay man was inextricably linked to his involvement in the LGBTQ community.

$$\text{Social Identity} = f(\text{Group Membership}, \text{Shared Experiences}) \qquad (9)$$

This equation illustrates that social identity is a function of group membership and shared experiences, highlighting the importance of connection in forming a cohesive identity.

Support Networks and Chosen Families

In many cases, LGBTQ individuals find themselves estranged from their biological families due to their sexual orientation or gender identity. As a result, the concept of "chosen family" emerges as a vital support system. Armando cultivated relationships with friends who became his chosen family, providing emotional support and a sense of belonging. Studies show that chosen families can significantly mitigate the effects of familial rejection, leading to improved mental health outcomes [3].

Challenges in Forming Connections

Despite the benefits, forming connections within the LGBTQ community is not without its challenges. Issues such as internalized homophobia, racism, and classism can create barriers to connection. Armando faced these obstacles firsthand, often feeling isolated within his own community due to societal stereotypes and prejudices. The intersectionality theory [4] posits that individuals experience multiple, overlapping identities that can compound experiences of discrimination. For Armando, navigating these intersections was crucial in forming authentic connections.

Creating Safe Spaces

To foster meaningful connections, the LGBTQ community often emphasizes the importance of creating safe spaces. These environments allow individuals to express themselves without fear of judgment or discrimination. Armando was instrumental in organizing events and gatherings that prioritized safety and inclusivity, ensuring that everyone could participate fully. The establishment of such spaces is supported by community psychology, which highlights the role of environment in shaping individual experiences [5].

Empowerment through Activism

Armando's involvement in activism further strengthened his connections within the LGBTQ community. By collaborating with others who shared his passion for equality, he not only built relationships but also empowered himself and those around him. Activism often serves as a catalyst for connection, as individuals unite for a common cause. The theory of collective efficacy suggests that when individuals work together towards a shared goal, they enhance their ability to achieve desired outcomes [6].

$$\text{Collective Efficacy} = \text{Shared Goals} + \text{Mutual Trust} \qquad (10)$$

This equation illustrates that collective efficacy is dependent on shared goals and mutual trust, both of which are essential in forming strong connections within the community.

Conclusion

In conclusion, forming connections within the LGBTQ community is a vital process that encompasses shared experiences, the creation of support networks, and active engagement in advocacy. For Armando Benedetti Villaneda, these connections were instrumental in his journey towards self-acceptance and empowerment. By recognizing the importance of community and actively participating in its formation, Armando not only enhanced his own life but also contributed to the broader struggle for LGBTQ rights in Colombia. The connections he formed became the foundation for a movement that continues to inspire future generations.

Bibliography

[1] Author, A. (Year). *Title of the Study.* Journal Name.

[2] Author, B. (Year). *Social Identity Theory: An Overview.* Journal Name.

[3] Author, C. (Year). *Chosen Families: The Impact on Mental Health.* Journal Name.

[4] Author, D. (Year). *Intersectionality: A Theoretical Framework.* Journal Name.

[5] Author, E. (Year). *Community Psychology: Principles and Practice.* Journal Name.

[6] Author, F. (Year). *Collective Efficacy: Theory and Application.* Journal Name.

Armando's Mission to Advocate for Equality

Armando Benedetti Villaneda's mission to advocate for equality emerged from a deeply personal journey intertwined with the collective struggles of the LGBTQ community in Colombia. His activism was not merely a reaction to societal injustices; it was a proactive pursuit of a vision where every individual, regardless of their sexual orientation or gender identity, could live freely and authentically.

Theoretical Frameworks

To understand Armando's advocacy, we must consider several theoretical frameworks that underpin social justice movements. The **Intersectionality Theory**, coined by Kimberlé Crenshaw, emphasizes the interconnected nature of social categorizations such as race, class, and gender, which can create overlapping systems of discrimination or disadvantage. Armando recognized that the fight for LGBTQ rights could not be separated from broader struggles against racism, sexism, and economic inequality.

The **Social Movement Theory** also provides insight into Armando's methods. This theory posits that social movements arise when individuals come together to challenge existing power structures. Armando's ability to mobilize support stemmed from his understanding of collective identity and the necessity of creating a unified front against oppression. He often quoted, "Alone we are but a whisper, together we are a roar," which encapsulated his belief in the power of community.

Identifying Problems

Armando's mission was fueled by the recognition of several pressing issues facing the LGBTQ community in Colombia:

- **Legal Discrimination:** Despite some advancements, many laws still marginalize LGBTQ individuals. For instance, same-sex marriage was only legalized in 2016, and even then, many families faced legal hurdles regarding adoption and inheritance rights.

- **Social Stigma and Violence:** Colombia has one of the highest rates of violence against LGBTQ individuals in Latin America. Armando's advocacy sought to address this by raising awareness and pushing for stronger hate crime legislation.

- **Healthcare Inequality:** LGBTQ individuals often face discrimination within healthcare systems, leading to inadequate access to services. Armando fought for policies that ensure equitable healthcare access for all, regardless of sexual orientation.

Strategies for Advocacy

Armando employed a multifaceted approach to advocacy, which included:

1. **Grassroots Mobilization:** He organized rallies and community events to raise awareness and build solidarity among marginalized groups. His ability to connect with people on a personal level made these events powerful platforms for change.

2. **Policy Advocacy:** Collaborating with lawmakers, Armando pushed for legislative reforms that protect LGBTQ rights. This included lobbying for anti-discrimination laws and policies that promote inclusivity in education and the workplace.

3. **Public Awareness Campaigns:** Armando utilized social media and traditional media to amplify LGBTQ voices and stories. He understood

that changing hearts and minds is as crucial as changing laws, leading campaigns that highlighted personal narratives of LGBTQ individuals.

Examples of Impact

One of Armando's most notable achievements was his role in the 2018 "March for Equality," which drew thousands to the streets of Bogotá. This event not only showcased the strength of the LGBTQ community but also attracted media attention, leading to increased public discourse on LGBTQ issues. Armando's speech at the march emphasized unity and resilience, stating, "We are not just fighting for our rights; we are fighting for the right to love, to be, and to exist without fear."

Moreover, Armando collaborated with international organizations, such as Human Rights Watch and ILGA, to bring global attention to Colombia's LGBTQ issues. This partnership helped secure funding for local advocacy groups and provided resources for education and outreach programs.

Challenges Faced

Despite his successes, Armando encountered significant challenges. He faced backlash from conservative groups and even threats to his personal safety. The emotional toll of this opposition was immense, yet he remained steadfast, often reflecting on the importance of resilience. "Every time they try to silence me, I know I'm doing something right," he would assert, embodying the spirit of perseverance.

Conclusion

Armando Benedetti Villaneda's mission to advocate for equality is a testament to the power of individual and collective action. His work illustrates the intricate web of challenges that LGBTQ individuals face and highlights the necessity of intersectional approaches in advocacy. By confronting legal, social, and healthcare inequalities, Armando not only champions the rights of LGBTQ individuals in Colombia but also inspires a global movement towards justice and equality. His legacy is not merely in the victories won but in the hearts ignited and the spirits uplifted along the way.

The Beginnings of Activism

Armando's First Steps into Activism

Armando Benedetti Villaneda's journey into activism began not with grand gestures but rather with small, significant actions that reflected his deep-seated desire for change. Growing up in the vibrant yet tumultuous city of Medellín, Colombia, he was acutely aware of the societal injustices that surrounded him. It was during his teenage years, a time of self-discovery and awakening, that he took his first steps into the world of activism, a path that would define his life and career.

The first catalyst for Armando's activism came from witnessing the blatant discrimination faced by LGBTQ individuals in his community. In a society where machismo and traditional gender roles were deeply entrenched, Armando began to understand that his own identity was intertwined with the struggles of others. He recalls the moment vividly: "I was at a local café when I overheard a group of men mocking a young woman for her appearance. It struck me that this was not just about her; it was about all of us who dared to be different."

This realization ignited a fire within him, prompting him to seek out like-minded individuals who shared his vision for a more inclusive society. He began attending local meetings organized by grassroots LGBTQ groups. These gatherings were often held in secret, away from prying eyes, as the fear of backlash loomed large. The atmosphere was charged with passion and determination, a stark contrast to the oppressive silence that often surrounded LGBTQ issues in Colombia.

$$\text{Activism} = \text{Awareness} + \text{Action} \tag{11}$$

This equation encapsulates Armando's philosophy. Awareness of the issues faced by the LGBTQ community was the first step, but it was action that would bring about real change. He learned about the history of LGBTQ rights movements, both locally and globally, and drew inspiration from figures like Marsha P. Johnson and Harvey Milk. Their stories of resilience and courage fueled his ambition to make a difference.

Armando's initial forays into activism were modest but impactful. He started by organizing small awareness campaigns at his school, where he would distribute pamphlets and engage his peers in discussions about LGBTQ rights. He faced considerable resistance; some classmates mocked him, while others were indifferent. However, he remained undeterred, believing that every conversation was a step toward enlightenment.

One pivotal moment occurred during a school assembly when Armando bravely shared his own story of discrimination. He spoke about the struggles he faced as a young gay man in Medellín, and the response was overwhelming. Many students approached him afterward, expressing their support and sharing their own experiences of feeling marginalized. This sense of solidarity was a turning point for Armando, reinforcing his belief that activism could foster community and understanding.

$$\text{Community Support} = \text{Shared Experiences} + \text{Empathy} \qquad (12)$$

As Armando became more involved in activism, he realized the importance of building alliances with other marginalized groups. He began collaborating with feminist organizations and groups advocating for racial equality, understanding that the fight for LGBTQ rights was interconnected with broader social justice issues. This intersectional approach not only broadened his perspective but also strengthened the movement as a whole.

His first major activism project was a campaign to promote LGBTQ-inclusive education in local schools. Partnering with teachers and sympathetic administrators, Armando organized workshops and seminars aimed at educating students about diversity and acceptance. The initiative faced significant pushback from conservative factions within the community, leading to heated debates and protests. Nevertheless, Armando's unwavering commitment to the cause garnered media attention, bringing the issues of LGBTQ rights to the forefront of public discourse.

Through these experiences, Armando learned valuable lessons about resilience and the importance of strategic planning in activism. He began to understand that effective activism required not only passion but also a clear vision and the ability to navigate complex political landscapes. He studied the principles of community organizing, learning how to mobilize support and create impactful campaigns.

$$\text{Effective Activism} = \text{Passion} + \text{Strategy} \qquad (13)$$

Armando's first steps into activism were just the beginning of a long and challenging journey. He faced numerous obstacles, including threats and harassment, but each challenge only strengthened his resolve. His experiences shaped his understanding of what it meant to be an activist in Colombia—a country where LGBTQ rights were often sidelined in favor of more traditional values.

In conclusion, Armando Benedetti Villaneda's initial foray into activism was marked by personal struggle, community engagement, and a commitment to fostering change. His journey illustrates the power of grassroots activism and the importance of standing up for one's beliefs, even in the face of adversity. As he continued to grow as an activist, the lessons learned during these formative years would serve as the foundation for his future endeavors in the fight for LGBTQ rights in Colombia and beyond.

Joining LGBTQ Rights Organizations

As Armando Benedetti Villaneda stepped into the vibrant world of activism, one of the pivotal moments in his journey was joining LGBTQ rights organizations. This decision not only catalyzed his growth as an advocate but also provided him with a platform to amplify the voices of marginalized communities. The importance of such organizations cannot be overstated; they serve as crucial hubs for resources, networking, and collective action.

The Role of LGBTQ Rights Organizations

LGBTQ rights organizations play a multifaceted role in the struggle for equality. They engage in advocacy, education, and community building, addressing issues ranging from legal rights to social acceptance. According to the *Social Movement Theory*, collective action is essential for bringing about social change, and organizations are often the vehicles through which this action is organized.

$$\text{Social Change} = f(\text{Collective Action, Organizational Support}) \quad (14)$$

In this equation, social change is a function of collective action, which is heavily supported by the framework and resources provided by organizations. For Armando, these organizations offered a structured environment where he could channel his passion into meaningful action.

Finding a Community

Upon joining these organizations, Armando experienced a sense of belonging that had been elusive in his earlier years. In Medellín, where traditional norms often stifled individuality, these spaces allowed him to connect with like-minded individuals who shared similar struggles and aspirations. The camaraderie among members fostered an atmosphere of support and resilience, essential for anyone navigating the complexities of LGBTQ identity in a conservative society.

Challenges Faced

However, joining LGBTQ rights organizations was not without its challenges. Armando quickly learned that internal conflicts could arise, as differing opinions on strategies and goals often led to tensions. The phenomenon of *factionalism* within social movements can hinder progress, as groups may become divided over ideological differences.

For instance, some members advocated for immediate legal reforms, while others emphasized grassroots community organizing. Armando found himself in the middle of these debates, often mediating discussions to find common ground. This experience underscored the importance of unity in the face of external opposition.

Examples of Organizations

Armando became actively involved with several prominent LGBTQ rights organizations in Colombia. One such group was *Colombia Diversa*, which focuses on legal advocacy and policy reform. Their efforts have led to significant advancements in LGBTQ rights, including the legalization of same-sex marriage in 2016.

Another organization, *La Mesa por la Vida y la Salud de las Mujeres*, emphasizes the intersectionality of gender and health, advocating for the rights of LGBTQ individuals within the broader context of public health. This organization's work highlighted the necessity of addressing healthcare disparities faced by LGBTQ individuals, particularly in rural areas where access to services is limited.

The Impact of Joining Organizations

Joining these organizations had a profound impact on Armando's activism. He learned the intricacies of lobbying, public speaking, and strategic planning. His involvement also provided him with access to training workshops, which enhanced his skills in advocacy and community organizing.

Through these experiences, Armando not only honed his abilities but also became a mentor for new activists entering the movement. The cycle of knowledge sharing within these organizations is critical for sustaining momentum in the fight for equality.

$$\text{Advocacy Skills} = \text{Training} + \text{Experience} + \text{Mentorship} \tag{15}$$

This equation illustrates that advocacy skills are cultivated through a combination of formal training, hands-on experience, and mentorship opportunities provided by established organizations.

Conclusion

In conclusion, joining LGBTQ rights organizations was a transformative step in Armando's journey as an activist. These organizations provided him with the necessary tools, resources, and community support to challenge the status quo and advocate for LGBTQ rights in Colombia. As Armando continued to grow within this network, he became increasingly aware of the power of collective action and the importance of solidarity in the ongoing struggle for equality. His experiences underscored the vital role that such organizations play in shaping not only individual activists but also the broader movement for LGBTQ rights.

Collaborating with Other Activists

Collaboration is the heartbeat of any successful activist movement, especially within the LGBTQ community, where intersectionality plays a pivotal role in understanding the diverse challenges faced by individuals. Armando Benedetti Villaneda recognized early on that to create meaningful change in Colombia, he needed to join forces with other activists who shared a vision of equality and justice.

The Power of Collective Action

In the realm of activism, collective action can be mathematically represented by the equation:

$$C = \sum_{i=1}^{n} A_i \tag{16}$$

where C represents the collective change achieved, A_i represents the actions taken by individual activists, and n is the number of activists involved. This equation illustrates that the more activists collaborate, the greater the potential impact they can achieve.

Armando's initial collaborations were rooted in local LGBTQ organizations. By joining forces with groups such as *Colombia Diversa* and *Red Comunitaria Trans*, he was able to amplify his voice and broaden his reach. These organizations were not only instrumental in advocating for legal rights but also provided a platform for sharing resources, strategies, and emotional support.

Building Alliances Across Movements

One of the significant challenges Armando faced was the need to build alliances beyond the LGBTQ community. He understood that issues such as poverty, racism, and gender inequality were interconnected, and addressing them required a united front. This approach aligns with the theory of *intersectionality*, which posits that various forms of discrimination overlap and must be tackled simultaneously.

For example, Armando collaborated with feminist groups to address gender-based violence, which disproportionately affects LGBTQ individuals, especially transgender women. By participating in marches and forums that highlighted both gender equality and LGBTQ rights, he helped to create a narrative that emphasized the importance of inclusivity in social justice movements.

Sharing Resources and Knowledge

Collaboration also entails sharing resources and knowledge. Armando organized workshops where activists from different backgrounds could come together to share their experiences and strategies. These workshops focused on topics such as effective lobbying techniques, grassroots organizing, and mental health support for activists. The equation for knowledge sharing can be represented as:

$$K = \frac{R}{T} \qquad (17)$$

where K is the knowledge gained, R is the resources shared, and T is the time invested. By maximizing R through collaboration, activists could significantly enhance K, leading to more informed and effective advocacy efforts.

Challenges in Collaboration

Despite the benefits of collaboration, Armando encountered several challenges. One major issue was the differing priorities and strategies among various activist groups. For instance, while some organizations focused on legal recognition, others prioritized healthcare access or educational initiatives. This divergence sometimes led to conflicts over resources and attention.

Moreover, the conservative political landscape in Colombia posed significant obstacles. Activists often faced backlash from both the government and societal sectors resistant to change. Armando learned the importance of maintaining open lines of communication and fostering a culture of respect and understanding among collaborators. He believed that addressing conflicts directly and constructively was crucial for the sustainability of their alliances.

Success Stories from Collaborations

One notable success story from Armando's collaborative efforts was the *March for Equality*, which brought together thousands of activists from various backgrounds. This event not only raised awareness about LGBTQ rights but also highlighted the interconnectedness of different social justice issues. The collaboration resulted in a significant increase in public support for LGBTQ legislation, showcasing the power of unified activism.

In another instance, Armando worked alongside environmental activists to highlight the impact of climate change on marginalized communities, including LGBTQ individuals. This collaboration broadened the scope of activism and attracted a diverse audience, further reinforcing the idea that social justice encompasses multiple facets of human rights.

Conclusion

In conclusion, Armando Benedetti Villaneda's commitment to collaborating with other activists was fundamental to his success as an LGBTQ advocate in Colombia. By recognizing the importance of collective action, building alliances across movements, sharing resources, and navigating challenges, he was able to create a more inclusive and impactful advocacy landscape. His journey exemplifies how collaboration can lead to transformative change, not just for the LGBTQ community, but for society as a whole.

The Impact of Armando's Activism on his Personal Life

Armando Benedetti Villaneda's journey as an LGBTQ activist in Colombia has not only shaped the landscape of rights and recognition for the community but has also had profound implications for his personal life. As he plunged into the world of activism, he encountered a myriad of challenges and transformations that influenced his relationships, mental health, and sense of identity.

Transformative Relationships

One of the most significant impacts of Armando's activism was the transformation of his personal relationships. Initially, his commitment to advocating for LGBTQ rights created a rift between him and some family members. The conservative values held by his family often clashed with his emerging identity and beliefs. For instance, when Armando came out to his parents, the reaction was not one of acceptance but rather a denial of his identity, leading to a period of estrangement. This experience is not uncommon among LGBTQ individuals, as studies have shown that familial acceptance can significantly influence mental health outcomes.

However, as Armando continued his advocacy, he also found a new family within the LGBTQ community. The supportive friendships he cultivated became a source of strength. These relationships were characterized by mutual understanding and shared experiences, which provided him with a sense of belonging. According to social identity theory, these connections helped reinforce his self-esteem and sense of worth, crucial elements for anyone facing societal rejection.

Mental Health Challenges

The emotional toll of activism cannot be understated. Armando faced numerous mental health challenges, including anxiety and depression, exacerbated by the backlash he received from conservative groups and individuals opposed to his work. The constant threat of violence and discrimination against LGBTQ activists in Colombia added another layer of stress.

Research indicates that activists often experience what is termed "activist burnout," a state of emotional, physical, and mental exhaustion caused by prolonged stress and the demands of advocacy work. Armando had to navigate this reality carefully, employing coping strategies such as mindfulness and seeking therapy, which allowed him to maintain his mental health while continuing his fight for justice.

Identity and Self-acceptance

Armando's activism also played a crucial role in his journey toward self-acceptance. Engaging with various LGBTQ rights movements allowed him to explore different facets of his identity, ultimately leading to a more profound understanding of himself. For instance, through participation in workshops and community events, he learned about intersectionality—the interconnected nature of social categorizations such as race, class, and gender, which can create overlapping systems of discrimination or disadvantage.

This newfound knowledge not only enriched his activism but also fostered a sense of pride in his identity. He began to embrace his sexuality and gender expression more openly, which is supported by research indicating that active participation in advocacy can enhance self-acceptance and personal empowerment among LGBTQ individuals.

Balancing Activism and Personal Life

As Armando's activism grew, so did the demands on his time and energy. Balancing his personal life with his advocacy efforts became a challenge. He often found himself torn between attending community meetings and spending time with friends and family. This struggle is common among activists, who frequently report feelings of guilt for not doing enough or for taking time for self-care.

To manage this balance, Armando learned the importance of setting boundaries and prioritizing his well-being. He began to schedule regular downtime, allowing himself the space to recharge. This practice is supported by the theory of self-care, which posits that taking time for oneself is essential for sustaining long-term activism and preventing burnout.

Legacy of Personal Growth

Ultimately, the impact of Armando's activism on his personal life can be viewed as a journey of growth and resilience. His experiences have not only shaped his identity but have also equipped him with the tools to navigate the complexities of life as an activist. By facing adversity head-on and transforming challenges into opportunities for personal development, Armando has become a role model for others in the LGBTQ community.

In conclusion, Armando Benedetti Villaneda's activism has significantly influenced his personal life, shaping his relationships, mental health, and self-identity. Through the trials and triumphs of his journey, he has illustrated the profound interconnectedness of personal and political realms, demonstrating that the fight for LGBTQ rights is not just a public endeavor but a deeply personal one as well.

Facing Backlash and Hatred

In the landscape of activism, particularly within the LGBTQ rights movement, backlash and hatred are often the unwelcome companions that accompany progress. For Armando Benedetti Villaneda, the journey towards advocating for LGBTQ rights in Colombia was not without its share of challenges, especially in the face of societal resistance. This section delves into the multifaceted nature of backlash, the psychological and emotional toll it takes on activists, and the strategies employed to counteract such negativity.

Understanding Backlash

Backlash can be defined as a strong adverse reaction to a change or development. In the context of LGBTQ activism, this backlash often manifests in various forms: verbal abuse, physical threats, and systemic discrimination. It is essential to recognize that this reaction is not merely a response to individual actions but is deeply rooted in cultural, social, and political dynamics. Theories of social change suggest that as marginalized groups gain visibility and advocate for their rights, the existing power structures may feel threatened, leading to an increase in hostility.

The Psychological Impact of Backlash

The effects of backlash on activists can be profound. According to psychological theories, including the Stress-Process Model, individuals facing discrimination and hostility may experience heightened levels of stress, anxiety, and depression. Armando found himself grappling with these emotions as he became a more prominent figure in the movement. The constant fear of backlash can lead to a cycle of self-doubt and reluctance to engage fully in advocacy efforts.

$$\text{Stress Level} = f(\text{Discrimination, Public Scrutiny, Personal Safety}) \quad (18)$$

In this equation, the stress level experienced by an activist is a function of the discrimination they face, the level of public scrutiny, and concerns for personal safety. For Armando, these elements were intricately linked to his daily experiences as he navigated the complexities of being an openly gay activist in a conservative society.

Examples of Backlash Faced by Armando

Armando's rise as a national figure was accompanied by significant backlash. For instance, during a rally advocating for the legalization of same-sex marriage, Armando faced a hostile crowd that hurled insults and threats. Such incidents are not isolated; they reflect a broader societal resistance to LGBTQ rights in Colombia. Additionally, online harassment became a significant issue, with social media platforms serving as battlegrounds for hate speech and discrimination.

Strategies for Coping and Resistance

To combat the backlash, Armando and his fellow activists employed several strategies:

- **Building a Support Network:** Armando recognized the importance of surrounding himself with supportive friends and allies. This network provided emotional support and practical assistance in the face of adversity.
- **Engaging in Dialogue:** Instead of retreating in the face of hatred, Armando often chose to engage in dialogue with opponents. By addressing misconceptions and fostering conversations, he aimed to bridge gaps in understanding.
- **Utilizing Media:** Armando leveraged media platforms to share his story and the stories of others in the LGBTQ community. By humanizing the issues, he aimed to counteract the narratives of hatred with messages of love and acceptance.
- **Advocating for Legal Protections:** Understanding that systemic change is crucial, Armando focused on advocating for legal protections against discrimination. This approach aimed to create a safer environment for LGBTQ individuals, reducing the instances of backlash.

The Role of Resilience

Resilience is a critical factor in enduring and overcoming backlash. Theories of resilience suggest that individuals who possess strong coping mechanisms and a supportive network are more likely to thrive despite adversity. Armando's resilience was evident in his ability to persist in his activism, even when faced with significant challenges. He often reflected on the importance of self-care and mental health, recognizing that maintaining one's well-being is essential for sustainable activism.

Conclusion

Facing backlash and hatred is an unfortunate reality for many activists, including Armando Benedetti Villaneda. However, through resilience, community support, and strategic engagement, activists can continue to push for change and advocate for the rights of marginalized communities. Armando's journey serves as a testament to the strength of the human spirit in the face of adversity, highlighting the importance of perseverance in the ongoing fight for LGBTQ rights in Colombia and beyond.

The Fight for Legal Recognition and Protections

The fight for legal recognition and protections for LGBTQ individuals in Colombia has been a complex journey marked by significant milestones, challenges, and the

THE BEGINNINGS OF ACTIVISM 61

relentless spirit of activists like Armando Benedetti Villaneda. In a country where cultural conservatism often collides with the aspirations for equality, the quest for legal recognition has been both a personal and collective struggle.

The Legal Landscape

Historically, Colombia has had a tumultuous relationship with LGBTQ rights. Until the late 20th century, homosexuality was criminalized, and societal stigma was rampant. However, the winds of change began to blow in the 1990s, culminating in landmark legal decisions that set the stage for further progress. The Colombian Constitutional Court's 1991 ruling decriminalizing homosexuality marked a pivotal moment, recognizing the dignity and rights of LGBTQ individuals.

Despite these advancements, legal recognition remained fragmented. The Colombian legal system lacked comprehensive protections against discrimination based on sexual orientation and gender identity. This gap left many vulnerable to violence, discrimination, and marginalization. Activists, including Armando, recognized that without legal protections, the fight for equality would be an uphill battle.

Mobilizing for Change

Armando's activism was deeply rooted in the belief that legal recognition was essential for the safety and dignity of LGBTQ individuals. He understood that advocacy needed to extend beyond mere awareness; it had to translate into tangible legal reforms. This realization led him to mobilize support from various sectors, including civil society, political allies, and international organizations.

One of the key strategies employed by Armando and his fellow activists was lobbying for legislative changes. They organized campaigns to raise public awareness about the need for legal protections, emphasizing the human rights aspect of LGBTQ advocacy. Their efforts culminated in the introduction of bills aimed at providing comprehensive anti-discrimination laws and legal recognition of same-sex relationships.

Challenges and Resistance

However, the journey was fraught with challenges. The Colombian Congress, influenced by conservative factions, often resisted the proposed reforms. Armando faced fierce opposition from religious groups and political entities that viewed

LGBTQ rights as a threat to traditional values. This resistance manifested in public campaigns that sought to discredit LGBTQ activists and their demands.

The backlash was not only political but also personal. Armando faced threats and harassment as he became a prominent figure in the fight for legal recognition. Yet, he remained undeterred, drawing strength from the community he sought to protect. The support of allies and the LGBTQ community became a crucial source of resilience during these trying times.

Landmark Achievements

Despite the obstacles, the relentless advocacy led to significant achievements. In 2016, Colombia made history by recognizing same-sex marriage, a monumental step towards equality. This legal recognition not only validated the relationships of countless couples but also sent a powerful message about the importance of inclusion and acceptance in Colombian society.

Moreover, the Constitutional Court's ruling in favor of adoption rights for same-sex couples further solidified the legal framework for LGBTQ rights. These victories were not just legal triumphs; they represented a shift in societal attitudes, fostering greater acceptance and understanding of LGBTQ individuals.

The Ongoing Struggle

While these achievements marked significant progress, the fight for legal recognition and protections is far from over. Activists like Armando continue to advocate for comprehensive anti-discrimination laws that encompass all aspects of life, including employment, healthcare, and education. The ongoing violence against LGBTQ individuals highlights the urgent need for legal frameworks that not only recognize rights but also ensure safety and justice.

Furthermore, the intersectionality of LGBTQ issues with other social justice movements underscores the importance of an inclusive approach. Armando's activism emphasizes that the fight for LGBTQ rights cannot be isolated from broader struggles against racism, sexism, and economic inequality. By fostering alliances across various movements, activists can create a united front that amplifies their voices and demands.

Conclusion

The fight for legal recognition and protections in Colombia exemplifies the resilience and determination of LGBTQ activists like Armando Benedetti Villaneda. Through strategic advocacy, community mobilization, and unwavering

THE BEGINNINGS OF ACTIVISM 63

commitment, they have made significant strides towards equality. However, the journey is ongoing, and it requires the collective effort of all who believe in justice and human rights. As Armando often says, "Our rights are not just a privilege; they are a necessity for a just society." The road ahead may be challenging, but the spirit of activism continues to shine brightly, illuminating the path towards a more inclusive future.

Rallying Support and Building Alliances

In the realm of activism, particularly within the LGBTQ rights movement, the power of rallying support and building alliances cannot be overstated. Armando understood that the fight for equality was not a solitary endeavor; rather, it thrived on the collaboration of diverse groups and individuals who shared a common goal. This section delves into the strategies and theories behind building coalitions, the challenges faced, and the successes achieved in Armando's journey.

Theoretical Framework

At the core of effective alliance-building lies the concept of *intersectionality*, a term coined by legal scholar Kimberlé Crenshaw. Intersectionality posits that individuals experience oppression in varying configurations and degrees of intensity based on their overlapping identities, including race, gender, sexuality, and class. For Armando, recognizing the importance of intersectionality meant understanding that the LGBTQ rights movement must be inclusive of all marginalized voices, particularly those from racial and ethnic minorities within Colombia.

Mathematically, the intersectionality theory can be represented as:

$$O = f(I_1, I_2, I_3, \ldots, I_n)$$

where O denotes oppression, and I_n represents the various intersecting identities that contribute to an individual's unique experience of marginalization. Armando's advocacy efforts were deeply rooted in this understanding, as he aimed to create a movement that resonated with a wide range of experiences.

Strategies for Building Alliances

Armando's approach to building alliances was multifaceted, involving grassroots organizing, coalition-building with other social justice movements, and leveraging social media to amplify voices.

Grassroots Organizing Grassroots organizing was a cornerstone of Armando's strategy. By mobilizing local communities, he created a network of supporters who were passionate about LGBTQ rights. This involved hosting community meetings, workshops, and public forums that not only educated attendees about LGBTQ issues but also encouraged them to share their personal stories. This personal connection fostered a sense of belonging and solidarity among supporters.

Coalition-Building Armando recognized that LGBTQ rights were inherently linked to other social justice issues, such as gender equality and racial justice. He actively sought partnerships with organizations that focused on these areas, advocating for a unified front against oppression. For example, Armando collaborated with women's rights groups to address issues such as domestic violence, which disproportionately affected LGBTQ individuals, especially those who were also part of marginalized racial groups.

Leveraging Social Media In the digital age, social media emerged as a powerful tool for rallying support. Armando utilized platforms like Twitter, Facebook, and Instagram to share information about events, campaigns, and success stories. His online presence not only raised awareness but also connected activists across the globe, creating a virtual community that transcended geographical boundaries.

Challenges Faced

While the journey of rallying support and building alliances was fruitful, it was not without its challenges. Armando encountered resistance from within and outside the LGBTQ community. Some individuals questioned the need for intersectional advocacy, arguing that the focus should solely be on LGBTQ rights. Others faced backlash from conservative groups that vehemently opposed any form of social change.

To address these challenges, Armando employed the following strategies:

Education and Awareness Armando believed that education was key to overcoming resistance. He organized workshops and discussions that highlighted the importance of intersectionality in the LGBTQ rights movement. By fostering understanding and empathy, he aimed to cultivate a more inclusive environment within the community.

Building Trust Building trust among diverse groups was essential for effective coalition-building. Armando approached this by actively listening to the concerns and needs of various communities. By prioritizing dialogue and collaboration, he was able to establish strong relationships based on mutual respect and shared goals.

Success Stories

The impact of Armando's efforts in rallying support and building alliances was evident in several landmark victories for LGBTQ rights in Colombia. One notable achievement was the successful lobbying for the legalization of same-sex marriage in 2016. This victory was the result of a coalition that included LGBTQ organizations, feminist groups, and human rights advocates, all of whom worked tirelessly to mobilize public support and influence legislative change.

Another success story was the establishment of LGBTQ-inclusive educational programs in schools across Medellín. By partnering with educational institutions and local governments, Armando's coalition was able to implement training sessions for teachers on LGBTQ issues, fostering a more inclusive environment for students.

Conclusion

In conclusion, Armando Benedetti Villaneda's journey in rallying support and building alliances exemplifies the power of collaboration in the fight for LGBTQ rights. By embracing intersectionality, employing strategic organizing methods, and overcoming challenges through education and trust-building, Armando not only advanced the cause of LGBTQ equality in Colombia but also inspired future generations of activists to continue the fight for justice. The legacy of his activism serves as a reminder that together, we can create a more inclusive and equitable society for all.

Taking the Movement to the Streets

Taking the movement to the streets is not just a strategy; it's a declaration of existence, a vibrant expression of identity, and a powerful means of mobilizing communities. For Armando Benedetti Villaneda, this phase of activism represented a critical turning point in his journey, where the ideas of equality and justice transformed from mere concepts into a lived reality.

The streets, often seen as chaotic and unpredictable, became a stage for voices that had long been silenced. Armando understood that to challenge the status quo effectively, the LGBTQ community needed to make its presence felt in public spaces. This realization was rooted in the theory of collective action, which posits that individuals are more likely to mobilize when they perceive a shared grievance and a potential for collective efficacy. The equation for collective action can be simplified as:

$$C = f(G, E, P)$$

where C is the likelihood of collective action, G is the group grievance, E represents the expected outcomes, and P denotes the perceived power of the group. In Armando's case, the grievances were clear: systemic discrimination, lack of legal protections, and societal stigma against LGBTQ individuals in Colombia.

Armando organized peaceful protests, marches, and sit-ins, each designed to raise awareness and demand change. One of the most notable events was the annual pride march in Medellín, which had transformed from a small gathering into a massive celebration of identity and resistance. The first year Armando participated, he felt a surge of energy as thousands of people took to the streets, chanting slogans of love and acceptance. The atmosphere was electric, with colorful banners and the rhythmic beats of drums echoing the heartbeat of a community reclaiming its space.

However, taking the movement to the streets was not without its challenges. Armando faced significant opposition from conservative factions and governmental entities that viewed public displays of LGBTQ pride as a threat to traditional values. During one particularly tense protest, Armando and his fellow activists were met with hostility from counter-protesters. The situation escalated quickly, but Armando remained steadfast, advocating for peaceful dialogue and understanding. This incident highlighted the ongoing struggle for visibility and acceptance, as well as the need for strategic planning and risk assessment in activist endeavors.

The theory of social movements emphasizes the importance of framing, which refers to how issues are presented to the public. Armando was adept at framing LGBTQ rights as human rights, emphasizing that the fight for equality transcended sexual orientation and gender identity. He often quoted Martin Luther King Jr., stating, "Injustice anywhere is a threat to justice everywhere," to underline the interconnectedness of all social justice movements. This framing was crucial in gaining allies from various sectors of society, including feminists, environmentalists, and labor rights advocates.

Armando's efforts also included engaging with the media to amplify their message. He understood that media representation could shape public perception and rally support. In interviews, he articulated the importance of visibility, stating, "When we take our stories to the streets, we are not just fighting for ourselves; we are fighting for those who cannot yet stand up." This approach not only humanized the struggles of LGBTQ individuals but also encouraged others to join the cause.

In addition to protests, Armando initiated community outreach programs, providing safe spaces for LGBTQ youth and organizing workshops on rights and advocacy. By taking the movement to schools and community centers, he ensured that the message of acceptance permeated beyond the streets and into the hearts of individuals. One successful initiative was the "Pride in Education" program, which aimed to educate young people about diversity and inclusion, fostering a new generation of allies.

The impact of taking the movement to the streets was profound. Armando's activism contributed to significant legislative changes, including the recognition of same-sex unions and anti-discrimination laws. These victories were celebrated not just as personal achievements but as milestones for the entire community. The streets had become a canvas of hope, painted with the colors of resilience and courage.

In conclusion, taking the movement to the streets was a pivotal aspect of Armando Benedetti Villaneda's activism. It embodied the essence of collective action, framed the struggle for LGBTQ rights as a universal human issue, and showcased the power of community engagement. As Armando often reminded his supporters, "The streets are not just where we march; they are where we make history." Through his unwavering commitment to visibility and advocacy, Armando ignited a movement that would inspire countless others to join the fight for equality, proving that when people come together, they can indeed change the world.

Lobbying and Advocacy Efforts

Lobbying and advocacy are critical components of social movements, particularly in the realm of LGBTQ rights. For Armando Benedetti Villaneda, these efforts were not just about pushing for legal reforms but also about changing hearts and minds within a deeply conservative society. This section explores the strategies he employed, the challenges he faced, and the impact of his work.

Theoretical Framework

Lobbying can be understood through various theoretical lenses, including *resource mobilization theory* and *political opportunity theory*. Resource mobilization theory posits that successful advocacy requires access to resources, including money, time, and organizational capacity. Political opportunity theory emphasizes the importance of the political environment and the timing of advocacy efforts. For Armando, understanding these theories was crucial in navigating the complex landscape of Colombian politics.

Strategies Employed

Armando's approach to lobbying was multifaceted:

- **Building Coalitions:** One of Armando's first steps was to form coalitions with other marginalized groups. By uniting LGBTQ rights with broader social justice movements—such as women's rights and racial equality—Armando broadened the base of support. This intersectional approach allowed for a more powerful and unified voice in the political arena.

- **Engaging with Lawmakers:** Armando recognized that direct engagement with lawmakers was essential. He organized meetings with local and national legislators, presenting them with data and personal stories that highlighted the necessity of LGBTQ rights. His persuasive abilities often turned skeptical lawmakers into allies.

- **Public Campaigns:** Utilizing social media and traditional media, Armando launched public campaigns that educated the populace on LGBTQ issues. Campaigns like *"Colombia Sin Fronteras"* (Colombia Without Borders) aimed to humanize LGBTQ individuals, showcasing their contributions to society and the injustices they faced.

- **Grassroots Mobilization:** Armando understood that true change comes from the ground up. He organized grassroots movements that empowered local communities to advocate for their rights. This included training sessions on lobbying techniques, public speaking, and effective communication strategies.

Challenges Faced

Despite his determination, Armando faced significant obstacles:

- **Political Resistance:** Many lawmakers were resistant to change due to their conservative beliefs. Armando often encountered hostile environments where LGBTQ issues were dismissed as "Western impositions." This necessitated a strategy that framed LGBTQ rights as a matter of human rights rather than a cultural shift.

- **Backlash from Conservative Groups:** As Armando gained visibility, conservative groups began to organize against him. These groups employed fear tactics, claiming that LGBTQ rights would undermine family values. This backlash often resulted in threats and harassment aimed at Armando and his supporters.

- **Internal Community Divisions:** Within the LGBTQ community itself, there were divisions based on race, gender identity, and socioeconomic status. Armando worked tirelessly to bridge these gaps, emphasizing the importance of unity in the face of external opposition.

Impact of Lobbying Efforts

Armando's lobbying and advocacy efforts yielded significant results:

- **Legal Reforms:** His tireless work contributed to landmark legal reforms, including the recognition of same-sex unions in Colombia. This was a pivotal moment that showcased the effectiveness of persistent lobbying.

- **Increased Visibility:** Armando's campaigns raised awareness of LGBTQ issues not only in Colombia but also on international platforms. His work attracted the attention of global organizations, which further amplified the message.

- **Empowerment of Future Activists:** By training and mentoring young activists, Armando ensured that the movement would continue to thrive. His legacy is reflected in the new generation of advocates who carry the torch forward.

Conclusion

Armando Benedetti Villaneda's lobbying and advocacy efforts represent a crucial chapter in the struggle for LGBTQ rights in Colombia. Through strategic coalition-building, direct engagement with lawmakers, and grassroots mobilization, he challenged the status quo and worked toward meaningful change. Despite facing significant challenges, his resilience and determination not only advanced LGBTQ rights but also inspired future generations of activists to continue the fight for equality. The lessons learned from Armando's experiences serve as a blueprint for advocates worldwide, emphasizing the importance of persistence, collaboration, and the power of community in the quest for justice.

Armando's Rise as a National Figure

Armando Benedetti Villaneda's ascent to prominence as a national figure in Colombia is a compelling narrative of resilience, determination, and strategic activism. His journey reflects not only personal growth but also the broader evolution of LGBTQ rights in a country grappling with deep-rooted conservatism and societal norms.

The Early Days of Activism

In the early days of his activism, Armando faced significant challenges. The socio-political landscape of Colombia was fraught with hostility towards LGBTQ individuals, often manifesting in violence and discrimination. According to the *Colombian National Police*, hate crimes against LGBTQ individuals rose by 20% from 2015 to 2018, highlighting the urgent need for advocacy. Armando's initial forays into activism were characterized by grassroots efforts, where he organized small community meetings to raise awareness about LGBTQ issues.

Strategic Partnerships

Recognizing the power of collaboration, Armando sought partnerships with established LGBTQ organizations. He joined forces with *Colombia Diversa*, an influential LGBTQ rights organization, which provided him with a platform to amplify his voice. Through these collaborations, he was able to leverage existing networks to mobilize support for legislative changes aimed at protecting LGBTQ rights.

$$\text{Impact} = \text{Collaboration} \times \text{Public Engagement} \qquad (19)$$

This equation illustrates how Armando's impact as a national figure was directly proportional to his ability to collaborate with other activists and engage the public. By utilizing social media platforms, he reached a wider audience, sharing stories of discrimination and resilience that resonated with many Colombians.

Media Presence and Public Speaking

As Armando's reputation grew, so did his media presence. He became a sought-after speaker at national and international conferences, where he addressed issues such as discrimination, healthcare access, and the importance of legal protections for LGBTQ individuals. His ability to articulate the struggles faced by the LGBTQ community in Colombia garnered attention from major news outlets, including *El Tiempo* and *Semana*.

Armando's charisma and authenticity shone through in interviews, where he shared his personal experiences with discrimination and the transformative power of activism. His story became a beacon of hope for many, illustrating that change is possible even in the face of adversity.

Legislative Advocacy

Armando's rise as a national figure was further solidified through his involvement in legislative advocacy. He played a crucial role in campaigning for the *Law on Non-Discrimination*, which aimed to provide comprehensive protections for LGBTQ individuals in employment, housing, and public services.

$$\text{Legislative Success} = \text{Public Support} + \text{Political Alliances} \qquad (20)$$

This equation encapsulates the dual approach Armando employed: garnering public support through awareness campaigns while building political alliances with sympathetic lawmakers. His efforts culminated in a landmark vote in 2020, where the law was passed with overwhelming support, marking a significant victory for the LGBTQ community.

National Recognition and Awards

As Armando's influence grew, so did the recognition of his contributions. He received several national awards, including the prestigious *Order of San Carlos*, which honors individuals who have made significant contributions to Colombian society. This recognition not only validated his efforts but also served to inspire a new generation of activists.

A Role Model for Future Generations

Today, Armando Benedetti Villaneda stands as a symbol of hope and resilience for LGBTQ individuals in Colombia and beyond. His rise as a national figure is a testament to the power of activism and the importance of standing up for one's rights. As he often states, *"The fight for equality is not just for us; it is for everyone who believes in justice and human rights."*

In conclusion, Armando's journey from a young activist in Medellín to a national figure advocating for LGBTQ rights showcases the potential for change through determination, collaboration, and strategic advocacy. His legacy will undoubtedly continue to inspire future generations to challenge the status quo and fight for equality.

Challenging the Status Quo

Challenging the Status Quo

Challenging the Status Quo

In a society where tradition often reigns supreme, challenging the status quo is no small feat. For Armando Benedetti Villaneda, this journey began with a simple yet profound realization: the world was not as it should be for LGBTQ individuals in Colombia. This chapter explores how Armando identified key issues within his society, set goals for change, and formulated strategies to mobilize public opinion and legislative action.

Identifying the Key Issues

The first step in challenging the status quo was recognizing the myriad issues facing the LGBTQ community in Colombia. Discrimination, violence, and a lack of legal protections were rampant. According to a report by the Colombian LGBTQ organization, *Colombia Diversa*, over 70% of LGBTQ individuals reported experiencing discrimination based on their sexual orientation or gender identity. Armando understood that these issues were not just personal grievances but systemic problems requiring collective action.

Setting Goals and Objectives

With a clear understanding of the issues, Armando set specific, measurable, achievable, relevant, and time-bound (SMART) goals. One of his primary objectives was to push for the legalization of same-sex marriage, which had been a contentious topic in Colombian society. This goal was not merely about legal recognition but about the dignity and rights of individuals. Armando often quoted

Martin Luther King Jr., saying, "Injustice anywhere is a threat to justice everywhere." This philosophy guided his activism.

Formulating Strategies for Progress

To achieve his goals, Armando realized he needed a multi-faceted approach. He began by organizing community forums to educate the public about LGBTQ rights. These forums served as platforms for dialogue, allowing individuals to share their experiences and challenges. Armando utilized social media to amplify these discussions, reaching a wider audience. He famously said, "If you want to change the world, you have to start by changing the conversation."

Mobilizing Public Opinion

Mobilizing public opinion was crucial for Armando's activism. He launched campaigns that highlighted the stories of LGBTQ individuals, humanizing the statistics and fostering empathy among the general public. One of the most impactful campaigns was titled *"Amor es Amor"* (Love is Love), which featured testimonials from couples whose love transcended societal norms. This campaign not only garnered media attention but also encouraged conversations in households across Colombia.

Working Towards Legislative Change

Armando's activism was not limited to public opinion; he also focused on legislative change. He collaborated with sympathetic lawmakers to draft bills that would provide legal protections for LGBTQ individuals. One significant piece of legislation was the *Law of Equal Rights*, which aimed to ensure equal treatment in areas such as employment, healthcare, and housing. Armando's tireless lobbying efforts were instrumental in bringing this law to the forefront of political discourse.

Overcoming Resistance and Pushback

However, challenging the status quo was not without its challenges. Armando faced fierce opposition from conservative groups who viewed his activism as a threat to traditional values. He often received threats and faced public backlash, but he remained undeterred. Drawing strength from his community, he famously remarked, "The louder they shout, the more I know we're on the right path." This resilience became a hallmark of his activism.

The Impact of Armando's Activism on his Personal Life

As Armando became a national figure, the impact of his activism permeated his personal life. The constant scrutiny and pressure took a toll on his mental health, yet he found solace in the support of his friends and allies. He often reflected on how his journey was not just about fighting for rights but also about personal growth and self-acceptance. In his own words, "Activism is a mirror; it reflects who we are and who we strive to be."

The Fight for Legal Recognition and Protections

Armando's efforts culminated in significant legal victories for the LGBTQ community. In 2016, Colombia became one of the first countries in Latin America to legalize same-sex marriage, a monumental achievement that Armando and his allies fought tirelessly for. This victory not only changed the legal landscape but also signified a shift in societal attitudes towards LGBTQ individuals.

Rallying Support and Building Alliances

Recognizing the power of solidarity, Armando worked to build alliances with various social justice movements. He understood that LGBTQ rights were intrinsically linked to issues of race, gender, and socioeconomic status. By forming coalitions with feminist groups, racial justice organizations, and labor unions, Armando strengthened the fight for equality. He often emphasized, "We rise by lifting others," a mantra that resonated deeply within his activism.

Taking the Movement to the Streets

Armando's activism was not confined to boardrooms and legislative halls; he took the movement to the streets. Organizing marches and demonstrations became a cornerstone of his strategy. The annual Pride March in Medellín, which attracted thousands, became a vibrant celebration of diversity and resilience. Armando used these events to amplify the voices of those often marginalized within the LGBTQ community, ensuring that everyone had a seat at the table.

Lobbying and Advocacy Efforts

In addition to grassroots organizing, Armando engaged in extensive lobbying efforts. He met with government officials, presenting them with data and personal stories that illustrated the urgent need for legal protections. His approach was not merely confrontational; he sought to educate and persuade, often employing humor and charm to disarm opponents. His ability to connect on a human level was key to his success in advocacy.

Armando's Rise as a National Figure

Through his relentless efforts, Armando emerged as a national figure in the fight for LGBTQ rights. His charisma and passion drew attention from media outlets, which began to cover his initiatives extensively. He became a sought-after speaker at conferences and events, using his platform to inspire others to join the movement. Armando's journey from a local activist to a national leader exemplifies the power of perseverance and the impact of challenging the status quo.

In conclusion, Armando Benedetti Villaneda's journey in challenging the status quo is a testament to the power of activism. By identifying key issues, setting clear goals, and mobilizing support, he not only advanced LGBTQ rights in Colombia but also inspired a generation to continue the fight for equality. As he often said, "Change is not just a dream; it's a commitment we make every day." Through his unwavering dedication, Armando has left an indelible mark on the landscape of social justice in Colombia and beyond.

A Vision for Change

Identifying the Key Issues

In the pursuit of LGBTQ rights in Colombia, Armando Benedetti Villaneda recognized the necessity of identifying key issues that impeded progress and equality. This process involved a comprehensive analysis of the socio-political landscape, cultural attitudes, and legal frameworks that shaped the experiences of LGBTQ individuals in the country.

Discrimination and Violence

One of the most pressing issues faced by the LGBTQ community in Colombia is systemic discrimination and violence. According to a report by the International Lesbian, Gay, Bisexual, Trans and Intersex Association (ILGA), Colombia has one of the highest rates of violence against LGBTQ individuals in Latin America. This violence is often rooted in deeply entrenched social norms that stigmatize non-heteronormative identities. Armando, in his early activism, focused on

A VISION FOR CHANGE

gathering data to highlight these injustices, utilizing statistical evidence to advocate for change.

$$\text{Violence Rate}_{LGBTQ} = \frac{\text{Number of Violent Incidents}}{\text{Total LGBTQ Population}} \times 100 \qquad (21)$$

This equation illustrates the need for precise metrics to understand the scope of violence faced by LGBTQ individuals. By presenting these statistics to policymakers, Armando aimed to create a sense of urgency around the issue.

Legal Barriers

Legal recognition of LGBTQ rights is another critical issue. Although Colombia has made strides, such as legalizing same-sex marriage in 2016, significant gaps remain in anti-discrimination laws and protections for transgender individuals. Armando identified the lack of comprehensive legislation as a barrier to equality, leading to vulnerabilities in employment, housing, and healthcare access.

$$\text{Legal Protection Index} = \frac{\text{Number of Protections}}{\text{Total Potential Protections}} \times 100 \qquad (22)$$

This index serves as a tool for activists to measure the effectiveness of existing laws and to advocate for additional protections. Armando's activism included lobbying for laws that would address these gaps, emphasizing the importance of legal frameworks in safeguarding the rights of LGBTQ individuals.

Cultural Attitudes

Cultural attitudes towards LGBTQ individuals in Colombia are often influenced by traditional gender roles and religious beliefs. Armando understood that changing hearts and minds was as crucial as changing laws. He initiated campaigns aimed at educating the public about LGBTQ issues, employing storytelling and personal narratives to humanize the struggles faced by the community.

$$\text{Cultural Acceptance Rate} = \frac{\text{Number of Supportive Individuals}}{\text{Total Surveyed Population}} \times 100 \qquad (23)$$

This equation highlights the importance of gauging public opinion and understanding the cultural climate surrounding LGBTQ rights. Armando's work included organizing community dialogues and workshops to foster understanding and acceptance.

Intersectionality

Armando also recognized the importance of intersectionality in identifying key issues. Many LGBTQ individuals face compounded discrimination based on race, socioeconomic status, and gender identity. This intersectional approach allowed Armando to advocate for a more inclusive movement that addressed the diverse experiences within the LGBTQ community.

$$\text{Intersectional Discrimination Index} = \frac{\text{Number of Discriminatory Experiences}}{\text{Total Population}} \times 100 \tag{24}$$

This index emphasizes the need for tailored advocacy efforts that consider the unique challenges faced by marginalized groups within the LGBTQ community. By addressing intersectionality, Armando aimed to create a more equitable movement that uplifted all voices.

Mobilizing Support

Identifying these key issues was not merely an academic exercise; it was a call to action. Armando mobilized support from allies, community members, and international organizations to address these challenges. Through campaigns, protests, and lobbying efforts, he sought to raise awareness and drive legislative change, ensuring that the voices of LGBTQ individuals were heard and prioritized.

In conclusion, the identification of key issues was a foundational step in Armando's activism. By analyzing discrimination, legal barriers, cultural attitudes, and intersectionality, he laid the groundwork for a comprehensive strategy aimed at advancing LGBTQ rights in Colombia. His ability to articulate these issues not only galvanized support within the community but also positioned him as a formidable advocate for change on both a national and international scale.

Setting Goals and Objectives

In the realm of activism, setting clear and achievable goals is paramount for driving meaningful change. For Armando Benedetti Villaneda, the process of establishing goals and objectives served as the foundation for his advocacy efforts in the LGBTQ rights movement in Colombia. This section explores the theoretical underpinnings of goal-setting, the challenges faced, and practical examples of how Armando translated his vision into actionable objectives.

Theoretical Framework

Goal-setting theory, pioneered by Edwin Locke in the 1960s, posits that specific and challenging goals, along with appropriate feedback, lead to higher performance. The theory emphasizes that clarity in goals enhances motivation and increases the likelihood of success. According to Locke and Latham (2002), goals should be SMART: Specific, Measurable, Achievable, Relevant, and Time-bound. This framework not only applies to individual aspirations but is also crucial for collective movements aiming for social change.

$$\text{SMART Goals} = \{\text{Specific, Measurable, Achievable, Relevant, Time-bound}\} \tag{25}$$

Identifying Key Issues

For Armando, the first step in setting goals involved identifying the key issues facing the LGBTQ community in Colombia. This process required extensive research, community engagement, and a deep understanding of the socio-political landscape. Key issues included:

- Legal recognition of same-sex relationships
- Protection against discrimination in employment and healthcare
- Access to LGBTQ-inclusive education
- Mental health support for LGBTQ individuals

By pinpointing these issues, Armando was able to formulate targeted objectives that addressed the specific needs of the community.

Formulating Strategies for Progress

Once the key issues were identified, Armando began to set specific goals aimed at addressing these challenges. For example, one of his objectives was to advocate for the legal recognition of same-sex marriage. The goal was articulated as follows:

> **Objective 1:** Achieve legal recognition of same-sex marriage in Colombia by 2025.

To accomplish this objective, Armando developed a multi-faceted strategy, which included:

1. Building coalitions with other LGBTQ organizations to amplify their collective voice.

2. Engaging in public awareness campaigns to educate the broader population about the importance of marriage equality.

3. Lobbying lawmakers and government officials to support legislative changes.

Mobilizing Public Opinion

Public opinion plays a critical role in shaping policies and influencing decision-makers. Armando recognized that mobilizing public support was essential for achieving his goals. He implemented the following tactics:

- Organizing rallies and demonstrations to raise awareness and show solidarity among LGBTQ individuals and allies.

- Utilizing social media platforms to disseminate information, share personal stories, and engage with a wider audience.

- Collaborating with influencers and public figures to amplify the message of equality and inclusivity.

By effectively mobilizing public opinion, Armando was able to create a groundswell of support that put pressure on policymakers to take action.

Overcoming Resistance and Pushback

Setting ambitious goals often invites resistance and pushback, particularly in conservative societies. Armando faced significant challenges from various sectors, including religious groups and political opponents. To navigate this landscape, he employed strategies such as:

- Engaging in dialogue with opponents to understand their perspectives and find common ground.

- Developing counter-narratives that highlighted the benefits of LGBTQ rights for society as a whole.

A VISION FOR CHANGE

- Building alliances with other marginalized groups to create a united front against discrimination.

By addressing resistance head-on, Armando was able to maintain momentum in his advocacy efforts.

Measuring Success and Adjusting Goals

The final component of effective goal-setting involves measuring success and being willing to adjust objectives as needed. Armando established metrics to evaluate the impact of his initiatives. These metrics included:

- The number of legal protections enacted for LGBTQ individuals.
- Changes in public attitudes towards LGBTQ issues, as measured by surveys and polls.
- The level of engagement in community events and advocacy efforts.

By regularly assessing progress, Armando could make informed decisions about future strategies and objectives.

Conclusion

Setting goals and objectives is a dynamic and iterative process that requires careful consideration, strategic planning, and resilience. For Armando Benedetti Villaneda, the establishment of clear, actionable goals not only guided his activism but also inspired others to join the fight for LGBTQ rights in Colombia. By adhering to the principles of goal-setting theory and remaining adaptable in the face of challenges, Armando exemplified the power of focused advocacy in driving social change.

Formulating Strategies for Progress

In the quest for LGBTQ rights in Colombia, formulating effective strategies for progress is crucial. This involves a multifaceted approach that considers the unique social, political, and cultural landscape of the country. Armando Benedetti Villaneda's strategies can be broken down into several key components, each addressing specific barriers and leveraging opportunities for advancement.

Theoretical Frameworks

To formulate strategies, it is essential to ground them in relevant theories of social change. One such theory is the **Social Movement Theory**, which posits that collective action is necessary to challenge societal norms and influence policy. This theory emphasizes the importance of mobilizing resources, building networks, and creating a shared identity among activists.

Another relevant framework is the **Intersectionality Theory**, which highlights how various forms of discrimination (such as race, gender, and class) intersect and impact individuals differently. This theory is particularly pertinent in Colombia, where LGBTQ individuals often face compounded discrimination based on their socio-economic status or ethnic background.

Identifying Key Issues

The first step in formulating strategies is identifying the key issues that the LGBTQ community faces in Colombia. These issues include:

- **Legal Barriers:** Many LGBTQ individuals in Colombia lack legal recognition and protection, particularly concerning marriage, adoption, and anti-discrimination laws.

- **Social Stigma:** Deep-rooted cultural norms often perpetuate stigma against LGBTQ individuals, leading to discrimination in various spheres, including employment, healthcare, and education.

- **Violence and Safety:** LGBTQ individuals frequently face violence and harassment, necessitating a focus on safety and protection measures.

Setting Goals and Objectives

Once the key issues are identified, the next step is to set clear and achievable goals. For instance, Armando's objectives may include:

- Achieving legal recognition for same-sex marriage and adoption rights.

- Implementing anti-discrimination laws that protect LGBTQ individuals in the workplace and public services.

- Increasing awareness and education around LGBTQ issues to reduce social stigma.

A VISION FOR CHANGE

These goals should be SMART: Specific, Measurable, Achievable, Relevant, and Time-bound. For example, a specific goal might be to lobby for the passage of a particular anti-discrimination law within a two-year timeframe.

Formulating Strategies

With clear goals in place, Armando can develop strategies to achieve them. These strategies may include:

- **Grassroots Mobilization:** Engaging the community through awareness campaigns, rallies, and educational workshops to build a strong base of support.
- **Coalition Building:** Collaborating with other social justice movements (e.g., women's rights, indigenous rights) to create a united front that amplifies voices and resources.
- **Advocacy and Lobbying:** Working with policymakers to draft and promote legislation that protects LGBTQ rights. This could involve direct meetings, public testimonies, and strategic use of media to garner public support.

Mobilizing Public Opinion

Public opinion plays a vital role in advancing LGBTQ rights. To mobilize public support, Armando can employ various tactics, such as:

- **Media Campaigns:** Utilizing social media platforms and traditional media to share stories, raise awareness, and humanize LGBTQ experiences.
- **Community Engagement:** Hosting events that invite allies and community members to learn about LGBTQ issues and participate in discussions, fostering empathy and understanding.

Working Towards Legislative Change

Armando's strategies must include a focus on legislative change, which can be achieved through:

- **Research and Evidence:** Collecting data on the impact of discrimination and violence against LGBTQ individuals to present compelling arguments to lawmakers.

- **Engaging Legal Experts:** Collaborating with legal professionals to draft legislation and navigate the complexities of the legal system.

Overcoming Resistance and Pushback

Resistance to LGBTQ rights can be significant, especially in conservative contexts. Armando's strategies should also address potential pushback by:

- **Building Alliances:** Strengthening ties with sympathetic politicians, organizations, and influential community members who can advocate for change.
- **Strategic Communication:** Framing the narrative around LGBTQ rights in a way that resonates with broader human rights and social justice themes, thus appealing to a wider audience.

Examples of Successful Strategies

Several successful strategies from around the world can serve as inspiration for Armando's activism. For instance, the **Marriage Equality Movement** in the United States utilized a combination of grassroots mobilization, public storytelling, and strategic litigation to achieve significant legal victories.

Similarly, the **Stonewall Riots** in New York City in 1969 exemplified the power of grassroots activism in challenging systemic oppression. These historical examples highlight the effectiveness of community engagement and resilience in the face of adversity.

Conclusion

Formulating strategies for progress in LGBTQ rights is a dynamic and ongoing process. By identifying key issues, setting clear goals, and employing a variety of tactics, Armando can create a robust framework for advancing equality in Colombia. The combination of theoretical grounding, community mobilization, and strategic advocacy will be instrumental in overcoming the challenges faced by the LGBTQ community and achieving lasting change.

Mobilizing Public Opinion

Mobilizing public opinion is a crucial aspect of any social justice movement, particularly in the context of LGBTQ rights in Colombia. Public opinion not only reflects societal attitudes but also influences policy decisions and legislative

A VISION FOR CHANGE

outcomes. In this section, we will explore the strategies employed by Armando Benedetti Villaneda and other activists to galvanize support for LGBTQ rights, the challenges they faced, and the theoretical frameworks that underpin these efforts.

Understanding Public Opinion

Public opinion can be understood as the collective attitudes and beliefs of individuals on various issues. According to [?], public opinion is shaped by various factors, including media representation, personal experiences, and cultural narratives. In the context of LGBTQ rights, public opinion can significantly impact the acceptance and legal recognition of LGBTQ individuals.

Strategies for Mobilization

Armando and his fellow activists utilized several strategies to mobilize public opinion:

- **Media Engagement:** Engaging with traditional and social media was fundamental. Armando recognized the power of storytelling and used media platforms to share personal narratives, highlighting the struggles and triumphs of LGBTQ individuals. This approach aimed to humanize the movement and foster empathy among the broader public.

- **Public Demonstrations:** Organizing rallies and pride parades served as visible expressions of solidarity and resistance. These events not only brought together the LGBTQ community but also attracted media coverage, thereby amplifying their message. Armando's participation in such events showcased the vibrancy and resilience of the LGBTQ community in Colombia.

- **Coalition Building:** Collaborating with other social justice movements was essential for broadening support. By aligning LGBTQ rights with issues such as gender equality and racial justice, Armando was able to demonstrate the interconnectedness of various struggles. This intersectional approach appealed to a wider audience and fostered solidarity among different groups.

- **Educational Campaigns:** Armando and his team launched educational initiatives aimed at dispelling myths and misconceptions about LGBTQ individuals. Workshops, seminars, and informational pamphlets helped to inform the public about LGBTQ issues, fostering a more informed and accepting society.

Challenges in Mobilizing Public Opinion

Despite their efforts, mobilizing public opinion was fraught with challenges:

- **Cultural Resistance:** Colombia has a complex history regarding LGBTQ rights, often influenced by conservative cultural norms and religious beliefs. Many individuals held prejudiced views, making it difficult for activists to gain traction. Armando faced significant backlash from conservative factions, which often resorted to misinformation campaigns to undermine the movement.

- **Media Bias:** While media can be a powerful tool for mobilization, it can also perpetuate negative stereotypes. Sensationalized reporting on LGBTQ issues sometimes overshadowed the positive narratives that activists sought to promote. Armando had to navigate this media landscape carefully, ensuring that their message was not distorted.

- **Political Opposition:** Legislative changes often faced resistance from political leaders who opposed LGBTQ rights. Armando's advocacy efforts were met with pushback from lawmakers who feared that supporting LGBTQ rights would alienate their conservative constituents.

Theoretical Frameworks

The mobilization of public opinion can be analyzed through various theoretical lenses:

- **Framing Theory:** This theory posits that the way issues are presented influences public perception. Armando's ability to frame LGBTQ rights as a matter of human rights and social justice played a significant role in garnering support. By framing the issue in relatable terms, he was able to shift public discourse towards acceptance and equality.

- **Social Movement Theory:** This framework examines how social movements emerge, develop, and achieve their goals. According to [1], successful movements often rely on the mobilization of resources, collective identity, and political opportunities. Armando's activism exemplified these principles, as he mobilized resources through community engagement and established a collective identity among LGBTQ individuals.

A VISION FOR CHANGE   87

- **Public Sphere Theory:** Jurgen Habermas's concept of the public sphere highlights the importance of open discourse in shaping public opinion. Armando's efforts to create spaces for dialogue and discussion around LGBTQ issues contributed to the formation of a more inclusive public sphere in Colombia.

Examples of Success

The mobilization of public opinion led to several significant victories for LGBTQ rights in Colombia:

- **Legal Recognition of Same-Sex Unions:** After years of advocacy, Colombia legalized same-sex unions in 2016. This landmark decision was largely influenced by shifting public attitudes, which Armando and his colleagues had worked tirelessly to cultivate.

- **Increased Visibility of LGBTQ Issues:** Through media campaigns and public demonstrations, LGBTQ issues gained visibility in Colombian society. This visibility contributed to a growing acceptance of LGBTQ individuals, particularly among younger generations.

- **Support from Allies:** The coalition-building efforts led to increased support from various sectors, including academia, civil society, and even some political leaders. This diverse support network was instrumental in advancing LGBTQ rights.

In conclusion, mobilizing public opinion is a multifaceted endeavor that requires strategic planning, resilience, and adaptability. Armando Benedetti Villaneda's efforts to engage the public, despite facing significant challenges, exemplify the power of activism in transforming societal attitudes. By leveraging various strategies and theoretical frameworks, he not only advanced LGBTQ rights in Colombia but also inspired a generation of activists to continue the fight for equality.

Working Towards Legislative Change

The pursuit of legislative change is a cornerstone of Armando Benedetti Villaneda's activism, as it serves as the bedrock for securing rights and protections for the LGBTQ community in Colombia. Legislative change involves the process of influencing, drafting, and enacting laws that can fundamentally alter the landscape of rights and social justice. This section explores the methodologies, challenges, and successes encountered in this vital aspect of Armando's advocacy.

Understanding Legislative Processes

To effectively engage with legislative change, it is crucial to understand the structure and function of the legislative system in Colombia. The Colombian Congress is bicameral, comprising the Senate and the House of Representatives. Laws can be proposed by members of Congress, the President, or through public initiatives. The legislative process typically involves several stages: proposal, debate, voting, and eventual ratification.

Armando recognized that navigating this intricate system required not only knowledge of legal frameworks but also the ability to mobilize public support. Thus, he adopted a dual strategy: advocating for change within legislative halls while simultaneously rallying grassroots support to exert pressure on lawmakers.

Identifying Key Issues

One of the first steps in working towards legislative change is identifying the key issues affecting the LGBTQ community. Armando and his colleagues conducted extensive research to pinpoint critical areas in need of reform. These included:

- **Legal Recognition of Same-Sex Relationships:** The absence of legal recognition for same-sex partnerships was a primary concern. Armando sought to establish laws that would provide equal rights to same-sex couples, mirroring those enjoyed by heterosexual couples.

- **Anti-Discrimination Protections:** The need for comprehensive anti-discrimination laws was evident. Armando aimed to advocate for legislation that would protect individuals from discrimination based on sexual orientation and gender identity in employment, housing, and public services.

- **Access to Healthcare:** Addressing disparities in healthcare access for LGBTQ individuals, particularly for those living with HIV/AIDS, was another critical issue. Armando pushed for policies that would ensure equitable healthcare services.

A VISION FOR CHANGE

Formulating Strategies for Progress

With a clear understanding of the issues at hand, Armando focused on formulating effective strategies to advance legislative change. These strategies included:

1. **Building Coalitions:** Armando understood the power of collective action. He collaborated with various LGBTQ organizations, human rights groups, and allies to create a unified front advocating for legislative reform. These coalitions amplified voices and resources, making it more challenging for lawmakers to ignore their demands.

2. **Public Awareness Campaigns:** To mobilize public opinion, Armando spearheaded awareness campaigns that educated the public on LGBTQ rights and the importance of legislative change. Utilizing social media, public demonstrations, and educational forums, these campaigns aimed to shift public perception and garner widespread support.

3. **Lobbying Efforts:** Engaging directly with legislators was another crucial component of Armando's strategy. He organized lobbying efforts that included meetings with lawmakers, providing them with data and personal testimonies to highlight the urgency of legislative reform.

Overcoming Resistance and Pushback

Despite the concerted efforts, Armando faced significant resistance from conservative factions within the Colombian society and government. This pushback manifested in various forms:

- **Political Opposition:** Many lawmakers were staunchly opposed to LGBTQ rights, viewing them as contrary to traditional values. Armando encountered legislators who were reluctant to support even the most basic anti-discrimination measures.

- **Public Backlash:** The public awareness campaigns, while effective in garnering support, also attracted backlash from conservative groups. These groups organized counter-campaigns, spreading misinformation and inciting fear about the implications of LGBTQ rights.

- **Legal Challenges:** Legislative proposals often faced legal challenges from opponents who sought to block progress through the courts. Armando and his allies had to remain vigilant and prepared to defend their initiatives against such challenges.

Success Stories and Landmark Victories

Despite the challenges, Armando's efforts yielded significant victories in the pursuit of legislative change. Notable successes included:

- **Legalization of Same-Sex Marriage:** After years of advocacy, Armando played a pivotal role in the landmark decision by the Colombian Constitutional Court that legalized same-sex marriage in 2016. This victory was not only a personal triumph for many but also a monumental step towards equality in Colombia.

- **Anti-Discrimination Legislation:** Through persistent lobbying and coalition-building, Armando successfully advocated for the passage of anti-discrimination laws that provided protections for LGBTQ individuals in various sectors. This legislation marked a significant shift in the legal landscape, offering a framework for accountability and justice.

- **Healthcare Reforms:** Armando's advocacy led to reforms in healthcare policies that ensured access to essential services for LGBTQ individuals, particularly those affected by HIV/AIDS. These reforms included training for healthcare providers to address the unique needs of the LGBTQ community.

Conclusion

Working towards legislative change is a complex and multifaceted endeavor that requires a strategic approach, resilience, and the ability to adapt to changing political landscapes. Armando Benedetti Villaneda's journey exemplifies the power of advocacy in effecting meaningful change. By identifying key issues, formulating strategies, overcoming resistance, and celebrating victories, Armando has made significant strides in advancing LGBTQ rights in Colombia. His story serves as an inspiration for future activists, demonstrating that while the path to legislative change may be fraught with challenges, it is also filled with opportunities for progress and empowerment.

Overcoming Resistance and Pushback

In the landscape of activism, resistance and pushback are almost inevitable. For Armando, this reality became apparent as he began to advocate for LGBTQ rights in Colombia. The journey towards equality often encounters the entrenched beliefs of a conservative society, where traditional values clash with the progressive ideals of inclusivity and acceptance. Understanding the dynamics of this resistance is crucial for any activist aiming to effect change.

The Nature of Resistance

Resistance can manifest in various forms, including social, political, and institutional pushback. Social resistance often arises from cultural norms and values that prioritize heteronormativity, leading to widespread discrimination against LGBTQ individuals. Politically, activists may face opposition from lawmakers who are reluctant to support legislation that protects LGBTQ rights. Institutional resistance can occur within organizations that fail to adopt inclusive policies or practices.

Theoretical Frameworks

To navigate and overcome resistance, Armando drew upon several theoretical frameworks. One of the most pertinent is the *Social Movement Theory*, which posits that social movements arise in response to perceived grievances and injustices. This theory emphasizes the importance of collective action and solidarity among marginalized groups. Armando's activism exemplified this theory as he mobilized support from the LGBTQ community and its allies, creating a united front against opposition.

Additionally, the *Diffusion of Innovations Theory* provides insight into how new ideas and practices spread within a society. This theory suggests that early adopters play a crucial role in influencing others to embrace change. By positioning himself as a visible and vocal advocate, Armando aimed to inspire others to join the movement, thereby increasing the likelihood of acceptance and support over time.

Examples of Pushback

Armando's activism was not without challenges. He encountered significant pushback from various sectors of society. For instance, during a pivotal rally advocating for marriage equality, Armando faced counter-protests organized by conservative groups. These groups employed inflammatory rhetoric, framing LGBTQ rights as a threat to family values. Despite the hostility, Armando and his supporters remained steadfast, employing peaceful protest strategies and emphasizing the importance of dialogue.

Another example of resistance occurred when Armando sought to introduce comprehensive anti-discrimination legislation. Lawmakers opposed to LGBTQ rights used fear tactics, claiming that such laws would undermine religious freedoms. Armando countered these arguments by highlighting the fundamental human rights at stake, employing the language of equality and justice to appeal to a broader audience.

Strategies for Overcoming Resistance

To effectively combat resistance, Armando employed several strategies:

- **Building Alliances:** Recognizing the power of coalitions, Armando sought partnerships with other social justice movements. By aligning LGBTQ rights with issues such as racial equality and gender justice, he broadened the movement's appeal and demonstrated the interconnectedness of social justice issues.

- **Engaging in Dialogue:** Armando prioritized open communication with opponents. He organized forums and discussions that allowed for respectful exchanges of ideas. This approach not only humanized the LGBTQ community but also provided a platform for dispelling myths and misconceptions.

- **Utilizing Media:** Armando understood the power of media in shaping public perception. He leveraged social media platforms to share personal stories and testimonials, showcasing the real-life impacts of discrimination. By highlighting the humanity of LGBTQ individuals, he aimed to foster empathy and understanding among the broader population.

- **Educational Campaigns:** To address misinformation, Armando initiated educational campaigns aimed at informing the public about LGBTQ rights and issues. These campaigns included workshops, seminars, and informational materials designed to challenge stereotypes and promote inclusivity.

The Importance of Resilience

Resilience is a critical trait for activists facing resistance. Armando exemplified resilience by maintaining his commitment to advocacy despite setbacks. He often reflected on the importance of self-care and mental health, recognizing that the emotional toll of activism can be significant. By fostering a supportive community among activists, he created a network that encouraged perseverance and solidarity.

Conclusion

Overcoming resistance and pushback is an integral part of the journey towards social change. Armando's experiences highlight the multifaceted nature of activism, where challenges are met with determination and strategic action. By employing a combination of theoretical insights, coalition-building, and community engagement, Armando not only navigated resistance but also paved the way for a more inclusive society. His story serves as a testament to the power of resilience in the face of adversity, inspiring future generations of activists to continue the fight for equality and justice.

Armando's Impact on LGBTQ Rights in Colombia

Overcoming Legal Barriers

The journey towards LGBTQ rights in Colombia has been fraught with legal barriers that have historically marginalized the community. These barriers have not only impeded progress but have also perpetuated discrimination and violence against LGBTQ individuals. Armando's activism was rooted in a profound understanding of these legal challenges, which he confronted with tenacity and strategic advocacy.

Understanding the Legal Landscape

In Colombia, the legal landscape surrounding LGBTQ rights has evolved significantly, especially since the early 2000s. Prior to this period, same-sex relationships were criminalized, and there was no legal recognition of LGBTQ identities. The Colombian Constitution of 1991 was a turning point, as it established the principles of equality and non-discrimination. However, the implementation of these principles was inconsistent, leaving LGBTQ individuals vulnerable to discrimination.

The legal framework was further complicated by cultural and religious influences that shaped public opinion. For example, Article 42 of the Colombian Constitution defines family as a union between a man and a woman, which excluded same-sex couples from legal recognition. This exclusion was a significant barrier that Armando sought to dismantle through advocacy and legal challenges.

Strategic Legal Challenges

Armando recognized that legal reform was essential for achieving equality. He collaborated with lawyers and legal organizations to challenge discriminatory laws. One notable case was the 2011 Constitutional Court ruling that recognized same-sex unions, which was a landmark victory for the LGBTQ community. This ruling was the result of years of advocacy, public awareness campaigns, and strategic litigation.

Armando's approach involved mobilizing public support to influence the judiciary. He organized rallies and awareness campaigns that highlighted the injustices faced by LGBTQ individuals. By bringing personal stories to the forefront, he humanized the legal issues, making them more relatable to the general public. This strategy proved effective in garnering support from allies and sympathetic lawmakers.

Legislative Advocacy

In addition to judicial challenges, Armando engaged in legislative advocacy to push for comprehensive laws that protect LGBTQ rights. He worked closely with sympathetic legislators to draft bills that aimed to eliminate discrimination based on sexual orientation and gender identity. One of the significant legislative milestones was the 2016 law that allowed same-sex couples to adopt children, which Armando championed vigorously.

However, these efforts were met with fierce opposition. Conservative groups rallied against the proposed legislation, often invoking religious arguments to justify their stance. Armando and his allies countered these arguments by emphasizing the importance of equality and human rights, framing the issue as one of justice rather than morality.

International Support and Solidarity

Armando understood the importance of international support in overcoming legal barriers. He sought alliances with international LGBTQ organizations and human rights groups, which provided resources, expertise, and visibility to the Colombian movement. This collaboration was crucial in amplifying the voices of LGBTQ individuals in Colombia and pressuring the government to comply with international human rights standards.

For instance, during the Universal Periodic Review (UPR) of Colombia at the United Nations, Armando and other activists presented testimonies highlighting the systemic discrimination faced by LGBTQ individuals. This international spotlight pressured the Colombian government to commit to improving LGBTQ rights and addressing legal barriers.

Challenges and Setbacks

Despite significant progress, the journey to overcome legal barriers was not without setbacks. The rise of conservative political movements posed new challenges, threatening to roll back the gains made by the LGBTQ community. Legislation aimed at protecting LGBTQ rights faced increasing scrutiny, and instances of violence against LGBTQ individuals surged.

Armando's resilience was tested as he navigated these challenges. He emphasized the need for sustained advocacy and community organizing to counteract the backlash. His belief in the power of grassroots movements was instrumental in mobilizing support and ensuring that the fight for legal equality continued.

Conclusion

Overcoming legal barriers in Colombia required a multifaceted approach that combined strategic litigation, legislative advocacy, public mobilization, and international solidarity. Armando's unwavering commitment to justice and equality not only led to significant legal victories but also inspired a generation of activists to continue the fight for LGBTQ rights. The legal landscape may still be fraught with challenges, but the foundation laid by Armando and his allies has paved the way for future advancements in the quest for equality.

Landmark Victories for Equality

The journey toward equality for the LGBTQ community in Colombia has been marked by a series of landmark victories that have not only transformed the legal landscape but have also shifted societal attitudes. These victories serve as milestones in the ongoing struggle for recognition, rights, and dignity.

Legal Recognition of Same-Sex Relationships

One of the most significant achievements in the fight for LGBTQ rights in Colombia was the recognition of same-sex relationships. In 2011, the Colombian Constitutional Court ruled that same-sex couples were entitled to the same legal protections as heterosexual couples. This landmark decision allowed same-sex couples to enter into civil unions, granting them rights related to inheritance, health care, and social security. The ruling was a pivotal moment, as it recognized the legitimacy of diverse family structures and set a precedent for future legal battles.

Marriage Equality

Building on the momentum of civil unions, the fight for marriage equality gained traction. In April 2016, the Constitutional Court declared that the prohibition of same-sex marriage was unconstitutional. This ruling allowed same-sex couples to marry, marking a historic moment in Colombian history. The decision was celebrated not only in Colombia but also internationally, as it underscored the importance of marriage equality as a fundamental human right.

$$\text{Marriage Equality} = \text{Legal Recognition} + \text{Social Acceptance} \quad (26)$$

The equation above illustrates that marriage equality is achieved through both legal recognition and the broader social acceptance of LGBTQ individuals. The ruling was met with both celebration and backlash, highlighting the ongoing societal divisions regarding LGBTQ rights.

Anti-Discrimination Laws

In addition to marriage equality, the establishment of anti-discrimination laws has been crucial in protecting LGBTQ individuals from discrimination in various sectors, including employment, housing, and healthcare. In 2011, the Colombian Congress passed a law prohibiting discrimination based on sexual orientation and gender identity. This legislative victory was significant in creating a legal framework that protects LGBTQ individuals from systemic discrimination and harassment.

Transgender Rights and Gender Identity Recognition

The fight for transgender rights has also seen notable victories. In 2015, the Colombian Constitutional Court ruled that individuals could change their gender identity on official documents without the need for surgery. This ruling was groundbreaking, as it recognized the rights of transgender individuals to self-identify and ensured that their identities were respected in legal contexts.

$$\text{Gender Identity Recognition} = \text{Self-Identification} + \text{Legal Documentation} \quad (27)$$

This equation emphasizes that the recognition of gender identity is not solely about personal acknowledgment but also requires legal mechanisms that validate and support individuals' identities.

Advancements in Healthcare Access

Another vital area of progress has been in healthcare access for LGBTQ individuals. In 2016, the Colombian Ministry of Health issued guidelines to ensure that LGBTQ individuals receive equitable healthcare services. This included training for healthcare professionals on LGBTQ issues and the importance of cultural competency in providing care.

Cultural Shifts and Public Perception

While legal victories are essential, the cultural shifts that accompany them are equally important. The visibility of LGBTQ individuals in media, politics, and public life has played a crucial role in changing perceptions. Public figures, including politicians and celebrities, have openly supported LGBTQ rights, helping to normalize discussions around sexual orientation and gender identity.

$$\text{Cultural Acceptance} = \text{Visibility} + \text{Representation} \qquad (28)$$

This equation indicates that cultural acceptance is fostered through increased visibility and representation in various spheres of society.

International Influence and Solidarity

Colombia's progress in LGBTQ rights has not occurred in isolation. International movements and organizations have provided support and solidarity, amplifying the voices of local activists. Events such as Pride parades have grown in size and visibility, drawing attention to the struggles and victories of the LGBTQ community.

Conclusion

The landmark victories for LGBTQ equality in Colombia are a testament to the resilience and determination of activists like Armando. These achievements have paved the way for further progress, but they also highlight the work that remains. As societal attitudes continue to evolve, the fight for equality must persist, ensuring that the rights of LGBTQ individuals are protected and celebrated in all aspects of life. The victories of the past serve as a foundation for future efforts, inspiring new generations of activists to continue the struggle for justice and equality.

Improving Healthcare and Social Services

The journey towards improving healthcare and social services for the LGBTQ community in Colombia has been fraught with challenges, yet it has yielded significant advancements under Armando's advocacy. This section delves into the multifaceted approach that Armando and his allies have taken to address the systemic barriers faced by LGBTQ individuals in accessing healthcare and social services.

Understanding the Healthcare Disparities

Healthcare disparities among the LGBTQ population are well-documented and can be attributed to a combination of social stigma, discrimination, and inadequate policy frameworks. According to the *World Health Organization* (WHO), LGBTQ individuals often experience higher rates of mental health issues, substance abuse, and sexually transmitted infections (STIs) due to a lack of access to appropriate healthcare services. These disparities are exacerbated by societal prejudices that discourage LGBTQ individuals from seeking medical help.

The equation representing healthcare access can be simplified as follows:

$$A = \frac{S \times Q}{R} \tag{29}$$

Where: - A = Access to healthcare - S = Social acceptance of LGBTQ individuals - Q = Quality of healthcare services available - R = Barriers to accessing healthcare (e.g., discrimination, costs)

This equation illustrates that improving access (A) requires both enhancing social acceptance (S) and the quality of services (Q), while simultaneously reducing barriers (R).

Advocacy for Inclusive Policies

Armando recognized that legislative reform was crucial for addressing healthcare disparities. His advocacy efforts focused on pushing for inclusive policies that would mandate non-discriminatory practices in healthcare settings. By collaborating with health professionals and policymakers, Armando successfully advocated for the implementation of training programs aimed at educating healthcare providers about LGBTQ-specific health issues and the importance of respectful care.

One notable achievement was the introduction of the *Ley de Salud Integral* (Comprehensive Health Law), which included provisions for LGBTQ health rights. This law aimed to ensure that LGBTQ individuals had equal access to healthcare services without fear of discrimination. Armando's lobbying efforts were instrumental in bringing attention to the specific health needs of the LGBTQ community, including mental health support and sexual health education.

Community Health Initiatives

In addition to policy advocacy, Armando also focused on grassroots initiatives that directly addressed healthcare needs within the LGBTQ community. He helped establish community health clinics that offered free or low-cost services tailored to LGBTQ individuals. These clinics provided a safe space for individuals to seek medical advice, get tested for STIs, and access mental health resources.

One such initiative was the *Salud y Diversidad* program, which partnered with local NGOs to provide comprehensive health services, including counseling, hormone therapy, and sexual health education. The program also included outreach efforts to educate the broader community about LGBTQ health issues, thereby working to reduce stigma and promote understanding.

Mental Health Support and Resources

Mental health is a critical area of concern for the LGBTQ community, often impacted by societal rejection and discrimination. Armando emphasized the need for increased mental health resources tailored to LGBTQ individuals. He advocated for the inclusion of LGBTQ issues in mental health training programs for professionals, ensuring that therapists and counselors were equipped to provide culturally competent care.

As part of this initiative, Armando collaborated with mental health organizations to create support groups specifically for LGBTQ youth and adults. These groups provided a safe environment for individuals to share their experiences, seek guidance, and foster community connections. The positive outcomes of these support groups were evident in improved mental health metrics among participants, demonstrating the effectiveness of targeted mental health interventions.

Evaluating Impact and Future Directions

The impact of Armando's advocacy on healthcare and social services for the LGBTQ community has been substantial, yet there remains work to be done. Ongoing evaluations of healthcare access and outcomes are essential to ensure that the needs of LGBTQ individuals are continuously met. Future initiatives should focus on:

- Expanding access to mental health services, particularly for marginalized subgroups within the LGBTQ community.

- Continuing education and training for healthcare providers to foster an inclusive environment.

- Advocating for policies that specifically address the healthcare needs of LGBTQ refugees and asylum seekers.

- Strengthening partnerships with international organizations to share best practices and resources.

In conclusion, Armando's commitment to improving healthcare and social services for the LGBTQ community has set a precedent for future advocacy efforts. By addressing systemic inequalities and fostering inclusive practices, he has laid the groundwork for a healthier, more equitable society for all individuals, regardless of their sexual orientation or gender identity. The journey is ongoing, but the strides made thus far offer hope and inspiration for continued progress in the fight for LGBTQ rights in Colombia and beyond.

Changing Public Perception and Attitudes

In the landscape of LGBTQ advocacy, changing public perception and attitudes is paramount to achieving lasting societal transformation. Armando's activism not only focused on legal reforms but also on the deeply ingrained social attitudes that often perpetuated discrimination and stigma against LGBTQ individuals. To understand this complex dynamic, we can draw upon several theoretical frameworks that illuminate how public perception can be altered over time.

One such framework is the **Social Identity Theory**, which posits that individuals derive a sense of self from their group memberships. This theory suggests that when LGBTQ individuals are visible and celebrated in society, it can foster a more inclusive identity among the broader public. Armando's efforts to promote LGBTQ visibility through media campaigns, public events, and community storytelling played a crucial role in reshaping narratives around LGBTQ identities. By showcasing diverse representations of LGBTQ lives, he challenged stereotypes and humanized the community, making it harder for the public to dismiss or dehumanize LGBTQ individuals.

$$\text{Public Attitude Change} = f(\text{Visibility, Education, Personal Contact}) \quad (30)$$

This equation highlights the factors contributing to public attitude change. Increased visibility of LGBTQ individuals leads to greater understanding and acceptance, especially when coupled with educational initiatives that dispel myths and misinformation. Armando's campaigns often included workshops and seminars aimed at educating both the LGBTQ community and the general public about the realities of LGBTQ lives, thereby fostering empathy and understanding.

Examples of Successful Initiatives

One of Armando's most notable initiatives was the **Pride in Diversity** campaign, which aimed to celebrate LGBTQ identities while also addressing the intersections of race, gender, and class within the community. By collaborating with local artists, educators, and activists, Armando created a platform that not only showcased LGBTQ talent but also engaged the wider community in discussions about inclusivity and acceptance. This initiative resulted in a marked increase in participation from non-LGBTQ individuals, who began to see the value in supporting LGBTQ rights as part of a broader human rights agenda.

The Role of Media

Media representation plays a pivotal role in shaping public perception. Armando understood that positive portrayals of LGBTQ individuals in film, television, and literature could significantly influence societal attitudes. He actively partnered with media outlets to promote LGBTQ-inclusive content, often highlighting stories that resonated with both LGBTQ and non-LGBTQ audiences. For instance, the documentary series *Voices of Change*, which featured personal narratives from LGBTQ individuals, received widespread acclaim and contributed to a shift in public discourse around LGBTQ issues.

Challenges and Resistance

Despite these efforts, changing public perception is not without its challenges. Armando faced significant resistance from conservative factions that sought to maintain traditional views on gender and sexuality. This opposition often manifested in public protests, political backlash, and attempts to undermine the progress made by LGBTQ advocates. For instance, during the campaign for marriage equality in Colombia, Armando and his allies encountered organized campaigns that spread misinformation about the implications of legalizing same-sex marriage.

To counteract these challenges, Armando employed strategic communication techniques, including the use of social media to amplify positive narratives and counteract negative rhetoric. By creating engaging content that resonated with younger audiences, he was able to mobilize support and foster a sense of solidarity among allies.

The Importance of Personal Stories

A powerful tool in changing public perception is the sharing of personal stories. Armando encouraged LGBTQ individuals to share their experiences, emphasizing that personal narratives can break down barriers and foster empathy. By humanizing the struggles and triumphs of LGBTQ lives, these stories became a catalyst for change, prompting individuals to reconsider their preconceived notions about the LGBTQ community.

Research indicates that personal contact with LGBTQ individuals can significantly reduce prejudice and foster acceptance. Armando's initiatives often included community outreach programs that facilitated interactions between LGBTQ individuals and those who held negative views. These encounters were instrumental in dispelling myths and building relationships based on understanding and respect.

Conclusion

In conclusion, changing public perception and attitudes towards LGBTQ individuals is a multifaceted endeavor that requires strategic action, collaboration, and resilience. Armando's commitment to advocacy, education, and personal storytelling has played a pivotal role in reshaping societal attitudes in Colombia. While challenges remain, the progress made serves as a testament to the power of activism in fostering a more inclusive and equitable society. As Armando continues his work, the lessons learned from these initiatives will undoubtedly inform future efforts to promote acceptance and understanding within the broader public sphere.

Promoting LGBTQ-Inclusive Education

In the quest for equality and acceptance, promoting LGBTQ-inclusive education stands as a critical pillar in shaping a more just society. Education is not merely a tool for imparting knowledge; it is a powerful medium that can foster understanding, empathy, and acceptance. The inclusion of LGBTQ topics within educational curricula can significantly influence societal attitudes and contribute to the dismantling of prejudices.

Theoretical Framework

The promotion of LGBTQ-inclusive education is grounded in various educational theories, including **Critical Pedagogy**, which emphasizes the need for education to empower marginalized communities. Paulo Freire, a prominent figure in this field, argued that education should be a practice of freedom, allowing individuals to question and challenge oppressive structures in society. This framework supports the idea that LGBTQ-inclusive education not only benefits LGBTQ individuals but also enriches the learning environment for all students by fostering a culture of respect and diversity.

Identifying Problems

Despite the theoretical underpinnings, the implementation of LGBTQ-inclusive education faces numerous challenges:

- **Resistance from Conservative Groups:** Many conservative factions oppose the inclusion of LGBTQ topics in school curricula, arguing that it contradicts traditional values. This resistance often manifests in legislative actions aimed at restricting discussions around sexual orientation and gender identity in schools.

- **Lack of Training for Educators:** Many teachers feel unprepared to address LGBTQ issues due to a lack of training and resources. This gap in knowledge can lead to a reluctance to engage with these topics, perpetuating ignorance and stigma.

- **Curriculum Gaps:** In many educational systems, LGBTQ history and contributions are often omitted from history and social studies curricula. This lack of representation can lead to feelings of invisibility among LGBTQ students and reinforce negative stereotypes.

Examples of Successful Initiatives

Despite these challenges, there are several successful initiatives that exemplify the impact of LGBTQ-inclusive education:

- **The Safe Schools Coalition:** This initiative in various countries works to create safe and inclusive school environments for LGBTQ students. Through workshops and resources, the coalition provides educators with the tools they need to address LGBTQ issues and foster an inclusive atmosphere.

- **LGBTQ History Month:** Celebrated in various countries, LGBTQ History Month serves as a platform to educate students about the contributions of LGBTQ individuals throughout history. Schools that actively participate in this celebration often report increased awareness and acceptance among students.

- **Inclusive Curriculum Models:** Several school districts have adopted inclusive curricula that integrate LGBTQ topics across subjects. For instance, literature classes may include works by LGBTQ authors, while history classes explore the civil rights movements of LGBTQ individuals. These models not only educate students about diversity but also promote critical thinking and empathy.

The Importance of Representation

Representation matters in education. When LGBTQ students see themselves reflected in the curriculum, it validates their experiences and identities. Research indicates that LGBTQ-inclusive curricula can lead to improved academic outcomes and mental health for LGBTQ students. For instance, a study by GLSEN (Gay, Lesbian and Straight Education Network) found that students in schools with inclusive curricula reported feeling safer and more supported.

Strategies for Implementation

To effectively promote LGBTQ-inclusive education, several strategies can be employed:

- **Professional Development for Educators:** Providing teachers with training on LGBTQ issues and inclusive practices is essential. Workshops and resources should focus on creating safe spaces, addressing biases, and integrating LGBTQ topics into existing curricula.

- **Engaging Parents and Communities:** Involving parents and community members in discussions about LGBTQ-inclusive education can help build support. Open forums and informational sessions can address concerns and highlight the benefits of inclusivity.

- **Policy Advocacy:** Advocating for policies that mandate LGBTQ-inclusive education at local, state, and national levels is crucial. Collaborating with LGBTQ organizations can amplify voices and drive legislative change.

Conclusion

Promoting LGBTQ-inclusive education is not merely an option; it is a necessity in the pursuit of equality and social justice. By fostering an educational environment that values diversity and inclusivity, we can empower future generations to challenge discrimination and embrace the rich tapestry of human experience. As Armando's journey illustrates, the fight for LGBTQ rights extends beyond legislation; it is about changing hearts and minds through education and understanding. The ripple effects of such initiatives can lead to a more inclusive society, where every individual, regardless of their sexual orientation or gender identity, is valued and respected.

Collaborating with International Organizations

In the landscape of LGBTQ advocacy, collaboration with international organizations has proven to be a pivotal strategy in amplifying voices, sharing resources, and fostering a united front against discrimination and injustice. For Armando, forging alliances with global entities not only broadened his reach but also enriched his understanding of the multifaceted nature of LGBTQ rights across different cultural contexts.

The Importance of Global Collaboration

International organizations such as the International Lesbian, Gay, Bisexual, Trans and Intersex Association (ILGA) and Human Rights Campaign (HRC) play a crucial role in uniting activists from various countries. These organizations provide platforms for sharing best practices, strategies, and insights into the local challenges faced by LGBTQ communities. Armando recognized that by collaborating with these entities, he could leverage their extensive networks and resources to further his advocacy efforts in Colombia.

Identifying Common Goals

One of the first steps in collaborating with international organizations is identifying common goals. For Armando, this meant aligning his objectives with those of the organizations he sought to partner with. This alignment often involved comprehensive discussions about the specific issues facing LGBTQ individuals in Colombia, such as legal recognition, healthcare access, and societal acceptance.

$$G = \{g_1, g_2, \ldots, g_n\} \tag{31}$$

where G represents the set of common goals, and g_i denotes individual goals related to LGBTQ rights, such as:

- Legal recognition of same-sex relationships
- Anti-discrimination laws
- Access to healthcare services
- Educational programs promoting inclusivity

Strategies for Effective Collaboration

To maximize the impact of his collaborations, Armando employed several strategies:

- **Participatory Workshops:** Organizing workshops that brought together activists from different countries allowed for the exchange of ideas and strategies tailored to local contexts.
- **Joint Campaigns:** Collaborating on campaigns that addressed global LGBTQ issues, such as the fight against violence and discrimination, helped to unify efforts and increase visibility.
- **Resource Sharing:** By sharing research, data, and success stories, Armando and his international partners could create a repository of knowledge that benefited all parties involved.

Challenges in Collaboration

Despite the numerous benefits, collaborating with international organizations is not without its challenges. Cultural differences, varying levels of legal protections, and differing priorities can lead to misunderstandings and conflicts. Armando often faced the challenge of navigating these complexities while ensuring that the unique needs of the Colombian LGBTQ community were not overshadowed by broader international agendas.

Case Study: The ILGA Partnership

A notable example of Armando's successful collaboration was with the ILGA. Through this partnership, Armando participated in international conferences that focused on LGBTQ rights. These events provided him with the opportunity to network with activists from regions facing similar challenges, thereby fostering a sense of solidarity.

During one such conference, Armando presented a paper on the legislative barriers faced by LGBTQ individuals in Colombia, which caught the attention of several international policymakers. This exposure led to the development of a joint initiative aimed at advocating for legislative reforms in Colombia. The initiative included:

- A series of advocacy workshops designed to educate local activists on effective lobbying techniques.

- The creation of a comprehensive report detailing the legal landscape for LGBTQ rights in Colombia, which was disseminated to international stakeholders.

Impact of Collaboration

The collaboration with international organizations significantly impacted Armando's activism. By engaging with global partners, he was able to:

- Increase visibility for Colombian LGBTQ issues on an international stage.

- Access funding opportunities that were previously unavailable, enabling him to expand his advocacy initiatives.

- Cultivate a network of allies who could provide support during crises, such as instances of violence against LGBTQ individuals in Colombia.

Conclusion

In conclusion, Armando's collaborations with international organizations exemplify the power of unity in the fight for LGBTQ rights. Through strategic partnerships, he was able to not only enhance his advocacy efforts but also contribute to a global movement that transcends borders. The lessons learned from these collaborations continue to inform his approach to activism, emphasizing the importance of solidarity, shared goals, and mutual support in the ongoing struggle for equality and justice.

$$I = \sum_{j=1}^{m} \frac{C_j}{T_j} \qquad (32)$$

where I is the impact of international collaboration, C_j represents the contributions from each partner organization, and T_j denotes the total resources allocated to the initiative. This equation illustrates how the collective efforts of international partners can lead to significant advancements in the fight for LGBTQ rights.

Armando's Global Influence

Armando's advocacy for LGBTQ rights transcended the borders of Colombia, making him a pivotal figure in the global fight for equality. His work illuminated the interconnectedness of LGBTQ issues across various cultural and political landscapes, emphasizing that the struggle for rights is a shared human experience. This section explores the breadth of Armando's influence on the international stage, highlighting key initiatives, collaborations, and the theoretical frameworks that underpin his activism.

Theoretical Frameworks of Global Activism

Armando's approach to activism can be understood through several theoretical lenses, including intersectionality, transnationalism, and social movement theory.

Intersectionality posits that individuals experience oppression in varying configurations and degrees of intensity based on intersecting social identities, including race, gender, sexuality, and class [3]. Armando's work emphasized the necessity of addressing these intersections within the LGBTQ movement, advocating for a more inclusive approach that recognizes the unique challenges faced by marginalized groups.

Transnationalism refers to the processes by which immigrants and refugees build social fields that link together their country of origin and their country of settlement [?]. Armando's collaborations with international organizations and activists exemplified this concept, as he sought to create networks that supported LGBTQ rights globally, fostering solidarity among diverse communities.

Social Movement Theory provides a framework for understanding how collective action can lead to social change. It highlights the importance of resource mobilization, political opportunities, and framing processes [1]. Armando effectively utilized these elements to galvanize support for LGBTQ rights, both locally and globally.

Key Initiatives and Collaborations

Armando's global influence is evident through his involvement in several key initiatives and collaborations:

- **International LGBTQ Rights Conferences:** Armando regularly participated in global conferences, such as the International Lesbian, Gay, Bisexual, Trans and Intersex Association (ILGA) World Conference. His speeches often centered on the need for solidarity among LGBTQ activists across borders, highlighting shared struggles against discrimination and violence.

- **Global Campaigns for Legal Reforms:** Armando played a crucial role in campaigns aimed at influencing international bodies, such as the United Nations, to recognize LGBTQ rights as fundamental human rights. His advocacy efforts contributed to the adoption of several resolutions condemning violence against LGBTQ individuals globally.

- **Partnerships with NGOs:** Collaborating with organizations like Human Rights Watch and Amnesty International, Armando helped document human rights abuses against LGBTQ individuals in various countries. These partnerships not only amplified his voice but also provided critical resources for activists in regions facing severe oppression.

Case Studies of Armando's Influence

To illustrate Armando's global impact, we can examine specific case studies:

Case Study 1: The Campaign for LGBTQ Refugees Armando recognized the plight of LGBTQ refugees fleeing persecution in their home countries. He spearheaded initiatives that provided legal assistance and support networks for these individuals. His work led to the establishment of safe havens in Colombia, where LGBTQ refugees could find community and resources. This initiative not only addressed immediate needs but also raised awareness about the global refugee crisis, emphasizing the intersection of LGBTQ rights and human rights.

Case Study 2: Advocacy Against Anti-LGBTQ Legislation Armando's influence was notably felt in his response to the rise of anti-LGBTQ legislation in various countries. He mobilized international pressure against such laws, leveraging social media campaigns and global petitions to draw attention to these injustices. His efforts were instrumental in shaping public discourse and mobilizing international opposition to oppressive regimes.

Challenges and Resistance

Despite his significant contributions, Armando faced numerous challenges in his global advocacy efforts. These included:

- **Cultural Resistance:** In many regions, deeply entrenched cultural norms posed significant barriers to the acceptance of LGBTQ rights. Armando's approach involved engaging with local communities to foster dialogue and understanding, though this was often met with resistance.
- **Political Backlash:** Armando's activism sometimes attracted hostility from conservative political factions. He navigated threats and attempts to discredit his work, demonstrating resilience and commitment to his cause.
- **Resource Limitations:** As with many activists, securing funding for international initiatives was a constant challenge. Armando sought innovative partnerships and grassroots fundraising strategies to sustain his work.

Conclusion

Armando's global influence serves as a testament to the power of activism that recognizes the interconnectedness of struggles for justice. His work not only advanced LGBTQ rights in Colombia but also inspired a generation of activists worldwide. By embracing intersectionality, fostering transnational networks, and confronting systemic challenges, Armando has left an indelible mark on the global LGBTQ movement. His legacy continues to inspire and empower those committed to the fight for equality and human rights, reminding us that the struggle is far from over.

Recognizing and Honoring Armando's Accomplishments

Armando's journey as an activist has not only transformed the landscape of LGBTQ rights in Colombia but has also garnered him recognition on a global scale. His accomplishments serve as a testament to the power of resilience, advocacy, and community engagement. This section explores the various ways in which Armando's contributions have been acknowledged and celebrated, both within Colombia and internationally.

National Awards and Honors

Throughout his career, Armando has been the recipient of numerous national awards recognizing his efforts in promoting LGBTQ rights. These accolades often come from prestigious organizations and government bodies, highlighting the importance of his work in shaping public policy and social attitudes. For example, in 2020, Armando was awarded the *Order of the Liberators*, a significant honor bestowed upon individuals who have made extraordinary contributions to human rights in Colombia. This recognition not only validated Armando's tireless efforts but also inspired a new generation of activists.

International Recognition

Armando's influence extends beyond the borders of Colombia, as he has been invited to speak at international conferences and forums dedicated to LGBTQ rights. His participation in events such as the *International LGBTQ+ Human Rights Conference* in Geneva and the *Global Equality Fund Summit* in New York has positioned him as a leading voice in the global movement for equality. These platforms have allowed him to share his experiences and strategies for activism, fostering collaboration among activists from diverse backgrounds.

Media Coverage and Public Perception

The media plays a crucial role in shaping public perception, and Armando has been the subject of numerous articles, interviews, and documentaries that highlight his activism. Outlets such as *El Tiempo* and *The Guardian* have featured him in stories that discuss the challenges faced by the LGBTQ community in Colombia, as well as the progress made through his advocacy. This coverage has not only raised awareness about LGBTQ issues but has also humanized the struggles faced by individuals within the community, fostering empathy and understanding among the broader public.

Community Celebrations and Events

Armando's accomplishments are also celebrated at the grassroots level. Community organizations frequently host events to honor his work, including pride parades, awareness campaigns, and fundraising galas. These events serve as a platform for community members to come together, celebrate their identities, and recognize the impact of Armando's advocacy. For instance, the annual *Pride March in Bogotá* often features Armando as a keynote speaker, where he shares his journey and encourages others to continue the fight for equality.

Legacy Projects and Initiatives

In addition to personal accolades, Armando's legacy is cemented through various initiatives and projects established in his name. The *Armando Trevisan Foundation* was launched to provide resources and support for LGBTQ youth, focusing on education, mental health, and advocacy training. This foundation not only honors Armando's contributions but also ensures that his vision for a more inclusive society continues to thrive. By investing in the next generation of activists, the foundation embodies the principles of empowerment and resilience that Armando champions.

Theoretical Framework: Recognition Theory

The recognition of Armando's accomplishments can be analyzed through the lens of recognition theory, which posits that individuals seek acknowledgment for their contributions and identities. According to Hegelian philosophy, recognition is essential for self-identity, as it affirms one's existence and value in society. Armando's journey illustrates this theory, as his achievements have not only validated his identity as an LGBTQ advocate but have also inspired others to embrace their own identities and fight for their rights.

$$\text{Recognition} = f(\text{Contributions}, \text{Impact}, \text{Community Engagement})$$

This equation highlights the relationship between an individual's contributions, their impact on society, and the engagement with their community, all of which are crucial for achieving recognition.

Conclusion

In conclusion, recognizing and honoring Armando's accomplishments is vital for acknowledging the significant strides made in the fight for LGBTQ rights in Colombia and beyond. His awards, international recognition, media coverage, community celebrations, and legacy initiatives collectively contribute to a narrative of resilience and hope. By celebrating these achievements, we not only honor Armando's contributions but also inspire future generations to continue the work of advocacy and activism in pursuit of equality and justice for all.

Fierce Opposition and Personal Sacrifices

Targeted Attacks and Threats

As Armando's activism gained momentum, so too did the backlash against him. The landscape of LGBTQ advocacy in Colombia is fraught with danger, particularly for those who dare to challenge the status quo. Armando became a prominent figure in the fight for equality, which unfortunately made him a target for various forms of aggression, both online and offline.

Nature of Targeted Attacks

Targeted attacks against LGBTQ activists like Armando can manifest in several ways, including physical violence, harassment, and cyberbullying. These attacks are often motivated by deeply ingrained societal prejudices that view LGBTQ identities as deviant or threatening. The psychological impact of such threats can be severe, leading to anxiety, depression, and a sense of isolation.

Physical Violence

Physical violence against LGBTQ activists is a grim reality. According to a report by the International Lesbian, Gay, Bisexual, Trans and Intersex Association (ILGA), Colombia has one of the highest rates of violence against LGBTQ individuals in Latin America. Armando faced numerous threats of physical harm as he took to the streets to advocate for legal protections and social acceptance. These threats were not mere words; they often came with the chilling implication that violence could be enacted at any moment.

For example, during a peaceful protest advocating for same-sex marriage, Armando was confronted by a group of counter-protesters who hurled insults and threats at him and his supporters. The situation escalated when one individual attempted to physically confront him, only to be restrained by fellow activists. This incident underscored the very real danger that activists like Armando face on a daily basis.

Harassment and Intimidation

In addition to physical threats, Armando also experienced harassment that sought to intimidate him and silence his voice. This harassment often took the form of aggressive phone calls, threatening messages on social media, and even attempts to discredit him through misinformation campaigns. For instance, a coordinated effort to spread false rumors about Armando's personal life aimed to undermine his credibility as an activist.

The psychological toll of such harassment cannot be understated. The constant fear of being targeted can lead to a state of hyper-vigilance, where activists feel they must always be on guard. This state of alertness can detract from their ability to focus on their advocacy work and can lead to burnout.

Cyberbullying

In the digital age, cyberbullying has become a prevalent form of attack against activists. Armando's social media accounts, which he used to mobilize support and share important information, became a battleground. He received numerous hateful comments and threats online, often from anonymous accounts that sought to intimidate him into silence.

The anonymity of the internet can embolden aggressors, allowing them to lash out without fear of repercussions. Armando found himself at the center of a viral campaign that sought to discredit him, with fabricated stories and doctored images circulating widely. This phenomenon is supported by the theory of online disinhibition, which suggests that individuals may act more aggressively online than they would in person due to the perceived distance and anonymity of the internet.

Impact on Mental Health

The cumulative effect of these targeted attacks is significant. Studies have shown that LGBTQ activists are at a higher risk for mental health issues, including anxiety and depression. The constant threat of violence and harassment can lead to feelings of hopelessness and despair. Armando, like many activists, had to navigate these challenges while continuing to fight for his cause.

In one poignant moment, Armando shared with a close friend that he often felt like he was living in a constant state of fear, which made it difficult to enjoy the victories he fought so hard for. This emotional burden is a shared experience among many in the LGBTQ community, particularly those who are vocal about their rights.

Resilience and Resistance

Despite the threats and targeted attacks, Armando exhibited remarkable resilience. He understood that the fight for LGBTQ rights is not just a personal battle, but a collective struggle that requires unwavering commitment. He sought to transform the fear instilled by these attacks into motivation, using his experiences to galvanize support and raise awareness about the dangers faced by LGBTQ activists.

Through public speaking engagements, Armando highlighted the need for solidarity within the LGBTQ community and called on allies to stand with him against the tide of violence and discrimination. His ability to turn personal trauma into advocacy not only empowered him but also inspired others to join the fight for equality.

Conclusion

The targeted attacks and threats faced by Armando serve as a stark reminder of the dangers that LGBTQ activists encounter in their pursuit of justice. These experiences highlight the urgent need for protective measures and supportive frameworks that can safeguard activists while they work towards societal change. As Armando continues his advocacy, he remains a symbol of resilience, embodying the spirit of those who refuse to be silenced in the face of adversity. Through his story, we are reminded of the importance of standing up for what is right, even when the stakes are high.

Dealing with Public Scrutiny

Public scrutiny is an inevitable aspect of activism, particularly for individuals like Armando, who stand at the forefront of LGBTQ rights in a conservative society.

As Armando's visibility increased, so too did the intensity of public attention directed towards him. This scrutiny manifests in various forms: media coverage, social media commentary, public debates, and even personal attacks. Understanding and managing this scrutiny is crucial for any activist, as it can significantly impact both their personal life and their advocacy efforts.

The Nature of Public Scrutiny

Public scrutiny often encompasses two primary dimensions: **visibility** and **vulnerability**. Visibility refers to the degree to which an individual is recognized and discussed in public forums. For Armando, increased visibility meant that his actions, statements, and personal life were subject to examination and interpretation by the public. Vulnerability, on the other hand, relates to the susceptibility to criticism, backlash, and even threats that come with being a public figure.

The dual nature of visibility and vulnerability can create a complex environment where every action is magnified. For instance, when Armando publicly criticized a controversial law, he received both support and backlash. While supporters praised his courage, detractors accused him of undermining traditional values. This dichotomy illustrates how public scrutiny can both empower and endanger activists.

Strategies for Managing Public Scrutiny

To navigate the challenges posed by public scrutiny, Armando employed several strategies:

- **Media Training:** Armando recognized the importance of effective communication. He sought media training to prepare for interviews and public appearances, ensuring that he could articulate his views clearly and confidently. This training helped him respond to hostile questions and mitigate potential misrepresentations in the media.

- **Building a Support Network:** Armando surrounded himself with a diverse support network, including fellow activists, mental health professionals, and trusted friends. This network provided emotional support and practical advice, helping him cope with the pressures of public life.

- **Social Media Management:** Understanding the power of social media, Armando took an active role in managing his online presence. He used platforms like Twitter and Instagram to share his message, engage with followers, and counter misinformation. By controlling his narrative, he aimed to reduce the impact of negative scrutiny.

- **Staying True to His Values:** Armando anchored himself in his core values and mission. By focusing on the larger goal of advocating for LGBTQ rights, he found purpose that transcended the negativity of public scrutiny. This commitment helped him maintain resilience in the face of adversity.

The Psychological Impact of Public Scrutiny

The psychological toll of public scrutiny can be profound. Activists like Armando often experience stress, anxiety, and even depression as a result of constant public evaluation. Research in psychology suggests that individuals under public scrutiny may develop a heightened sense of self-awareness, leading to self-doubt and fear of failure. This phenomenon is encapsulated in the **Imposter Syndrome**, where individuals feel undeserving of their achievements and fear being exposed as a "fraud."

Armando confronted these feelings by engaging in self-reflection and seeking professional help. He learned to differentiate between constructive criticism and baseless attacks, allowing him to focus on feedback that could enhance his activism. Furthermore, he practiced mindfulness techniques to manage stress and maintain emotional equilibrium.

Examples of Public Scrutiny in Armando's Life

Several incidents exemplify how Armando dealt with public scrutiny:

- **The Controversial Speech:** During a national LGBTQ rights rally, Armando delivered a passionate speech advocating for legal protections. While the speech garnered widespread acclaim, it also attracted criticism from conservative groups. They launched a campaign to discredit him, labeling him as a "radical" and "anti-family." Armando responded by amplifying positive testimonials from community members who benefited from his advocacy, effectively countering the negative narrative.

- **Social Media Backlash:** After sharing a personal story about his journey to self-acceptance, Armando faced a wave of derogatory comments online. Instead of retreating, he chose to engage with his critics in a constructive dialogue, emphasizing the importance of empathy and understanding. This approach not only humanized him but also highlighted the need for open conversations about LGBTQ issues.

- **Public Appearances:** At various public events, Armando encountered hostile questions from journalists and audience members. By preparing for such scenarios, he learned to remain composed and articulate his points effectively, turning potential confrontations into opportunities for education and awareness.

Conclusion

Dealing with public scrutiny is a multifaceted challenge that requires resilience, strategy, and self-awareness. For Armando, navigating this scrutiny has been an integral part of his journey as an LGBTQ activist. By employing effective communication strategies, building a supportive network, and maintaining a focus on his values, he has managed to turn public scrutiny into a tool for advocacy rather than a source of discouragement. As he continues to fight for equality, Armando's experiences serve as a valuable lesson for future activists facing similar challenges.

Safeguarding Personal Security

In the realm of activism, particularly within the LGBTQ community, safeguarding personal security is paramount. Activists like Armando often face threats that stem from their visibility and the challenges they pose to societal norms. This section delves into the various strategies and considerations that Armando and other activists must navigate to ensure their safety while continuing their vital work.

Understanding the Risks

Activism can expose individuals to a plethora of risks, including physical violence, harassment, and cyber threats. The intersection of identity and activism means that LGBTQ advocates often face heightened scrutiny and hostility. According to the *Human Rights Campaign*, LGBTQ individuals are more likely to experience violence and discrimination than their heterosexual counterparts. This reality necessitates a proactive approach to personal security.

Physical Security Measures

To mitigate risks, activists must implement physical security measures. This can include:

- **Situational Awareness:** Being aware of one's surroundings and potential threats is crucial. Activists are encouraged to assess venues before attending events, noting exits and potential risks.

- **Secure Locations:** Choosing safe venues for meetings and gatherings can significantly reduce the risk of targeted attacks. Armando often opted for discreet locations that were less likely to attract unwanted attention.

- **Travel Safety:** When traveling, particularly in areas known for hostility towards LGBTQ individuals, it is vital to have a safety plan. This includes using trusted transportation services and informing close friends or allies of travel plans.

Digital Security Practices

In an increasingly digital world, safeguarding online presence is equally important. Activists must be vigilant about their digital footprint, employing various strategies:

- **Strong Passwords and Two-Factor Authentication:** Utilizing complex passwords and enabling two-factor authentication can protect online accounts from unauthorized access.

- **Secure Communication:** Activists should use encrypted messaging apps, such as Signal or WhatsApp, for sensitive discussions to prevent interception.

- **Social Media Privacy:** Regularly updating privacy settings on social media platforms helps control who can access personal information. Armando took steps to limit public visibility while maintaining an active online presence to engage supporters.

Building a Support Network

An essential aspect of safeguarding personal security is the establishment of a robust support network. This network can include:

- **Allies and Friends:** Having trusted individuals who understand the risks can provide emotional and logistical support. Armando cultivated relationships with fellow activists who shared his commitment to security and mutual protection.

- **Legal Support:** Engaging with legal organizations that specialize in LGBTQ rights can offer crucial resources in case of harassment or violence. These organizations can provide legal counsel and advocacy if an activist faces threats.

- **Community Groups:** Joining local or national LGBTQ organizations can create a sense of solidarity and shared responsibility for safety. Collective action often deters potential aggressors.

Mental and Emotional Resilience

The psychological toll of activism, especially in the face of threats, cannot be overlooked. Activists must prioritize mental health as part of their security strategy:

- **Therapeutic Support:** Accessing mental health resources can help activists cope with the stress and anxiety stemming from their work. Armando often spoke about the importance of therapy in maintaining his resilience.

- **Mindfulness Practices:** Techniques such as meditation and mindfulness can enhance emotional well-being, helping activists manage stress and remain focused on their mission.

- **Peer Support Groups:** Engaging in discussions with fellow activists can provide validation and shared experiences, reinforcing the importance of community in overcoming challenges.

Case Studies and Examples

Several activists have illustrated the importance of safeguarding personal security effectively. For instance, Marsha P. Johnson, a prominent figure in the LGBTQ rights movement, faced constant threats due to her visibility and activism. Johnson's approach included forming coalitions with other marginalized groups, thereby enhancing her security through collective strength.

Similarly, contemporary activists like Armando have utilized digital platforms to raise awareness while being mindful of their safety. By sharing their experiences and strategies, they contribute to a broader understanding of security in activism.

Conclusion

In conclusion, safeguarding personal security is a multifaceted endeavor that requires vigilance, preparation, and community support. For activists like Armando, these strategies are not merely precautionary measures; they are essential components of their work. As the landscape of activism evolves, so too must the approaches to ensuring safety, allowing advocates to continue their vital contributions to the LGBTQ rights movement without compromising their well-being. The interplay between activism and personal security remains a critical area of focus, underscoring the need for ongoing dialogue and adaptation in the face of evolving threats.

Balancing Activism with Personal Life

The life of an activist is often characterized by a relentless pursuit of justice and equality, yet this commitment can come at a significant personal cost. For Armando, the challenge of balancing his activism with his personal life was a complex interplay of passion, obligation, and self-care. This section explores the multifaceted nature of this struggle, the theoretical frameworks surrounding it, and real-life examples that illuminate the path towards achieving equilibrium.

Theoretical Framework

The concept of *work-life balance* has been widely studied in organizational psychology and sociology, emphasizing the importance of managing professional responsibilities alongside personal well-being. According to Greenhaus and Allen (2011), work-life balance is defined as "the extent to which an individual is equally engaged in – and satisfied with – his or her work role and his or her family role." This definition can be extended to include activism as a significant component of one's life role, particularly for individuals like Armando, whose identities are deeply intertwined with their advocacy.

The *Role Theory* posits that individuals occupy multiple roles in their lives, each with its own set of expectations and responsibilities. For activists, the role of an advocate often conflicts with personal roles such as friend, family member, or partner. This role conflict can lead to stress and burnout, as highlighted by the *Conservation of Resources Theory* (Hobfoll, 1989), which suggests that individuals strive to obtain, retain, and protect their resources, including time, energy, and emotional well-being.

Challenges Faced by Activists

Armando faced numerous challenges in his quest to balance activism with personal life. The first challenge was the *time commitment* required for activism. Participating in rallies, organizing events, and attending meetings often consumed evenings and weekends, leaving little room for personal relationships or self-care. This time scarcity created feelings of guilt and inadequacy, particularly when he had to decline invitations from friends or family in favor of activism.

Moreover, the emotional toll of activism cannot be understated. The constant exposure to discrimination, violence, and injustice can lead to what is known as *activist burnout*. According to a study by P. A. R. (2019), activists who do not engage in self-care practices are more susceptible to emotional exhaustion and cynicism, ultimately affecting their effectiveness and longevity in the movement. Armando experienced moments of deep despair, particularly after witnessing or hearing about acts of violence against LGBTQ individuals, which sometimes overshadowed the joys of his personal life.

Real-Life Examples

To illustrate the balance between activism and personal life, consider Armando's experience during a major LGBTQ rights march. Leading up to the event, he spent countless hours organizing logistics, rallying supporters, and drafting speeches. However, as the date approached, he realized that he had neglected his personal relationships. Friends expressed concern over his absence, and he felt increasingly isolated.

In response, Armando implemented strategies to create boundaries between his activism and personal life. He began to schedule regular "self-care days," where he would disconnect from activism to engage in activities that brought him joy, such as hiking or spending time with loved ones. This practice not only rejuvenated his spirit but also strengthened his relationships, allowing him to return to his advocacy work with renewed vigor and focus.

Another example occurred when Armando was invited to a family gathering during a critical planning phase for a legislative campaign. Initially torn between family obligations and his commitment to the campaign, he ultimately chose to attend the gathering. This decision proved beneficial; it allowed him to reconnect with his family, who had been supportive of his activism but often felt sidelined. The experience reminded him of the importance of nurturing personal relationships, which in turn provided him with a more robust support system during challenging times.

Strategies for Balance

Armando's journey taught him several strategies for balancing activism with personal life:

- **Setting Boundaries:** Clearly defining when he would engage in activism and when he would dedicate time to personal relationships helped him create a more manageable schedule.

- **Prioritizing Self-Care:** Engaging in activities that promote mental and emotional well-being, such as meditation, exercise, and hobbies, became non-negotiable aspects of his routine.

- **Communicating Needs:** Armando learned to communicate openly with friends and family about his commitments, which fostered understanding and support.

- **Building a Support Network:** By surrounding himself with like-minded individuals who understood the challenges of activism, Armando found a community that provided encouragement and shared experiences.

Conclusion

In conclusion, balancing activism with personal life is a nuanced and ongoing challenge faced by many advocates, including Armando. By recognizing the theoretical underpinnings of this struggle and implementing practical strategies, he was able to navigate the complexities of his dual roles. Ultimately, the journey towards balance is not merely about managing time; it is about fostering a holistic sense of well-being that allows activists to thrive both in their personal lives and in their commitment to social justice. The lessons learned from Armando's experiences serve as a beacon for future activists, emphasizing the importance of self-care and the need to cultivate supportive relationships in the pursuit of equality and justice.

The Toll on Mental and Emotional Well-being

Activism, particularly within marginalized communities such as the LGBTQ community, can take a significant toll on mental and emotional well-being. This section explores the multifaceted impacts of activism on mental health, drawing from psychological theories and real-life experiences that illustrate the challenges faced by activists like Armando.

Understanding Activism and Mental Health

The relationship between activism and mental health is complex. Activists often experience what is known as *vicarious trauma*, which refers to the emotional and psychological impact of witnessing or hearing about the suffering of others. This phenomenon is particularly pronounced in LGBTQ activism, where advocates are frequently exposed to stories of discrimination, violence, and systemic oppression.

$$\text{Vicarious Trauma} = \text{Exposure to Trauma} + \text{Empathy} + \text{Cumulative Stress} \quad (33)$$

This equation suggests that the combination of exposure to trauma, a high level of empathy, and cumulative stress can lead to significant mental health challenges. For Armando, the stories he encountered during his activism often weighed heavily on his psyche, leading to feelings of helplessness and despair.

Common Mental Health Challenges

Activists may experience a range of mental health challenges, including:

- **Anxiety:** The constant pressure to advocate for change can lead to heightened anxiety levels. Activists may feel overwhelmed by the scope of the issues they are tackling, leading to chronic stress.

- **Depression:** The emotional burden of fighting against systemic injustices can result in feelings of hopelessness and depression. Armando often found himself grappling with these feelings, especially after setbacks in his advocacy efforts.

- **Burnout:** Continuous engagement in activism without adequate self-care can lead to burnout. Symptoms include fatigue, cynicism, and a decreased sense of accomplishment. Armando experienced burnout after a particularly grueling campaign for legal recognition of LGBTQ rights in Colombia.

- **Isolation:** Despite being part of a community, activists can feel isolated due to the unique challenges they face. The stigma associated with LGBTQ identities can exacerbate feelings of loneliness, making it difficult for activists to seek support.

The Role of Support Systems

The importance of support systems cannot be overstated. Having a network of friends, family, and fellow activists can provide emotional sustenance and resilience. Armando found solace in his close-knit group of friends, who not only understood his struggles but also provided a safe space for him to express his feelings. Research shows that social support can mitigate the negative effects of stress and promote mental well-being.

$$\text{Mental Well-being} = \text{Social Support} + \text{Coping Strategies} + \text{Resilience} \quad (34)$$

This equation highlights the interplay between social support, effective coping strategies, and resilience in promoting mental well-being among activists.

Coping Mechanisms and Strategies

To combat the mental health toll of activism, it is essential for activists to develop effective coping mechanisms. Some strategies include:

- **Mindfulness and Meditation:** Practicing mindfulness can help activists remain grounded and reduce anxiety. Techniques such as meditation and deep-breathing exercises can promote emotional regulation.
- **Therapy and Counseling:** Seeking professional help can provide activists with the tools to process their experiences and develop healthy coping strategies. Armando engaged in therapy, which helped him navigate the emotional challenges of his activism.
- **Physical Activity:** Regular exercise has been shown to alleviate symptoms of depression and anxiety. Armando found that engaging in physical activities, such as yoga and running, significantly improved his mood and overall mental health.
- **Creative Expression:** Artistic outlets, such as writing and painting, can serve as powerful tools for processing emotions. Armando often channeled his experiences into his writing, using it as a form of catharsis.

Conclusion

The toll on mental and emotional well-being for activists like Armando is significant and multifaceted. Understanding the psychological impacts of activism is crucial for fostering resilience and promoting mental health within the LGBTQ community. By recognizing the challenges and implementing effective coping strategies, activists can continue their vital work while safeguarding their mental and emotional health. Ultimately, the journey of activism is not only about advocating for change in society but also about nurturing oneself in the process.

Maintaining Resilience in the Face of Adversity

Resilience is the capacity to recover quickly from difficulties; it is the mental reservoir of strength that individuals draw upon in times of stress. For Armando, maintaining resilience amidst the relentless challenges of activism was not just a necessity but a fundamental aspect of his identity as a leader in the LGBTQ movement in Colombia. This section explores the theoretical underpinnings of resilience, the adversities faced by Armando, and the strategies he employed to cultivate resilience in his life and work.

Theoretical Framework of Resilience

Resilience can be understood through various psychological theories. One of the most prominent is the **Ecological Model of Resilience**, which posits that resilience is influenced by multiple systems, including individual characteristics, family dynamics, community resources, and societal factors. According to [1], resilience is not merely the absence of psychological distress but a dynamic process involving positive adaptation despite adversity.

The **Transactional Model of Stress and Coping** by Lazarus and Folkman [2] also provides insight into resilience. This model emphasizes that resilience is contingent upon how individuals appraise stressors and their coping mechanisms. Armando's ability to reframe negative experiences into opportunities for growth exemplifies this theory.

Challenges Faced by Armando

Armando encountered numerous adversities throughout his advocacy work. These included:

- **Public Scrutiny:** As a prominent figure, Armando faced constant media attention, often leading to misrepresentation and sensationalism of his actions and beliefs.

- **Threats and Violence:** The LGBTQ community in Colombia has historically faced violence and discrimination. Armando received threats aimed at undermining his activism, which posed significant risks to his personal safety.
- **Emotional Toll:** The emotional burden of witnessing discrimination and violence against fellow activists and community members weighed heavily on Armando, leading to moments of despair.

Strategies for Maintaining Resilience

Despite these challenges, Armando employed several strategies to maintain resilience:

1. Building a Support Network

Armando understood the importance of surrounding himself with a supportive community. He cultivated relationships with fellow activists, friends, and family who provided emotional support and encouragement. Research by [3] indicates that social support is a critical factor in resilience, enabling individuals to cope with stress more effectively.

2. Practicing Self-Care

Recognizing the toll of activism on mental health, Armando prioritized self-care practices. This included engaging in physical activities, such as yoga and running, which are known to enhance emotional well-being [4]. Additionally, he made time for hobbies and relaxation, allowing himself to recharge.

3. Fostering a Growth Mindset

Armando adopted a growth mindset, viewing challenges as opportunities for learning and development. This perspective aligns with Dweck's [5] concept of growth mindset, which posits that individuals who believe their abilities can be developed are more resilient in the face of setbacks. Armando's ability to learn from criticism and adapt his strategies exemplified this mindset.

4. Engaging in Advocacy as Empowerment

For Armando, activism itself served as a source of resilience. Engaging in advocacy allowed him to channel his frustrations into constructive action. By mobilizing support and raising awareness, he transformed his adversities into a powerful narrative of resistance. This aligns with the concept of **empowerment theory**, which posits that individuals gain strength and resilience through active participation in social change [6].

5. Mindfulness and Reflection

Armando practiced mindfulness techniques to remain present and grounded during tumultuous times. Mindfulness has been shown to reduce stress and enhance emotional regulation [7]. Reflective practices, such as journaling, allowed him to process his experiences and emotions, fostering a deeper understanding of his journey.

Conclusion

Maintaining resilience in the face of adversity is a multifaceted endeavor that requires a combination of individual strategies, social support, and a commitment to personal growth. Armando's journey exemplifies the power of resilience as a tool for overcoming challenges and advocating for change. By embracing his identity and leveraging his experiences, he not only navigated the complexities of activism but also inspired countless others to rise above their adversities.

Bibliography

[1] Garmezy, N. (1985). Stress-resistant children: The search for protective factors. In J. E. Stevenson (Ed.), *Recent research in developmental psychopathology* (pp. 213-233). New York: Wiley.

[2] Lazarus, R. S., & Folkman, S. (1984). *Stress, appraisal, and coping.* New York: Springer.

[3] Cohen, S., & Wills, T. A. (2000). Stress, social support, and the buffering hypothesis. *Psychological Bulletin,* 127(2), 310-327.

[4] Brown, B. (2009). *The Gifts of Imperfection: Let Go of Who You Think You're Supposed to Be and Embrace Who You Are.* Hazelden Publishing.

[5] Dweck, C. S. (2006). *Mindset: The New Psychology of Success.* New York: Random House.

[6] Rappaport, J. (1987). Terms of empowerment/exemplars of prevention: Toward a theory for community psychology. *American Journal of Community Psychology,* 15(2), 121-148.

[7] Kabat-Zinn, J. (1990). *Full Catastrophe Living: Using the Wisdom of Your Body and Mind to Face Stress, Pain, and Illness.* New York: Delacorte Press.

The Importance of a Support System

In the journey of activism, particularly within the LGBTQ community, the significance of a robust support system cannot be overstated. A support system encompasses individuals and groups that provide emotional, psychological, and practical assistance to activists. For Armando, this network was not merely a safety net; it was the very foundation upon which he built his resilience and capacity to confront adversity.

Theoretical Framework

The concept of a support system can be analyzed through various psychological and sociological lenses. One relevant theory is the **Social Support Theory**, which posits that social relationships provide individuals with emotional comfort, tangible assistance, and informational support. According to Cohen and Wills (1985), social support can mitigate stress and improve well-being, which is particularly crucial for those facing discrimination and hostility.

The equation for understanding the impact of social support on mental health can be represented as:

$$M = f(S, C) \tag{35}$$

where M represents mental health, S denotes the level of social support, and C indicates coping mechanisms. This relationship suggests that higher levels of social support (S) can lead to improved mental health outcomes (M) when combined with effective coping strategies (C).

Problems Faced Without a Support System

Without a supportive network, activists like Armando often encounter numerous challenges. The lack of emotional and practical support can lead to feelings of isolation, burnout, and even depression. For instance, in moments of intense backlash from conservative factions, the absence of allies can exacerbate stress levels, making it difficult for activists to maintain their resolve.

Armando experienced this firsthand during his early activism days, where he faced significant backlash from both societal structures and individuals. The attacks were not only verbal but also targeted his character and integrity. In such scenarios, the support system acts as a buffer, helping to mitigate the effects of such stressors.

Examples of Support Systems in Action

1. **Friendship Networks:** Armando's close friends played a pivotal role in his life, providing emotional support during challenging times. They would often gather to discuss their experiences, share coping strategies, and offer encouragement. This camaraderie fostered a sense of belonging, critical for maintaining mental health.

2. **LGBTQ Organizations:** Joining LGBTQ rights organizations not only provided Armando with a platform for advocacy but also connected him to a broader community of like-minded individuals. These organizations often host

workshops, support groups, and events that facilitate networking and collaboration among activists.

3. **Family Support:** While many LGBTQ individuals face rejection from their families, Armando's experience was different. His family, though initially hesitant, eventually became a significant source of support. They attended rallies with him, offered financial assistance for his initiatives, and provided a safe space for discussions about identity and activism.

Building and Maintaining a Support System

Creating a support system involves active engagement and nurturing of relationships. Armando's approach included:

- **Open Communication:** Regularly sharing his thoughts and feelings with his friends and family helped to strengthen their bonds. This transparency created an environment where everyone felt comfortable expressing their concerns and experiences.

- **Mutual Aid:** Armando emphasized the importance of reciprocity within his support network. He made it a point to offer help to others in his community, fostering a culture of mutual support that enriched everyone's experience.

- **Seeking Professional Help:** Recognizing the limits of peer support, Armando also sought professional counseling. This move not only provided him with additional coping strategies but also emphasized the importance of mental health care within activist circles.

Conclusion

In conclusion, the importance of a support system in the life of an activist cannot be overstated. For Armando, it was a lifeline that provided the emotional and practical support necessary to navigate the complexities of activism. By fostering strong relationships, engaging with community organizations, and prioritizing mental health, activists can build a resilient foundation that empowers them to continue their fight for equality and justice. The interplay of social support, coping strategies, and resilience forms a crucial triad that enhances the overall effectiveness of activism, ensuring that voices like Armando's resonate louder and longer in the quest for change.

Armando's Personal Triumphs amidst Struggles

Armando's journey as an LGBTQ activist has been marked by both challenges and significant personal triumphs. In this section, we will explore how he navigated his struggles and emerged victorious in various aspects of his life, ultimately shaping him into a resilient leader within the LGBTQ community.

Navigating Identity and Acceptance

One of Armando's most profound personal triumphs came from his ability to navigate the complexities of his identity. Growing up in a conservative society that often stigmatized LGBTQ individuals, Armando faced immense pressure to conform to traditional gender roles. However, he found strength in embracing his true self, which allowed him to connect with others who shared similar experiences.

This journey of self-acceptance was not without its difficulties. Armando faced rejection from some family members and friends, which led to feelings of isolation. Nevertheless, he discovered that vulnerability could be a source of strength. By openly sharing his experiences, he not only fostered connections with others but also inspired those around him to embrace their identities. The theory of *intersectionality*, developed by Kimberlé Crenshaw, emphasizes the importance of understanding how various aspects of identity—such as race, gender, and sexual orientation—intersect. Armando's recognition of his multifaceted identity allowed him to advocate for inclusivity within the LGBTQ community.

Building a Support Network

Armando's triumphs were also rooted in his ability to build a robust support network. During his formative years, he surrounded himself with friends who became like family, providing emotional support and encouragement. This community was instrumental in helping him navigate the challenges he faced as an LGBTQ individual.

The concept of *social capital*, as outlined by Pierre Bourdieu, underscores the value of social networks in achieving personal and collective goals. Armando utilized his social capital to amplify his voice and advocate for change. By collaborating with allies and fellow activists, he was able to leverage their strengths and resources, creating a powerful coalition dedicated to promoting LGBTQ rights.

Achievements in Advocacy

Armando's activism led to significant milestones that marked his personal triumphs. One notable achievement was his involvement in the successful campaign for legal recognition of same-sex partnerships in Colombia. This victory was not only a legal triumph but also a personal one, as it validated the experiences and relationships of countless LGBTQ individuals.

Furthermore, Armando's efforts in raising awareness about LGBTQ health issues contributed to improved healthcare access for marginalized communities. He organized workshops and seminars that educated healthcare professionals on LGBTQ-specific needs, thus fostering a more inclusive healthcare environment. The *Health Belief Model* suggests that individuals are more likely to engage in health-promoting behavior if they perceive a threat to their health and believe that a specific action can reduce that threat. Armando's advocacy helped bridge the gap between the LGBTQ community and healthcare providers, ultimately leading to better health outcomes.

Resilience in the Face of Adversity

Despite facing backlash and threats from conservative groups, Armando demonstrated remarkable resilience. He understood that adversity could serve as a catalyst for growth and change. His ability to maintain focus on his goals, even when faced with hostility, was a testament to his strength as an activist.

The psychological concept of *post-traumatic growth* describes how individuals can experience positive change following adversity. Armando exemplified this notion as he transformed his struggles into motivation for further activism. Each challenge he faced reinforced his commitment to fighting for equality and justice, inspiring others to join him in the struggle.

Inspiration and Legacy

Armando's personal triumphs extend beyond his individual achievements; they have also inspired a new generation of activists. By sharing his story and advocating for others, he has created a legacy of resilience and empowerment. His journey illustrates the importance of authenticity and the impact of collective action in the pursuit of social justice.

In conclusion, Armando's personal triumphs amidst struggles have shaped him into a formidable advocate for LGBTQ rights. His experiences highlight the significance of self-acceptance, the power of community, and the resilience required to overcome adversity. As he continues to inspire others, Armando's legacy serves as a reminder that personal triumphs can emerge from the darkest of struggles, paving the way for a more inclusive and equitable society.

The Legacy of Activism and Future Aspirations

The legacy of Armando's activism is not merely a collection of victories or defeats; it is a tapestry woven from the threads of resilience, courage, and an unwavering commitment to justice. His journey reflects a broader narrative of LGBTQ rights in Colombia and serves as an inspiration for future generations of activists.

Armando's activism has laid a foundation for significant advancements in legal recognition and social acceptance of LGBTQ individuals in Colombia. One of the most profound impacts of his work is seen in the legislative changes that have occurred since he began advocating for LGBTQ rights. For instance, the legalization of same-sex marriage in 2016 can be traced back to the groundwork laid by Armando and his contemporaries. This landmark victory was not just a legal triumph; it was a cultural shift that challenged long-standing prejudices and opened doors for discussions on equality and human rights.

However, the legacy of activism is also fraught with challenges. While significant strides have been made, the struggle for LGBTQ rights in Colombia is far from over. Issues such as discrimination in employment, healthcare access, and violence against LGBTQ individuals persist. Armando has often highlighted that the fight for equality is ongoing and that complacency can lead to regression. He emphasizes the importance of vigilance and continuous advocacy to ensure that the rights gained are not only preserved but expanded.

Armando's future aspirations reflect a vision that transcends national boundaries. He envisions a world where LGBTQ rights are universally recognized as human rights, where individuals can live authentically without fear of persecution. This vision is grounded in the theory of intersectionality, which posits that various forms of discrimination—such as those based on gender, race, and sexual orientation—are interconnected. Armando's advocacy incorporates this theory, acknowledging that the fight for LGBTQ rights must also address issues of gender equality, racism, and economic justice.

To achieve these aspirations, Armando believes in the power of grassroots movements and community engagement. He advocates for the mobilization of young activists who can bring fresh perspectives and energy to the movement. By mentoring emerging leaders and fostering collaboration among diverse social justice movements, Armando aims to create a more inclusive and effective advocacy landscape.

In terms of practical steps, Armando's future aspirations include the establishment of educational programs that promote LGBTQ inclusivity in schools. He argues that changing hearts and minds begins with education and that young people must be equipped with the knowledge and tools to challenge discrimination. This aligns with the principles of critical pedagogy, which emphasizes the role of education in fostering social change.

Furthermore, Armando envisions the creation of safe spaces for LGBTQ individuals, particularly in rural areas where access to resources and support is limited. He believes that community centers can serve as hubs for advocacy, education, and mental health support, providing a lifeline for those who may feel isolated or marginalized.

In conclusion, the legacy of Armando's activism is a testament to the power of resilience and the importance of continued advocacy. His aspirations for the future are rooted in a vision of inclusivity, intersectionality, and community empowerment. As he often states, "The fight for equality is not just about one group; it is about the dignity and rights of all people." By embracing this holistic approach, Armando hopes to inspire a new generation of activists who will carry the torch forward, ensuring that the legacy of activism is not only remembered but actively cultivated for years to come.

$$L = \sum_{i=1}^{n}(E_i - D_i) \tag{36}$$

Where L represents the legacy of activism, E_i signifies the achievements in equality, and D_i denotes the challenges faced. This equation encapsulates the ongoing struggle; it is a reminder that while progress has been made, the journey is far from complete. The future of LGBTQ rights hinges on the collective efforts of individuals committed to the cause, echoing Armando's belief that every voice matters in the chorus for change.

Armando's Impact on Future Generations

Armando's legacy as an LGBTQ activist extends far beyond the immediate victories he achieved in his lifetime. His influence resonates deeply within the hearts and minds of future generations, inspiring them to continue the fight for equality, justice, and acceptance. This section explores the multifaceted impact of Armando's work on emerging activists and the broader LGBTQ community.

The Ripple Effect of Activism

Armando's activism created a ripple effect that empowered countless individuals to embrace their identities and advocate for their rights. By sharing his personal journey, he demonstrated that vulnerability can be a powerful tool for change. His story, filled with challenges and triumphs, serves as a blueprint for those who may feel isolated or marginalized. The theory of social learning posits that individuals learn behaviors through observation and imitation (Bandura, 1977). Armando's courage in the face of adversity provided a model for others to follow, fostering a sense of community and solidarity.

Mentorship and Support

Armando actively engaged in mentorship, recognizing the importance of guiding young activists as they navigated their own paths. He established programs aimed at nurturing the next generation of leaders, emphasizing the significance of support networks. Research indicates that mentorship plays a crucial role in the development of leadership skills and self-efficacy (Eby et al., 2013). By investing time and resources in mentoring, Armando ensured that his knowledge and experiences would be passed down, creating a legacy of empowered individuals ready to challenge injustice.

Advocacy for Intersectionality

Armando's commitment to intersectionality highlighted the interconnectedness of various social justice movements. He understood that the fight for LGBTQ rights could not be separated from issues of race, gender, and class. This holistic approach is essential in contemporary activism, as it fosters inclusivity and acknowledges the diverse experiences within the community. Future generations of activists are increasingly recognizing the importance of intersectionality, as evidenced by movements that advocate for the rights of LGBTQ individuals of color, transgender individuals, and those with disabilities.

Cultural Shifts and Changing Narratives

Armando's work contributed to significant cultural shifts in societal attitudes towards LGBTQ individuals. By challenging stereotypes and advocating for representation in media, education, and politics, he helped reshape narratives that had long marginalized queer identities. Theories of cultural hegemony (Gramsci, 1971) explain how dominant cultural narratives can suppress alternative voices. Armando's activism played a crucial role in dismantling these hegemonic structures, paving the way for future generations to express their identities openly and authentically.

Global Influence and Solidarity

Armando's impact transcended borders, as he collaborated with international organizations to address global LGBTQ issues. His efforts to create solidarity among activists worldwide fostered a sense of shared purpose and collective action. The concept of transnational activism (Tilly, 2004) emphasizes the importance of cross-border collaboration in achieving social change. Future generations of activists have embraced this model, recognizing that the fight for LGBTQ rights is a global struggle that requires solidarity and cooperation.

Empowerment through Education

Education was a cornerstone of Armando's advocacy. He believed that informed individuals are empowered individuals. By advocating for LGBTQ-inclusive curricula and educational programs, he laid the groundwork for future generations to learn about their rights and the history of the LGBTQ movement. The impact of education on social justice is well-documented, as it fosters critical thinking and awareness (Freire, 1970). Armando's legacy is evident in the increasing number of educational institutions that prioritize inclusivity and diversity in their programs.

Inspiring Activism through Art and Expression

Armando utilized art as a medium for activism, understanding its power to evoke emotions and inspire change. His writings, performances, and visual art challenged societal norms and sparked conversations about LGBTQ rights. The role of art in social movements is profound, as it can mobilize communities and convey complex messages in accessible ways (Bourriaud, 2002). Future generations of activists continue to harness the power of art, using it as a tool for expression and advocacy.

A Vision for an Inclusive Future

Armando's vision for the future was rooted in inclusivity and equality. He believed that the fight for LGBTQ rights was intrinsically linked to the broader struggle for human rights. His unwavering commitment to social justice serves as a guiding principle for future activists, encouraging them to remain steadfast in their pursuit of equality for all marginalized communities. The principles of social justice advocacy emphasize the need for systemic change, urging future generations to challenge oppressive structures and advocate for a more equitable society (Rawls, 1971).

Conclusion

In conclusion, Armando's impact on future generations of LGBTQ activists is profound and far-reaching. Through mentorship, advocacy for intersectionality, cultural shifts, global solidarity, education, artistic expression, and a vision for inclusivity, he has left an indelible mark on the movement. As future activists draw inspiration from his life and work, they carry forward the torch of advocacy, ensuring that the fight for equality continues with renewed vigor and determination. Armando's legacy is not merely a reflection of past struggles; it is a call to action for all who believe in justice and equality.

Bibliography

[1] Bandura, A. (1977). *Social Learning Theory*. Prentice-Hall.

[2] Eby, L. T., Allen, T. D., Evans, S. C., Ng, T. W., & DuBois, D. L. (2013). Does Mentoring Matter? A Multidisciplinary Meta-Analytic Review of the Mentoring Literature. *Journal of Vocational Behavior*, 83(2), 106-116.

[3] Gramsci, A. (1971). *Selections from the Prison Notebooks*. International Publishers.

[4] Tilly, C. (2004). *Social Movements, 1768-2004*. Paradigm Publishers.

[5] Freire, P. (1970). *Pedagogy of the Oppressed*. Continuum.

[6] Bourriaud, N. (2002). *Relational Aesthetics*. Les presses du réel.

[7] Rawls, J. (1971). *A Theory of Justice*. Harvard University Press.

Armando's Other Advocacies

Armando's Other Advocacies

Armando's Other Advocacies

In the landscape of social justice, the interconnectedness of various movements is paramount. Armando recognized early on that the fight for LGBTQ rights could not be isolated from other social justice issues. His approach to activism was characterized by a commitment to intersectionality and inclusivity, which he believed were essential for meaningful progress.

Intersectionality and Inclusivity

The concept of intersectionality, first coined by Kimberlé Crenshaw, emphasizes how different forms of discrimination can overlap and compound, creating unique challenges for individuals at the intersection of multiple marginalized identities. Armando's advocacy was deeply rooted in this understanding, as he sought to address the complexities of identity that many individuals face.

$$\text{Intersectionality} = f(\text{Race, Gender, Sexual Orientation, Class, Ability}) \quad (37)$$

This equation illustrates that the experience of oppression cannot be understood through a singular lens; rather, it is a multifaceted phenomenon influenced by various social identities. Armando's work aimed to dismantle the barriers that these intersecting identities create, advocating for a more inclusive movement that recognizes the unique struggles of all individuals.

Advocating for Gender Equality

Armando's commitment to gender equality was evident in his collaborations with feminist organizations. He understood that the fight for LGBTQ rights was inextricably linked to the broader struggle for gender equality. His activism included organizing workshops and seminars that highlighted the importance of dismantling patriarchal structures that oppress not only women but also LGBTQ individuals.

For instance, during a campaign in Bogotá, Armando partnered with local women's rights groups to address issues such as domestic violence and reproductive rights, emphasizing that these issues disproportionately affect LGBTQ individuals. Through these collaborations, he aimed to foster solidarity among various social justice movements.

Fighting Against Racism and Xenophobia

Armando's advocacy also extended to combating racism and xenophobia, particularly within the LGBTQ community. He recognized that many LGBTQ individuals from racial and ethnic minorities faced additional layers of discrimination. His efforts included organizing anti-racist workshops and forums that educated community members about the importance of embracing diversity within the LGBTQ movement.

One notable initiative was the "Unity in Diversity" campaign, which aimed to amplify the voices of LGBTQ individuals from marginalized racial backgrounds. This campaign not only highlighted their stories but also sought to create a platform for dialogue about the intersections of race and sexuality.

Embracing LGBTQ Rights as Human Rights

Armando firmly believed that LGBTQ rights are fundamentally human rights. This belief guided his approach to advocacy, as he sought to frame the struggle for LGBTQ rights within the broader context of human rights. He often quoted the Universal Declaration of Human Rights, particularly Article 1, which states:

> "All human beings are born free and equal in dignity and rights."

By invoking this principle, Armando aimed to challenge the notion that LGBTQ rights were a niche issue, instead positioning them as a critical component of the global human rights agenda. He participated in international conferences, where he advocated for the inclusion of LGBTQ rights in discussions about human rights violations worldwide.

Armando's Efforts for Inclusivity within the LGBTQ Community

Inclusivity was a cornerstone of Armando's advocacy. He worked tirelessly to ensure that the LGBTQ community was a safe and welcoming space for individuals of all backgrounds. This involved addressing the specific needs of marginalized groups within the community, including transgender individuals, people of color, and those from low-income backgrounds.

Armando initiated programs that provided resources and support for these groups, including access to healthcare, legal assistance, and mental health services. His efforts were instrumental in creating a more equitable environment within the LGBTQ community, fostering a sense of belonging for all.

Collaborating with Other Movements and Organizations

Collaboration was key to Armando's approach to advocacy. He understood that the fight for LGBTQ rights could not be won in isolation; it required solidarity with other movements. Armando frequently collaborated with organizations focused on environmental justice, labor rights, and immigrant rights, recognizing that these issues were interconnected.

For example, during the "March for Our Lives" event, Armando joined forces with gun control advocates, highlighting how violence disproportionately affects marginalized communities, including LGBTQ individuals. This collaboration not only broadened the reach of his advocacy but also reinforced the idea that collective action is essential for social change.

Addressing Global LGBTQ Issues

Armando's advocacy was not confined to Colombia; he recognized the global nature of the struggle for LGBTQ rights. He collaborated with international activists and organizations to address issues such as violence, discrimination, and the plight of LGBTQ refugees and asylum seekers.

One of his notable projects was the "Global LGBTQ Solidarity Network," which aimed to connect activists across borders. This network facilitated the sharing of resources, strategies, and support, empowering LGBTQ activists in regions where their rights were severely restricted. Armando's global perspective underscored the importance of solidarity in the fight for justice.

Speaking Out on Violence and Discrimination Worldwide

Armando was a vocal advocate against violence and discrimination faced by LGBTQ individuals worldwide. He used his platform to raise awareness about the alarming rates of violence against LGBTQ individuals in various countries, particularly in regions where anti-LGBTQ laws were prevalent.

He organized awareness campaigns that highlighted personal stories of survivors of violence, emphasizing the urgent need for global action. Through social media and public speaking engagements, Armando sought to mobilize support for international initiatives aimed at protecting LGBTQ individuals from violence and persecution.

The Fight for LGBTQ Refugees and Asylum Seekers

Recognizing the dire circumstances faced by LGBTQ refugees and asylum seekers, Armando dedicated a significant portion of his advocacy to this issue. He collaborated with organizations that provided legal assistance and support services to those fleeing persecution due to their sexual orientation or gender identity.

One impactful initiative was the "Safe Haven Project," which aimed to provide safe spaces for LGBTQ refugees in Colombia. This project not only offered shelter but also facilitated access to healthcare, legal resources, and community support, helping individuals rebuild their lives in a new country.

Armando's Impact on Global LGBTQ Advocacy

Through his tireless efforts, Armando made significant contributions to global LGBTQ advocacy. His work inspired countless individuals to join the movement, fostering a sense of unity and purpose among activists worldwide. He was recognized internationally for his contributions, receiving awards and honors that celebrated his commitment to social justice.

Armando's impact extended beyond his immediate community, as he became a symbol of hope and resilience for LGBTQ individuals facing adversity globally. His belief in the power of collective action and solidarity continues to resonate within the LGBTQ movement.

Addressing Cultural Differences and Challenges

Armando understood that cultural differences could pose challenges in the fight for LGBTQ rights. He approached these challenges with sensitivity and respect, recognizing that advocacy must be tailored to the cultural context in which it operates. This involved engaging in dialogue with local communities and understanding their unique struggles and perspectives.

Through cultural competency training programs, Armando sought to educate activists on the importance of respecting cultural differences while advocating for LGBTQ rights. This approach fostered a more inclusive and respectful movement, allowing for greater collaboration and understanding among diverse groups.

Empowering LGBTQ Activists Across Borders

Empowerment was a central theme in Armando's advocacy. He believed in the importance of equipping LGBTQ activists with the tools and resources they needed to effect change in their own communities. This involved providing training, mentorship, and support to emerging activists, particularly in regions where LGBTQ rights were under threat.

Armando organized workshops and training sessions that focused on advocacy strategies, grassroots organizing, and coalition building. By empowering individuals to take action, he aimed to create a ripple effect of change that would extend far beyond his own efforts.

Armando's Legacy

Armando's commitment to intersectionality and inclusivity has left an indelible mark on the LGBTQ movement. His advocacy has inspired a new generation of activists who understand the importance of addressing the interconnectedness of social justice issues. As his work continues to influence the movement, Armando's legacy serves as a reminder that true progress requires collaboration, empathy, and a commitment to inclusivity.

In conclusion, Armando's other advocacies reflect his unwavering dedication to social justice in all its forms. By recognizing the interconnectedness of various movements and advocating for inclusivity, he has made significant strides in advancing LGBTQ rights while fostering solidarity among diverse communities. His work serves as a powerful reminder that the fight for justice is a collective endeavor, one that requires the voices and efforts of all individuals committed to creating a more equitable world.

Intersectionality and Inclusivity

Recognizing the Interconnectedness of Social Justice Movements

The struggle for LGBTQ rights cannot be viewed in isolation; rather, it exists within a broader tapestry of social justice movements that intersect and influence one another. This interconnectedness is vital to understanding the complexities of advocacy and the holistic approach required for effective change.

The theory of intersectionality, coined by legal scholar Kimberlé Crenshaw, posits that individuals experience oppression in varying degrees based on overlapping social identities, including race, gender, sexual orientation, and class. This framework helps activists recognize that the fight for LGBTQ rights is inextricably linked to other social justice causes, such as racial equality, gender justice, and economic rights.

$$O = f(I_1, I_2, I_3, \ldots, I_n) \tag{38}$$

Where O represents the overall oppression faced by an individual, and $I_1, I_2, \ldots, I_n$ are the various intersecting identities (e.g., gender, race, sexual orientation). This equation illustrates that oppression is not a singular experience but a complex function of multiple identities and societal structures.

For instance, consider the case of Black LGBTQ individuals, who face unique challenges due to the intersection of racism and homophobia. Their experiences highlight the necessity for advocacy that addresses both racial and sexual identity issues simultaneously. This dual struggle is exemplified in the work of organizations like the *Black LGBTQ+ Coalition*, which actively fights against anti-Black racism while promoting LGBTQ rights.

Similarly, the feminist movement has historically intersected with LGBTQ advocacy, particularly in the fight against gender-based violence. The concept of *gender justice* encompasses the rights of all individuals, regardless of their sexual orientation or gender identity, and seeks to dismantle patriarchal structures that perpetuate violence and discrimination.

The global context further complicates these interconnections. In many countries, LGBTQ rights are tied to broader human rights issues, including freedom of expression and assembly. Activists like Armando have worked alongside environmentalists, anti-racist groups, and women's rights organizations to create a united front against systemic injustices. For example, the *Global Fund for Women* has partnered with LGBTQ organizations to ensure that women's rights initiatives are inclusive of transgender and non-binary individuals, recognizing that gender equality cannot be achieved without addressing the specific needs of all gender identities.

Moreover, the economic dimensions of social justice cannot be overlooked. The LGBTQ community often faces economic disparities, such as higher rates of unemployment and poverty, particularly among marginalized groups within the community. Advocacy for economic justice, including fair wages and employment protections, is essential for creating a more equitable society. The *LGBTQ Economic Coalition* works to address these disparities by promoting policies that ensure economic opportunities for all, regardless of sexual orientation or gender identity.

In conclusion, recognizing the interconnectedness of social justice movements is crucial for effective advocacy. Armando's journey exemplifies how LGBTQ activism can benefit from collaboration with other social justice movements, creating a more inclusive and powerful force for change. By understanding and embracing these connections, activists can work toward a future where all individuals, regardless of their intersecting identities, can live freely and authentically.

Advocating for Gender Equality

Advocating for gender equality is a fundamental aspect of Armando's activism, reflecting the interconnectedness of various social justice movements. Gender equality is not merely a women's issue; it is a human rights issue that affects everyone, regardless of gender identity or expression. The pursuit of gender equality is rooted in the belief that all individuals should have equal rights, responsibilities, and opportunities, which aligns closely with the core values of the LGBTQ movement.

Theoretical Framework

The theoretical underpinnings of gender equality advocacy can be traced back to various feminist theories that have evolved over the decades. One of the most prominent theories is the *liberal feminist theory*, which argues for equality through legal reforms and policy changes. This approach emphasizes the importance of equal access to education, employment, and political participation. In contrast, *radical feminist theory* critiques the patriarchal structures that perpetuate gender-based oppression and advocates for a complete societal overhaul. Furthermore, *intersectional feminism* posits that the experiences of gender inequality cannot be understood in isolation from other forms of discrimination, such as race, class, and sexual orientation.

Identifying Key Issues

In Colombia, gender inequality manifests in various forms, including violence against women, economic disparities, and limited access to education. According to a report by the National Administrative Department of Statistics (DANE), women earn approximately 20% less than men for similar work, highlighting the persistent wage gap. Moreover, Colombia has one of the highest rates of femicide in Latin America, with women disproportionately affected by gender-based violence. These issues are compounded for LGBTQ individuals, particularly transgender women, who face heightened risks of violence and discrimination.

Armando's Initiatives

Armando has actively engaged in various initiatives aimed at addressing these disparities. One notable example is his collaboration with local NGOs to create awareness campaigns that educate communities about gender-based violence and the importance of consent. These campaigns utilize art, theatre, and social media to reach diverse audiences, emphasizing that gender equality benefits everyone.

In addition, Armando has worked to promote inclusive policies within LGBTQ organizations, ensuring that women's voices are heard and represented in decision-making processes. He has advocated for the inclusion of gender equality training in LGBTQ rights organizations, emphasizing that understanding gender dynamics is crucial for effective advocacy.

Collaborative Efforts

Armando understands that achieving gender equality requires collaboration across various movements. He has partnered with women's rights organizations to address issues such as reproductive rights and access to healthcare. This collaboration is critical, as it fosters a holistic approach to advocacy that recognizes the intersectionality of gender, sexuality, and class.

For instance, during the 2020 International Women's Day march in Bogotá, Armando joined forces with feminist groups to demand not only women's rights but also the rights of LGBTQ individuals. This intersectional approach highlights the importance of solidarity in the fight for equality, illustrating that gender equality and LGBTQ rights are inextricably linked.

Challenges and Resistance

Despite the progress made, advocating for gender equality in Colombia is fraught with challenges. Armando and his allies often face backlash from conservative factions that resist changes to traditional gender roles. This resistance is evident in the political landscape, where anti-feminist rhetoric has gained traction. Additionally, the COVID-19 pandemic exacerbated existing inequalities, with reports indicating an increase in domestic violence and economic instability for women.

Armando's response to these challenges has been to amplify the voices of marginalized groups within the gender equality movement, particularly those who are often overlooked, such as transgender individuals and women of color. By creating safe spaces for dialogue and support, he fosters resilience and empowerment among these communities.

The Path Forward

Looking ahead, Armando envisions a future where gender equality is fully realized, not just in Colombia but globally. He advocates for comprehensive education that addresses gender stereotypes from an early age, promoting a culture of respect and equality. Furthermore, he emphasizes the need for policies that support work-life balance, parental leave, and equitable pay, which are essential for achieving gender parity in the workplace.

In conclusion, Armando's advocacy for gender equality is an integral part of his broader mission for social justice. By recognizing the interconnectedness of gender and LGBTQ rights, he not only addresses the unique challenges faced by individuals in these communities but also contributes to a more equitable society for all. As he continues to champion these causes, Armando remains committed to fostering a world where everyone, regardless of gender identity, can thrive without fear of discrimination or violence.

Fighting Against Racism and Xenophobia

Racism and xenophobia are deeply rooted issues that affect not only individuals but also entire communities and societies. These forms of discrimination manifest in various ways, from overt acts of violence and hate speech to systemic inequalities that marginalize entire groups. Armando's advocacy recognizes that the fight for LGBTQ rights cannot be separated from the broader struggle against racism and xenophobia. This section explores the interconnectedness of these issues, the theoretical frameworks that inform this understanding, and the practical steps taken to combat these injustices.

Understanding Racism and Xenophobia

Racism can be defined as the belief that one race is inherently superior to another, leading to discrimination and prejudice based on racial identity. Xenophobia, on the other hand, refers to the fear or hatred of that which is perceived to be foreign or strange, often targeting immigrants and individuals from different cultural backgrounds. Both racism and xenophobia create barriers to equality and justice, perpetuating cycles of oppression.

Theoretical frameworks such as Critical Race Theory (CRT) provide a lens through which to understand the complexities of racism. CRT posits that racism is not merely an individual prejudice but a systemic issue embedded in the fabric of society. This perspective highlights the importance of recognizing how laws, policies, and institutional practices can perpetuate racial inequalities. Armando's activism draws on these theories to advocate for a more inclusive approach to LGBTQ rights that acknowledges and addresses the intersections of race, ethnicity, and sexual orientation.

The Intersectionality of Oppression

Intersectionality, a term coined by Kimberlé Crenshaw, refers to the ways in which different forms of discrimination intersect and overlap. For LGBTQ individuals of color, the experience of racism and xenophobia compounds the challenges they face in society. Armando emphasizes the importance of intersectional advocacy, which recognizes that the fight for LGBTQ rights must also include the fight against racism and xenophobia.

For example, LGBTQ individuals from immigrant backgrounds often face unique challenges, such as the threat of deportation or exclusion from both their cultural communities and the broader LGBTQ community. Armando has worked to amplify the voices of these individuals, creating spaces where their experiences are validated and their needs are addressed.

Practical Steps in the Fight Against Racism and Xenophobia

Armando's advocacy includes several practical steps aimed at combating racism and xenophobia within the LGBTQ movement. These steps include:

- **Education and Awareness:** Armando emphasizes the need for educational programs that address racism and xenophobia within LGBTQ organizations. Workshops and training sessions can help members understand their own biases and the importance of inclusivity.

- **Coalition Building:** Forming alliances with organizations that focus on racial justice and anti-xenophobia efforts is crucial. Armando has collaborated with various grassroots organizations to create a united front against discrimination.

- **Advocacy for Policy Change:** Armando advocates for policies that protect marginalized communities from discrimination. This includes lobbying for comprehensive immigration reform that respects the rights of LGBTQ immigrants and refugees.

- **Support for Victims:** Establishing support networks for individuals who experience racism and xenophobia is vital. Armando has been instrumental in creating safe spaces for individuals to share their experiences and access resources.

Case Studies and Examples

Armando's commitment to fighting racism and xenophobia is illustrated through several case studies:

- **The March for Equality:** During a recent march for LGBTQ rights, Armando organized a segment specifically addressing anti-Black racism within the LGBTQ community. This initiative highlighted the importance of acknowledging and addressing the unique struggles faced by Black LGBTQ individuals.

- **Community Dialogues:** Armando facilitated community dialogues that brought together LGBTQ individuals and those from immigrant backgrounds. These dialogues aimed to foster understanding and solidarity, allowing participants to share their experiences and build connections.

- **Advocacy Campaigns:** Armando has led campaigns that focus on the intersection of LGBTQ rights and racial justice. For instance, a campaign aimed at raising awareness about the disproportionate rates of violence faced by LGBTQ people of color garnered significant media attention and community support.

Challenges and Resistance

Despite the progress made, Armando's advocacy against racism and xenophobia is met with challenges. Resistance often comes from within the LGBTQ community, where some may prioritize sexual orientation over racial justice. This can lead to feelings of alienation among LGBTQ individuals of color who feel their experiences are marginalized.

Furthermore, systemic racism and xenophobia persist in society, making it difficult to enact meaningful change. Armando acknowledges that the fight against these injustices requires ongoing commitment and resilience. He emphasizes the importance of listening to and uplifting the voices of those most affected by these issues.

Conclusion

Fighting against racism and xenophobia is an essential component of Armando's advocacy for LGBTQ rights. By recognizing the interconnectedness of these struggles, Armando works to create a more inclusive movement that honors the diversity within the LGBTQ community. Through education, coalition building, and advocacy for policy change, he aims to dismantle the barriers that perpetuate discrimination and oppression. Armando's efforts serve as a reminder that true equality can only be achieved when all voices are heard and valued, regardless of race or background.

Embracing LGBTQ Rights as Human Rights

The discourse surrounding LGBTQ rights has evolved significantly over the past few decades, increasingly framing these rights as fundamental human rights. This paradigm shift is essential for fostering a more inclusive society where all individuals, regardless of their sexual orientation or gender identity, are afforded the same rights and protections as their heterosexual and cisgender counterparts.

Theoretical Framework

The foundation of LGBTQ rights as human rights is rooted in various international human rights treaties and declarations. The Universal Declaration of Human Rights (UDHR), adopted by the United Nations General Assembly in 1948, asserts in Article 1 that "All human beings are born free and equal in dignity and rights." This principle is echoed in numerous treaties, including the International Covenant on Civil and Political Rights (ICCPR) and the Convention on the Elimination of All Forms of Discrimination Against Women (CEDAW), which advocate for the protection of individuals from discrimination based on various characteristics, including sexual orientation and gender identity.

The theory of intersectionality, introduced by Kimberlé Crenshaw, further enriches the understanding of LGBTQ rights within the human rights framework. Intersectionality posits that individuals experience multiple, overlapping identities that can compound discrimination. For LGBTQ individuals, factors such as race, class, and disability can intersect with their sexual orientation or gender identity, leading to unique challenges that must be addressed in advocacy efforts.

Problems and Challenges

Despite the growing recognition of LGBTQ rights as human rights, significant challenges remain. In many regions, particularly in parts of Africa, Asia, and the Middle East, LGBTQ individuals face legal penalties, social ostracism, and violence. For example, in countries like Uganda and Nigeria, anti-LGBTQ laws are not only enforced but are often accompanied by violent backlash from both state and non-state actors. This raises critical questions about the effectiveness of international human rights frameworks, which may not always translate into tangible protections for marginalized communities.

Moreover, the backlash against LGBTQ rights in various parts of the world highlights the ongoing struggle for recognition. In the United States, for instance, the reversal of protections for transgender individuals in healthcare and military service, as well as the rise of anti-LGBTQ legislation in several states, demonstrates the fragility of hard-won rights. These developments underscore the need for continued advocacy and vigilance in the face of resistance.

Examples of Advocacy and Progress

In contrast to the challenges, there are numerous examples of successful advocacy that demonstrate the potential for LGBTQ rights to be embraced as human rights. The landmark case of Obergefell v. Hodges (2015) in the United States Supreme Court, which legalized same-sex marriage nationwide, serves as a pivotal example of how legal frameworks can evolve to recognize LGBTQ rights. This decision was not merely a legal victory; it symbolized a broader societal acceptance of LGBTQ individuals and their relationships.

Internationally, organizations such as ILGA (International Lesbian, Gay, Bisexual, Trans and Intersex Association) work tirelessly to advocate for LGBTQ rights, providing resources and support to activists around the globe. Their annual reports highlight both progress and setbacks, serving as a vital tool for understanding the global landscape of LGBTQ rights.

Conclusion

Embracing LGBTQ rights as human rights is not just a matter of legal recognition; it is a fundamental aspect of promoting dignity, equality, and justice for all individuals. As the movement continues to evolve, it is crucial to address the intersectional nature of discrimination and to advocate for comprehensive protections that encompass the diverse experiences of LGBTQ individuals. By framing LGBTQ rights within the broader human rights discourse, advocates can foster a more inclusive society that recognizes and celebrates diversity in all its forms.

$$\text{LGBTQ Rights} \subset \text{Human Rights} \tag{39}$$

This equation symbolizes the integral relationship between LGBTQ rights and the broader framework of human rights, emphasizing that the fight for equality is a universal struggle that transcends borders and identities.

Armando's Efforts for Inclusivity within the LGBTQ Community

Armando Trevisan's advocacy within the LGBTQ community has always been characterized by a commitment to inclusivity. He recognizes that the LGBTQ community is not monolithic; it encompasses a diverse range of identities, experiences, and cultural backgrounds. This understanding has shaped his approach to activism, leading him to address the unique challenges faced by various subgroups within the community.

Recognizing Intersectionality

At the core of Armando's efforts is the concept of intersectionality, a term coined by legal scholar Kimberlé Crenshaw in the late 1980s. Intersectionality posits that individuals experience oppression and discrimination in varying degrees based on their intersecting identities, including race, gender, sexuality, and socioeconomic status. Armando has consistently advocated for a framework that acknowledges these intersections, arguing that true inclusivity can only be achieved when the voices of the most marginalized are amplified.

For instance, Armando has collaborated with LGBTQ organizations that focus on the experiences of LGBTQ people of color, transgender individuals, and those with disabilities. He has often stated, "Our fight for equality is not just about sexual orientation; it is about dismantling all forms of oppression that affect our communities." This holistic view has allowed him to build coalitions that address the multifaceted nature of discrimination.

Creating Safe Spaces

Armando's advocacy also emphasizes the importance of creating safe spaces within the LGBTQ community. He has organized numerous workshops and forums aimed at fostering dialogue among diverse groups. These gatherings provide platforms for individuals to share their stories, discuss their challenges, and collaborate on solutions. For example, during a workshop titled "Voices of Diversity," participants from various backgrounds shared personal narratives that highlighted the intersection of race and sexuality. This initiative not only educated attendees but also fostered a sense of belonging and understanding.

Armando believes that safe spaces are crucial for healing and empowerment. He has stated, "When we create environments where everyone feels valued, we can harness the full potential of our community." His efforts have led to the establishment of support networks that cater to specific needs, such as mental health resources for LGBTQ youth or legal assistance for undocumented LGBTQ immigrants.

Advocating for Policy Change

Recognizing that inclusivity must also manifest in policy, Armando has been a staunch advocate for legislative changes that protect the rights of all LGBTQ individuals. He has worked tirelessly to lobby for anti-discrimination laws that address the specific needs of marginalized groups within the community. For example, he played a pivotal role in the campaign for the inclusion of gender identity and expression in anti-discrimination legislation in Colombia.

Armando's advocacy extends beyond local efforts; he has also engaged with international organizations to promote global standards for LGBTQ rights. He has been involved in initiatives that seek to align local policies with international human rights frameworks, emphasizing that inclusivity should be a global priority.

Promoting Education and Awareness

Education is another cornerstone of Armando's strategy for inclusivity. He has initiated educational programs that aim to raise awareness about the diverse identities within the LGBTQ community. These programs often include workshops in schools and community centers, focusing on topics such as the importance of pronouns, understanding non-binary identities, and the history of LGBTQ rights movements.

For example, Armando collaborated with local schools to implement an LGBTQ-inclusive curriculum, which has been met with both support and resistance. He firmly believes that educating young people about diversity in sexual orientation and gender identity is essential for fostering a more inclusive society. As he often remarks, "Change begins with education; when we teach acceptance, we pave the way for a more equitable future."

Building Alliances Across Movements

Armando understands that inclusivity within the LGBTQ community cannot be achieved in isolation. He has actively sought to build alliances with other social justice movements, recognizing that the fight for LGBTQ rights is intertwined with struggles against racism, sexism, and economic inequality. By collaborating with feminist organizations, anti-racist groups, and labor unions, Armando has worked to create a united front for social justice.

One notable example of this collaboration was the "March for Equality and Justice," where LGBTQ activists joined forces with anti-racist and feminist groups to address the systemic inequalities affecting multiple communities. This event not only highlighted the interconnectedness of various struggles but also demonstrated the power of solidarity in advocating for change.

Challenges and Resistance

Despite his efforts, Armando has faced challenges in promoting inclusivity within the LGBTQ community. Resistance often arises from within the community itself, as some individuals may hold onto traditional views that exclude certain identities. Armando has encountered pushback when advocating for the inclusion of transgender rights and the visibility of LGBTQ people of color. He approaches these challenges with patience and a willingness to engage in dialogue, believing that education and understanding can bridge divides.

In conclusion, Armando Trevisan's efforts for inclusivity within the LGBTQ community exemplify a comprehensive and intersectional approach to activism. Through recognizing the interconnectedness of identities, creating safe spaces, advocating for policy change, promoting education, and building alliances, he has made significant strides in fostering a more inclusive environment. His work serves as a reminder that true equality can only be achieved when all voices are heard and valued within the movement.

Collaborating with Other Movements and Organizations

In the quest for social justice, the LGBTQ movement has increasingly recognized the importance of collaboration with other social movements and organizations. This intersectional approach not only amplifies the voices of marginalized communities but also fosters a more comprehensive understanding of the systemic issues at play. Armando's advocacy has exemplified the power of these collaborations, demonstrating how unity across movements can lead to significant progress.

Theoretical Framework

The concept of intersectionality, coined by Kimberlé Crenshaw, serves as a foundational theory for understanding the interconnectedness of social identities and the unique challenges faced by individuals at their intersections. Intersectionality posits that various forms of discrimination—such as those based on race, gender, sexuality, and class—do not operate independently but are interconnected and compound one another. This theoretical framework underlines the necessity for LGBTQ activists to collaborate with organizations focused on racial justice, gender equality, and economic rights, among others.

Challenges of Collaboration

Despite the clear benefits, collaboration among movements is not without its challenges. One significant problem is the potential for competing priorities. For instance, while LGBTQ organizations may prioritize marriage equality, feminist groups might focus on reproductive rights. Such differences can lead to tension and fragmentation within coalitions. Furthermore, resource allocation can become contentious, as organizations vie for funding and attention, often leading to the marginalization of smaller or less visible groups.

Another challenge is the risk of tokenism, where organizations may superficially include LGBTQ voices without genuinely integrating their concerns into the broader agenda. This can result in a lack of meaningful engagement and ultimately undermine the goals of both movements.

Successful Collaborations: Case Studies

Armando's work has illustrated the effectiveness of collaboration through various initiatives that unite LGBTQ rights with other social justice causes. One notable example is the partnership between LGBTQ organizations and immigrant rights groups. Recognizing that many LGBTQ individuals are also immigrants facing discrimination, these organizations have collaborated to advocate for comprehensive immigration reform that includes protections for LGBTQ asylum seekers.

This collaboration has led to the development of joint campaigns, such as the "Safe Haven" initiative, which provides resources and legal assistance to LGBTQ refugees fleeing persecution. By pooling their expertise and resources, these organizations have been able to create a more robust support system for vulnerable populations.

Another example can be seen in the collaboration between LGBTQ activists and environmental justice organizations. As climate change disproportionately affects marginalized communities, including LGBTQ individuals, these groups have come together to advocate for policies that address both environmental sustainability and social equity. This partnership has resulted in joint advocacy efforts, such as the "Green Pride" campaign, which emphasizes the need for inclusive environmental policies that consider the unique needs of LGBTQ communities.

The Role of Solidarity in Activism

Armando emphasizes that solidarity is a crucial element in the fight for justice. Solidarity involves recognizing the shared struggles among different marginalized groups and actively supporting one another's causes. This principle has guided Armando's approach to collaboration, as he seeks to build alliances that transcend single-issue activism.

For instance, during the annual Pride celebrations, Armando has organized events that highlight the struggles of people of color within the LGBTQ community, fostering dialogue and understanding among diverse groups. By creating spaces for intersectional discussions, Armando has helped to cultivate a sense of community and shared purpose among activists from various backgrounds.

Conclusion

In conclusion, the collaboration between LGBTQ organizations and other social movements is essential for creating a more inclusive and effective advocacy landscape. By embracing intersectionality and prioritizing solidarity, activists like Armando can address the complex realities faced by individuals at the intersections of multiple identities. Through successful collaborations, the LGBTQ movement can continue to push for comprehensive social change, ensuring that the rights and dignity of all individuals are upheld.

This collaborative approach not only strengthens individual movements but also paves the way for a more equitable society, where the struggles of one group are recognized as part of the broader fight for justice. Armando's legacy serves as a testament to the power of unity and the importance of working together to achieve meaningful change.

Addressing Global LGBTQ Issues

Collaboration with International Activists and Organizations

In the realm of LGBTQ advocacy, the importance of collaboration with international activists and organizations cannot be overstated. The interconnectedness of social justice movements across borders necessitates a collective approach to address the myriad challenges faced by LGBTQ individuals worldwide. Armando's commitment to fostering these collaborations serves as a cornerstone of his activism, significantly amplifying the impact of his efforts.

Theoretical Framework

The theoretical underpinning for international collaboration in LGBTQ activism can be traced to the principles of *intersectionality* and *global citizenship*. Intersectionality, as coined by Kimberlé Crenshaw, emphasizes the interconnected nature of social categorizations such as race, class, and gender, which create overlapping systems of discrimination or disadvantage. In the context of LGBTQ rights, recognizing that individuals experience oppression differently based on their unique identities is crucial for effective advocacy.

Global citizenship, on the other hand, posits that individuals have a responsibility to engage with global issues, transcending national boundaries to promote human rights and social justice. This framework encourages activists like Armando to collaborate with international organizations, sharing knowledge, resources, and strategies to combat discrimination and violence against LGBTQ individuals on a global scale.

Challenges in Collaboration

Despite the theoretical benefits of collaboration, several challenges persist in the practical application of international LGBTQ advocacy. One significant problem is the disparity in legal protections and cultural acceptance of LGBTQ rights across different countries. For instance, while many Western nations have made substantial progress in legalizing same-sex marriage and protecting LGBTQ rights, several countries in Africa and the Middle East continue to enforce harsh penalties for homosexuality.

This disparity often leads to a lack of unified strategy among activists, as the priorities and methods of advocacy can vary significantly based on local contexts. Moreover, language barriers and differing cultural understandings of gender and sexuality can hinder effective communication and collaboration among activists from diverse backgrounds.

Armando's Collaborative Efforts

Armando has actively sought partnerships with various international organizations, such as *ILGA World* (International Lesbian, Gay, Bisexual, Trans and Intersex Association) and *OutRight Action International*. These organizations focus on promoting LGBTQ rights globally and provide a platform for activists to share resources and strategies.

For example, during a conference organized by ILGA World, Armando presented a case study on the successful advocacy strategies employed in Colombia, highlighting how local activists mobilized public opinion and leveraged social media to effect change. This experience not only provided valuable insights for activists from other regions but also fostered a spirit of solidarity and shared purpose.

Case Studies of Successful Collaborations

One notable example of successful international collaboration is the *Global Equality Fund*, which provides financial support to LGBTQ organizations in countries where rights are under threat. Armando played a pivotal role in advocating for the inclusion of Colombian LGBTQ organizations in the fund's initiatives, ensuring that local activists received the necessary resources to continue their work despite facing systemic challenges.

Another example can be found in the *Human Rights Campaign*'s partnership with LGBTQ activists in Colombia to address the issue of violence against transgender individuals. By pooling resources and expertise, they launched a campaign that not only raised awareness but also pressured the Colombian government to implement protective measures for marginalized communities.

The Future of International Collaboration

Looking ahead, the future of international collaboration in LGBTQ advocacy appears promising, albeit fraught with challenges. The rise of digital activism has enabled activists to connect and collaborate across borders more easily than ever before. Social media platforms serve as vital tools for sharing information, mobilizing support, and amplifying marginalized voices.

However, as Armando emphasizes, it is crucial for activists to remain vigilant against potential backlash from conservative forces that seek to undermine progress. The ongoing struggle for LGBTQ rights in various regions underscores the need for sustained collaboration and solidarity among activists globally.

In conclusion, Armando's collaboration with international activists and organizations exemplifies the power of unity in the fight for LGBTQ rights. By embracing an intersectional approach and fostering global citizenship, activists can work together to dismantle oppressive systems and create a more equitable world for all.

Speaking Out on Violence and Discrimination Worldwide

The global landscape of LGBTQ rights is marred by a pervasive culture of violence and discrimination that transcends borders. Armando recognized early on that the struggles faced by LGBTQ individuals are not confined to his home country of Colombia; rather, they are part of a larger tapestry of human rights violations occurring around the world. In this section, we will explore the various forms of violence and discrimination that LGBTQ individuals face globally, the theoretical frameworks that help us understand these issues, and the ways in which Armando has used his platform to speak out against these injustices.

Understanding Violence and Discrimination

Violence against LGBTQ individuals manifests in numerous forms, including physical assault, psychological abuse, and systemic discrimination. According to the *International Lesbian, Gay, Bisexual, Trans and Intersex Association (ILGA)*, over 70 countries still criminalize same-sex relations, and in some regions, LGBTQ individuals face the death penalty. This legal framework not only legitimizes violence but also perpetuates societal norms that dehumanize LGBTQ individuals.

Theoretical frameworks such as Judith Butler's *Gender Trouble* provide a lens to understand how societal norms around gender and sexuality contribute to violence. Butler argues that gender is performative; thus, when individuals fail to conform to traditional gender norms, they become targets for violence. This theory highlights the intersection of gender identity and societal expectations, illustrating how deviations from the norm can lead to severe repercussions.

Examples of Global Violence

Armando has consistently highlighted specific cases of violence against LGBTQ individuals worldwide. For instance, the brutal murder of Marielle Franco, a Brazilian politician and LGBTQ advocate, in 2018 sent shockwaves through the community. Franco's assassination was not only a targeted act of violence against her as a woman of color but also a broader attack on LGBTQ rights in Brazil, a country already grappling with high rates of violence against sexual minorities. In her memory, Armando has advocated for justice and accountability, emphasizing that such acts of violence are not isolated incidents but part of a systemic issue.

Another notable example is the ongoing persecution of LGBTQ individuals in Chechnya, where reports of detention, torture, and extrajudicial killings have emerged. Activists, including Armando, have raised their voices against these atrocities, calling for international intervention and support for those fleeing persecution. The plight of Chechen LGBTQ individuals illustrates the urgent need for global solidarity and action against state-sponsored violence.

The Role of Advocacy

Armando's advocacy extends beyond merely raising awareness; he actively engages in campaigns that seek to hold perpetrators accountable and push for legislative changes. He has collaborated with international organizations like Human Rights Watch and Amnesty International to document cases of violence and discrimination. By compiling reports and testimonials, these organizations provide concrete evidence of the human rights violations faced by LGBTQ individuals, which Armando uses to advocate for change.

The concept of *intersectionality*, coined by Kimberlé Crenshaw, is crucial in understanding how various forms of discrimination overlap. Armando emphasizes that LGBTQ rights cannot be viewed in isolation from issues of race, gender, and socioeconomic status. For instance, LGBTQ individuals from marginalized communities often face compounded discrimination, making it imperative to adopt an intersectional approach in advocacy efforts.

Mobilizing Public Opinion

Armando has harnessed the power of social media to mobilize public opinion against violence and discrimination. By sharing stories of survivors and highlighting the experiences of LGBTQ individuals worldwide, he has fostered a sense of global community and solidarity. Campaigns such as #LoveIsLove and #EndHomophobia have gained traction, encouraging individuals to speak out against injustices and support their LGBTQ peers.

Moreover, Armando has participated in international forums, such as the United Nations Human Rights Council, where he has delivered powerful speeches calling for the protection of LGBTQ rights. These platforms allow him to amplify the voices of those who are often silenced and to advocate for policies that promote equality and justice.

Conclusion

In conclusion, Armando's commitment to speaking out against violence and discrimination worldwide is a testament to his belief in the universality of human rights. By employing theoretical frameworks, sharing poignant examples, and mobilizing public opinion, he has made significant strides in advocating for LGBTQ rights on a global scale. The fight against violence and discrimination is ongoing, but through collective action and unwavering determination, Armando and countless others continue to pave the way for a more inclusive and just world for all individuals, regardless of their sexual orientation or gender identity.

The Fight for LGBTQ Refugees and Asylum Seekers

The plight of LGBTQ refugees and asylum seekers is a pressing global issue that intersects with human rights, international law, and social justice. Many individuals fleeing persecution due to their sexual orientation or gender identity face immense challenges in their journey for safety and acceptance. This section delves into the complexities of this struggle, the theoretical frameworks that inform our understanding, the problems faced by these individuals, and examples of advocacy efforts aimed at addressing their needs.

Theoretical Frameworks

To comprehend the fight for LGBTQ refugees and asylum seekers, it is essential to consider several theoretical frameworks:

- **Intersectionality:** Coined by Kimberlé Crenshaw, intersectionality provides a lens to understand how various forms of discrimination overlap. LGBTQ individuals often face multiple layers of oppression based on race, gender, and socioeconomic status, which can exacerbate their vulnerability as refugees.

- **Human Rights Theory:** At its core, the fight for LGBTQ asylum seekers is rooted in human rights. The Universal Declaration of Human Rights asserts that everyone is entitled to fundamental rights and freedoms without discrimination. This principle underpins the legal arguments for asylum based on sexual orientation and gender identity.

- **Queer Theory:** This framework challenges normative definitions of gender and sexuality, advocating for a broader understanding of identity. Queer theory informs advocacy by highlighting the need for policies that recognize the fluidity of gender and sexuality, rather than confining individuals to binary categories.

Problems Faced by LGBTQ Refugees

LGBTQ refugees and asylum seekers encounter numerous obstacles that complicate their quest for safety:

- **Legal Barriers:** Many countries do not recognize sexual orientation or gender identity as valid grounds for asylum. This lack of legal recognition forces LGBTQ individuals to present their cases within a framework that may not adequately capture their experiences of persecution.

- **Cultural Stigma:** In many regions, societal attitudes towards LGBTQ individuals remain hostile. This stigma can lead to discrimination within refugee camps, as well as difficulty in accessing essential services such as healthcare and legal aid.

- **Mental Health Challenges:** The trauma of persecution, combined with the stress of displacement, can severely impact the mental health of LGBTQ refugees. Issues such as depression, anxiety, and PTSD are prevalent among this population, necessitating targeted mental health support.

- **Economic Hardship:** Many LGBTQ refugees arrive in new countries with limited resources and face barriers to employment due to discrimination. This economic instability can hinder their ability to secure housing and integrate into their new communities.

Examples of Advocacy Efforts

Several organizations and movements have emerged to address the needs of LGBTQ refugees and asylum seekers:

- **The International Refugee Assistance Project (IRAP):** This organization provides legal assistance to refugees, including those fleeing persecution based on sexual orientation and gender identity. IRAP's work highlights the importance of legal representation in navigating complex asylum processes.

- **Rainbow Railroad:** A Canadian non-profit, Rainbow Railroad assists LGBTQ individuals in escaping violence and persecution in their home countries. By facilitating safe passage and resettlement, the organization exemplifies a proactive approach to addressing the needs of LGBTQ refugees.

- **The United Nations High Commissioner for Refugees (UNHCR):** The UNHCR has increasingly recognized the unique challenges faced by LGBTQ asylum seekers. Their guidelines advocate for the inclusion of sexual orientation and gender identity in refugee determinations, reflecting a growing understanding of the complexities involved.

- **Local Grassroots Organizations:** Many grassroots organizations around the world are dedicated to supporting LGBTQ refugees at the community level. These groups often provide vital resources such as legal aid, mental health services, and social support networks.

Conclusion

The fight for LGBTQ refugees and asylum seekers is a multifaceted struggle that requires a concerted effort from activists, policymakers, and society at large. By employing theoretical frameworks such as intersectionality and human rights theory, advocates can better understand and address the unique challenges faced by this vulnerable population. As the global landscape continues to evolve, it is imperative that we remain committed to ensuring that LGBTQ refugees receive the protection, support, and dignity they deserve. The journey towards equality and justice for LGBTQ individuals must include a steadfast commitment to those seeking refuge from persecution, as their stories are integral to the broader narrative of human rights.

$$\text{Asylum Success Rate} = \frac{\text{Number of Approved Asylum Applications}}{\text{Total Asylum Applications}} \times 100 \quad (40)$$

Armando's Impact on Global LGBTQ Advocacy

Armando's influence on global LGBTQ advocacy is a testament to the power of intersectional activism and the importance of solidarity across borders. His work transcended local issues, resonating with activists and movements worldwide, and he became a symbol of hope and resilience for marginalized communities.

Theoretical Framework

To understand Armando's impact, we must consider the theoretical frameworks that underpin his advocacy. One such framework is *intersectionality*, a term coined by Kimberlé Crenshaw, which emphasizes that individuals experience oppression in varying configurations and degrees of intensity based on their intersecting social identities, such as race, gender, sexuality, and class. Armando's advocacy highlighted how LGBTQ rights are inextricably linked to other social justice movements, fostering a more inclusive approach to activism.

Addressing Global Issues

Armando's commitment to addressing global LGBTQ issues was evident in his collaboration with international organizations such as *ILGA* (International Lesbian, Gay, Bisexual, Trans and Intersex Association) and *OutRight Action International*. These partnerships allowed him to amplify the voices of LGBTQ individuals facing persecution in countries with draconian anti-LGBTQ laws.

For instance, Armando participated in the *Global LGBTQ Rights Conference* held in Amsterdam in 2019, where he presented a paper on the challenges faced by LGBTQ refugees and asylum seekers. He highlighted the legal barriers that prevent these individuals from seeking safety, using statistical data to underscore the urgency of the situation:

$$\text{Refugee Acceptance Rate} = \frac{\text{Number of Accepted LGBTQ Refugees}}{\text{Total Number of LGBTQ Refugees}} \times 100 \quad (41)$$

This equation illustrates the disparity in acceptance rates, emphasizing the need for policy reform and international cooperation.

Speaking Out Against Violence and Discrimination

Armando's advocacy included speaking out against violence and discrimination faced by LGBTQ individuals globally. He utilized social media platforms to raise awareness and mobilize support, reaching millions of followers. His viral campaign, *#SafeSpacesForAll*, called attention to the violence faced by LGBTQ individuals in countries like Brazil, where reports indicated a significant increase in hate crimes.

According to the *Brazilian Forum on Public Security*, the number of LGBTQ homicides rose by 30% in the last year, prompting Armando to take action. He organized a series of international vigils, connecting activists from different countries to honor victims and demand justice.

Empowering LGBTQ Activists Across Borders

Armando's impact extended to empowering LGBTQ activists across borders. He established mentorship programs that paired experienced activists with emerging leaders in countries facing severe repression. This initiative not only provided guidance but also fostered a sense of global community among LGBTQ activists.

One notable success was the *LGBTQ Leadership Exchange Program*, which allowed activists from Central America to connect with their counterparts in Europe. Participants shared strategies, resources, and experiences, leading to collaborative projects that addressed local issues while drawing on global best practices.

Addressing Cultural Differences and Challenges

Armando recognized the importance of addressing cultural differences and challenges within the LGBTQ movement. He advocated for culturally sensitive approaches that respect local traditions while promoting human rights. In his travels, he often emphasized the need for dialogue between LGBTQ activists and traditional leaders, fostering understanding and collaboration.

For example, during a conference in Kenya, Armando facilitated discussions between LGBTQ activists and tribal elders, resulting in a joint declaration that recognized the rights of LGBTQ individuals within the context of local customs. This approach not only advanced LGBTQ rights but also helped bridge divides within communities.

Armando's Global Influence

Armando's global influence is reflected in numerous accolades and recognition from international bodies. He was awarded the *Global LGBTQ Advocacy Award* in 2021 for his tireless efforts to promote equality and justice. His work inspired a new generation of activists, who continue to build on his legacy.

In addition, Armando's writings, including his influential book *"Beyond Borders: The Global Fight for LGBTQ Rights"*, have become essential reading for activists and scholars alike. The book explores the interconnectedness of LGBTQ struggles worldwide and offers a roadmap for future advocacy.

Conclusion

In conclusion, Armando's impact on global LGBTQ advocacy is profound and multifaceted. By embracing intersectionality, addressing global issues, empowering activists, and fostering cultural sensitivity, he has set a standard for what it means to be a global advocate for LGBTQ rights. His legacy serves as a reminder that the fight for equality is not confined by borders; it is a shared struggle that requires solidarity, resilience, and unwavering commitment.

Addressing Cultural Differences and Challenges

In the realm of LGBTQ advocacy, cultural differences and challenges present both obstacles and opportunities. These variations arise from the diverse sociopolitical landscapes, cultural norms, and historical contexts that shape the experiences of LGBTQ individuals across the globe. Understanding and addressing these differences is crucial for effective advocacy and the promotion of inclusive policies.

Theoretical Frameworks

To navigate cultural differences, it is essential to employ theoretical frameworks that acknowledge intersectionality. Intersectionality, as coined by Kimberlé Crenshaw, provides a lens through which we can understand how various social identities, including race, gender, sexuality, and class, intersect to create unique experiences of oppression and privilege. In the context of LGBTQ advocacy, intersectionality emphasizes that not all LGBTQ individuals face the same challenges; rather, their experiences are influenced by their cultural and social backgrounds.

$$E = \sum_{i=1}^{n} \frac{P_i \cdot V_i}{C_i} \tag{42}$$

Where: - E = Effectiveness of advocacy - P_i = Perceived relevance of the issue - V_i = Value of the cultural context - C_i = Cultural barriers encountered

This equation illustrates that the effectiveness of advocacy efforts is contingent on the perceived relevance of issues within specific cultural contexts and the barriers that advocates may encounter.

Cultural Norms and Attitudes

Cultural norms significantly influence attitudes towards LGBTQ individuals. In many cultures, traditional beliefs around gender and sexuality can lead to discrimination and violence against LGBTQ individuals. For instance, in certain regions of Africa and the Middle East, homosexuality is criminalized, and LGBTQ individuals face severe repercussions. This cultural backdrop necessitates a tailored approach to advocacy that respects local customs while promoting universal human rights.

For example, the work of organizations like *OutRight Action International* highlights the importance of culturally sensitive advocacy. They engage local activists who understand the nuances of their communities, ensuring that campaigns resonate with local values while challenging harmful practices. This approach fosters solidarity and builds trust within communities that may otherwise resist external interventions.

Globalization and Cultural Exchange

Globalization has facilitated the exchange of ideas and practices across borders, leading to both positive and negative outcomes for LGBTQ advocacy. On one hand, global networks have enabled activists to share strategies and successes, fostering a sense of solidarity. For instance, the global Pride movement has inspired local Pride events in countries where LGBTQ visibility was previously absent.

On the other hand, globalization can also lead to cultural imperialism, where Western ideals of LGBTQ rights are imposed on non-Western cultures. This imposition can result in backlash and resistance, as local communities may perceive these efforts as a threat to their cultural identity. Therefore, it is essential for advocates to engage in dialogue that respects cultural differences while promoting universal rights.

Case Studies

One notable example of addressing cultural differences in LGBTQ advocacy is the work done in Latin America. In Colombia, activists have successfully navigated the complexities of a predominantly Catholic society to promote LGBTQ rights. The *Colombian LGBTQ Federation* has utilized community-based approaches, incorporating traditional values of family and community to foster acceptance. This strategy has led to significant legal advancements, including the legalization of same-sex marriage in 2016.

Conversely, in regions like Eastern Europe, LGBTQ activists face substantial challenges due to entrenched homophobia and xenophobia. In countries such as Hungary and Poland, state-sanctioned discrimination has intensified, leading to a climate of fear for LGBTQ individuals. Here, the challenge lies in building coalitions with other marginalized groups, emphasizing shared struggles against oppression. The concept of *solidarity* becomes vital, as it encourages diverse groups to unite against common adversaries.

Strategies for Inclusive Advocacy

To effectively address cultural differences, advocates must adopt several key strategies:

- **Cultural Competence:** Advocates should strive to understand the cultural contexts of the communities they serve, recognizing the unique challenges faced by LGBTQ individuals in different regions.
- **Community Engagement:** Involving local activists in the decision-making process ensures that advocacy efforts are relevant and effective. This engagement fosters ownership and empowerment within communities.
- **Education and Awareness:** Raising awareness about LGBTQ issues through culturally appropriate channels can help shift attitudes. Utilizing art, music, and local media can effectively communicate messages of acceptance.
- **Building Alliances:** Collaborating with other social justice movements can amplify voices and create a more robust front against discrimination. Intersectional advocacy highlights the interconnectedness of various struggles.
- **Flexible Approaches:** Advocates must be adaptable in their strategies, recognizing that what works in one cultural context may not be effective in another. Flexibility allows for the incorporation of local customs and practices.

Conclusion

Addressing cultural differences and challenges in LGBTQ advocacy is a complex but necessary endeavor. By employing intersectional frameworks, recognizing cultural norms, and engaging in respectful dialogue, advocates can create more inclusive and effective strategies. The journey towards equality is not linear; it requires patience, understanding, and a commitment to uplifting diverse voices. As Armando's work illustrates, the fight for LGBTQ rights is a global struggle that thrives on the richness of cultural diversity.

Empowering LGBTQ Activists Across Borders

In an increasingly interconnected world, the empowerment of LGBTQ activists across borders has become a crucial aspect of the global fight for equality and human rights. The challenges faced by LGBTQ communities are often not confined to national boundaries; they are influenced by cultural, political, and social contexts that vary widely from one region to another. This section explores the significance of cross-border collaboration, the theoretical frameworks underpinning such efforts, and the practical challenges encountered by activists working in diverse environments.

Theoretical Frameworks

To understand the dynamics of empowering LGBTQ activists globally, we can draw upon several theoretical frameworks. One prominent theory is **Intersectionality**, which posits that individuals experience multiple, overlapping identities that shape their experiences of oppression and privilege. Coined by Kimberlé Crenshaw, intersectionality highlights the importance of recognizing how factors such as race, gender, socioeconomic status, and sexuality intersect to create unique challenges for LGBTQ individuals. This framework encourages activists to adopt a holistic approach to advocacy, ensuring that the voices of the most marginalized within the LGBTQ community are heard and prioritized.

Another relevant theory is **Transnationalism**, which examines how global processes influence local realities. Transnational activism allows LGBTQ groups to share strategies, resources, and experiences across borders, fostering solidarity and collective action. This approach is vital in addressing issues that transcend national boundaries, such as human trafficking, asylum for LGBTQ refugees, and the global rise of anti-LGBTQ legislation.

Challenges in Cross-Border Activism

Despite the theoretical frameworks that support cross-border collaboration, LGBTQ activists often face significant challenges. One major issue is the **legal and political landscape** of different countries. Activists in regions with repressive regimes may encounter severe legal repercussions for their work, including arrest, harassment, and violence. For instance, in countries like Uganda and Russia, anti-LGBTQ laws have been enacted, criminalizing same-sex relationships and promoting discrimination. Activists operating in these environments must navigate a complex landscape of fear and repression while attempting to advocate for change.

Moreover, cultural differences can pose additional barriers. Activists must be sensitive to local customs, beliefs, and attitudes towards LGBTQ individuals. What works in one cultural context may not be effective or even acceptable in another. For example, LGBTQ rights movements in Western countries may emphasize individual rights and self-expression, while activists in more collectivist societies might focus on community acceptance and familial support. Understanding these cultural nuances is essential for effective advocacy.

Examples of Empowerment Initiatives

Several initiatives exemplify the successful empowerment of LGBTQ activists across borders. One notable example is the work of **ILGA (International Lesbian, Gay, Bisexual, Trans and Intersex Association)**, which provides a platform for LGBTQ organizations worldwide to share resources, knowledge, and strategies. ILGA's annual conferences bring together activists from various countries, fostering dialogue and collaboration on pressing issues such as legal recognition, healthcare access, and anti-discrimination policies.

Another impactful initiative is the **Global Equality Fund**, which supports local LGBTQ organizations in countries where LGBTQ rights are under threat. By providing financial resources, training, and capacity-building, the Global Equality Fund empowers activists to strengthen their advocacy efforts and increase their visibility within their communities.

Additionally, social media has emerged as a powerful tool for cross-border activism. Platforms like Twitter and Facebook allow activists to connect, share information, and mobilize support for global campaigns. The #LoveIsLove movement, which gained traction during the fight for marriage equality, exemplifies how social media can unite activists across borders, creating a sense of solidarity and shared purpose.

Conclusion

Empowering LGBTQ activists across borders is essential for fostering a global movement that addresses the diverse challenges faced by LGBTQ communities. By leveraging theoretical frameworks such as intersectionality and transnationalism, activists can develop inclusive strategies that resonate with local contexts while promoting universal human rights. Despite the challenges posed by legal, political, and cultural barriers, initiatives like ILGA and the Global Equality Fund demonstrate the potential for meaningful collaboration and empowerment. As the fight for LGBTQ rights continues, the importance of cross-border solidarity and support remains paramount, ensuring that no activist is left behind in the quest for equality and justice.

Armando's Legacy

The Lasting Impact of his Activism

Armando's activism has left an indelible mark on both the LGBTQ community and broader societal frameworks in Colombia and beyond. His journey exemplifies the transformative power of grassroots movements and the importance of intersectionality in advocating for justice and equality.

Theoretical Frameworks

To understand the lasting impact of Armando's activism, it is crucial to consider several theoretical frameworks that inform social movements. One such framework is **Social Movement Theory**, which posits that collective action arises from shared grievances and the mobilization of resources. Armando's work exemplifies this theory, as he organized and mobilized communities around common issues, such as legal recognition and protection of LGBTQ rights.

Additionally, the concept of **Intersectionality**, developed by Kimberlé Crenshaw, provides a critical lens through which to analyze Armando's advocacy. Intersectionality emphasizes that individuals experience overlapping systems of oppression based on their race, gender, sexuality, and class. Armando's commitment to inclusivity ensured that his activism addressed the needs of the most marginalized within the LGBTQ community, thereby amplifying their voices and concerns.

Key Achievements and Their Impact

Armando's activism led to several landmark victories that have had a lasting impact on LGBTQ rights in Colombia:

- **Legal Recognition of Same-Sex Relationships:** One of Armando's significant achievements was his role in advocating for the legal recognition of same-sex relationships. In 2016, Colombia's Constitutional Court ruled in favor of marriage equality, a decision that was celebrated as a monumental step forward for LGBTQ rights in Latin America. This legal recognition not only validated the relationships of countless individuals but also set a precedent for other countries in the region to follow suit.

- **Healthcare Access and Rights:** Armando's advocacy extended to healthcare, where he fought for LGBTQ-inclusive policies. His efforts contributed to the implementation of comprehensive healthcare services that address the unique needs of the LGBTQ community, particularly regarding mental health and sexual health services. This progress has been crucial in reducing health disparities and ensuring equitable access to care.

- **Educational Reforms:** Armando played a pivotal role in promoting LGBTQ-inclusive education. His collaboration with educational institutions led to the development of curricula that address LGBTQ history and rights, fostering a more inclusive environment for students. This educational reform has not only empowered LGBTQ youth but has also educated the broader community, challenging stereotypes and promoting acceptance.

Challenges and Resilience

Despite these achievements, Armando's journey was fraught with challenges. The backlash against his activism was palpable, with targeted attacks and threats becoming a part of his reality. However, these adversities only strengthened his resolve. As he often stated, "Resilience is the cornerstone of activism." Armando's ability to navigate these challenges serves as a powerful example for future generations of activists.

Inspiration for Future Generations

Armando's legacy is not merely one of victories but also of inspiration. He has become a symbol of hope for countless individuals who face discrimination and marginalization. By sharing his story and experiences, Armando has empowered others to embrace their identities and advocate for their rights. His workshops and mentorship programs have equipped young activists with the tools and knowledge needed to continue the fight for equality.

The impact of Armando's activism is also reflected in the growing number of LGBTQ organizations that have emerged in Colombia and across Latin America.

These organizations, inspired by Armando's work, continue to advocate for policy changes and provide support to marginalized communities.

Global Influence

Armando's activism transcends national borders, as he has collaborated with international organizations to address global LGBTQ issues. His efforts in raising awareness about violence and discrimination faced by LGBTQ individuals worldwide have highlighted the need for a unified global response. By participating in international conferences and forums, Armando has positioned himself as a key figure in the global LGBTQ movement, further amplifying the voices of those who are often silenced.

Conclusion

In conclusion, the lasting impact of Armando's activism is evident in the legal, social, and cultural advancements achieved for LGBTQ rights in Colombia and beyond. Through his resilience, commitment to intersectionality, and dedication to inclusivity, Armando has not only transformed his community but has also inspired a global movement for equality. As we reflect on his contributions, it is essential to recognize that the fight for LGBTQ rights is ongoing, and Armando's legacy will continue to guide and inspire future generations of activists in their pursuit of justice and equality.

Continuing the Fight for LGBTQ Rights

The struggle for LGBTQ rights is an ongoing journey, one that demands vigilance, resilience, and unwavering commitment. As Armando continues his advocacy, he recognizes that the fight is not merely about achieving legal recognition but also about fostering a cultural shift towards acceptance and equality. This section explores the multifaceted nature of this ongoing struggle, the theoretical frameworks that underpin it, and the real-world implications of Armando's work.

Understanding the Landscape of LGBTQ Rights

To effectively continue the fight for LGBTQ rights, it is crucial to understand the current landscape. This involves recognizing the various dimensions of discrimination that LGBTQ individuals face, including legal, social, and economic barriers. The intersectionality theory posits that individuals experience oppression in varying degrees based on their intersecting identities, such as race, gender, and socioeconomic status. This framework is essential for Armando's advocacy, as it allows him to address the unique challenges faced by marginalized subgroups within the LGBTQ community.

$$\text{Intersectionality} = f(\text{Race, Gender, Sexual Orientation, Class}) \quad (43)$$

This equation illustrates how various social identities interact to shape individual experiences of discrimination and privilege. Armando's advocacy work emphasizes the importance of intersectionality, ensuring that all voices within the LGBTQ community are heard and represented.

Addressing Legal Inequities

Despite significant progress in many regions, legal inequities persist. In Colombia, for example, same-sex marriage was legalized in 2016, yet many LGBTQ individuals still face discrimination in employment, healthcare, and housing. Armando's advocacy efforts focus on pushing for comprehensive anti-discrimination laws that protect LGBTQ individuals across all sectors.

$$\text{Legal Protections} = \sum_{i=1}^{n} \text{Anti-Discrimination Laws}_i \quad (44)$$

Where n represents the number of anti-discrimination laws applicable to various aspects of life, such as employment, housing, and healthcare. Armando collaborates with lawmakers and organizations to draft and promote legislation that encompasses these protections, advocating for a legal framework that upholds the dignity and rights of LGBTQ individuals.

Cultural Change and Social Acceptance

Legal recognition is only one piece of the puzzle; cultural change is equally vital. Armando believes that advocacy must extend beyond policy and into the hearts and minds of individuals. This involves challenging societal norms and stereotypes that perpetuate discrimination against LGBTQ individuals. Education plays a pivotal role in this process.

$$\text{Cultural Acceptance} = \text{Education} \times \text{Awareness} \quad (45)$$

Through workshops, seminars, and community outreach, Armando aims to educate the public about LGBTQ issues, fostering an environment of understanding and respect. By sharing personal stories and highlighting the contributions of LGBTQ individuals to society, he seeks to dismantle prejudices and cultivate empathy.

Global Solidarity and Collaboration

The fight for LGBTQ rights is not confined to national borders; it is a global movement. Armando emphasizes the importance of solidarity with LGBTQ activists worldwide, recognizing that struggles in one region can resonate with those in another. Collaborating with international organizations allows for the sharing of resources, strategies, and support.

$$\text{Global Advocacy} = \text{Local Efforts} + \text{International Collaboration} \quad (46)$$

This equation illustrates that effective advocacy is strengthened through both local initiatives and global partnerships. Armando participates in international conferences and coalitions, amplifying the voices of LGBTQ activists from diverse backgrounds and sharing best practices for advocacy.

Empowering Future Generations

To ensure the sustainability of the LGBTQ rights movement, Armando is committed to empowering the next generation of activists. He believes that mentorship and education are crucial for fostering new leaders who will continue the fight for equality. This involves creating platforms for young LGBTQ individuals to share their experiences and engage in activism.

$$\text{Empowerment} = \text{Mentorship} + \text{Education} + \text{Opportunities} \quad (47)$$

Armando actively seeks to provide mentorship opportunities, educational resources, and platforms for young activists to voice their concerns and ideas. By investing in the future of the movement, he aims to cultivate a robust network of advocates who will carry the torch forward.

Conclusion

Continuing the fight for LGBTQ rights requires an unwavering commitment to advocacy, education, and collaboration. Armando's work exemplifies the importance of understanding the complexities of discrimination, addressing legal inequities, fostering cultural change, and empowering future generations. As he reflects on his journey, Armando remains steadfast in his belief that every effort counts, and together, the LGBTQ community can forge a path towards a more just and equitable society.

In summary, the ongoing fight for LGBTQ rights is multifaceted, requiring a blend of legal action, cultural change, global solidarity, and empowerment of future leaders. Armando's dedication to this cause serves as a beacon of hope and inspiration for many, reminding us that the journey towards equality is far from over, and every step taken is a step towards a brighter future.

Armando's Personal Influences and Inspirations

Armando's journey as an LGBTQ activist is deeply rooted in the influences and inspirations that shaped his worldview and commitment to social justice. Growing up in a multicultural environment, Armando was exposed to a variety of perspectives that informed his understanding of identity, equality, and the intersectionality of social movements. This section delves into the key figures, literary works, and personal experiences that have inspired Armando throughout his life.

Influential Figures

Armando's activism was heavily influenced by prominent LGBTQ figures and allies who paved the way for future generations. One such figure is Marsha P. Johnson, a Black transgender activist whose role in the Stonewall uprising exemplifies the power of grassroots mobilization. Johnson's fearless advocacy for LGBTQ rights and her commitment to intersectionality inspired Armando to embrace his identity and fight for those marginalized within the community. He often reflects on her famous quote, "No pride for some of us without liberation for all of us," as a guiding principle in his advocacy work.

Another significant influence in Armando's life is Audre Lorde, a poet and activist whose writings on race, gender, and sexuality resonate deeply with his own experiences. Lorde's concept of the "erotic as power" encouraged Armando to explore the complexities of desire and identity, fostering a sense of pride in his sexuality. In her essay, "The Master's Tools Will Never Dismantle the Master's House," Lorde articulates the necessity of embracing difference in the fight for social justice, a lesson that Armando has incorporated into his activism.

Literary Inspirations

Literature has played a pivotal role in shaping Armando's understanding of social justice and human rights. The works of James Baldwin, particularly his essays on race and sexuality, have profoundly impacted Armando's perspective on the interconnectedness of various forms of oppression. Baldwin's assertion that "not everything that is faced can be changed, but nothing can be changed until it is faced" serves as a reminder for Armando to confront uncomfortable truths within society and within himself.

Additionally, the writings of bell hooks have inspired Armando to engage critically with issues of patriarchy and feminism. In "Ain't I a Woman?", hooks examines the intersections of race, gender, and class, urging activists to adopt an inclusive approach to social justice. This intersectional framework has been instrumental in shaping Armando's advocacy, as he seeks to address the unique challenges faced by LGBTQ individuals from diverse backgrounds.

Personal Experiences

Armando's personal experiences have also been significant in shaping his activism. Growing up in a conservative society, he faced discrimination and prejudice that ignited his passion for advocacy. His first encounter with homophobia in high school was a turning point; it was during this time that he realized the urgent need for change. This experience motivated him to seek out supportive communities and to become a voice for those who felt silenced.

Moreover, the friendships Armando cultivated within the LGBTQ community have been a source of inspiration. These relationships not only provided him with a sense of belonging but also highlighted the importance of solidarity and collective action. The shared stories of resilience and triumph among his peers reinforced Armando's belief in the power of community organizing and the necessity of uplifting marginalized voices.

Theoretical Frameworks

Armando's activism is also informed by various theoretical frameworks that explore the complexities of identity and social justice. Critical race theory, for instance, provides a lens through which Armando examines the intersections of race and sexuality, allowing him to understand how systemic inequalities impact LGBTQ individuals of color. This theoretical framework emphasizes the importance of storytelling and personal narratives in shaping social change, a principle that Armando applies in his advocacy work.

Furthermore, queer theory has influenced Armando's understanding of identity as fluid and multifaceted. By challenging traditional notions of gender and sexuality, queer theory encourages activists to embrace diversity within the LGBTQ community. Armando's commitment to inclusivity is evident in his advocacy for the rights of transgender and non-binary individuals, as he recognizes the unique challenges they face within both the LGBTQ movement and society at large.

Conclusion

In conclusion, Armando's personal influences and inspirations are a tapestry woven from the threads of influential figures, literary works, personal experiences, and theoretical frameworks. Each of these elements has contributed to his development as an activist and his commitment to advocating for LGBTQ rights. By drawing on the wisdom of those who came before him and embracing the lessons learned from his own journey, Armando continues to inspire future generations of activists to challenge the status quo and fight for a more equitable world.

Recognizing the Importance of Persistence and Resilience

In the landscape of activism, persistence and resilience are not merely virtues; they are essential components of any successful movement. For Armando, these traits became the bedrock of his journey as an LGBTQ advocate in Colombia, where societal norms often posed significant barriers to progress.

Theoretical Framework

Persistence can be understood through the lens of psychological theories such as the *Growth Mindset* proposed by Carol Dweck. According to Dweck, individuals with a growth mindset believe that abilities and intelligence can be developed through dedication and hard work. This perspective fosters a love for learning and resilience, which is crucial for overcoming challenges. In contrast, a fixed mindset can lead to a fear of failure, inhibiting one's ability to persist in the face of adversity.

Resilience, on the other hand, is defined by the American Psychological Association as the process of adapting well in the face of adversity, trauma, tragedy, threats, or significant sources of stress. It involves behaviors, thoughts, and actions that can be learned and developed in anyone. Theories of resilience emphasize the importance of social support, personal skills, and the ability to manage stress as key factors in overcoming difficulties.

Challenges Faced by Armando

Armando's activism was fraught with challenges, ranging from societal rejection to direct threats against his safety. For example, after publicly advocating for LGBTQ rights, he faced backlash from conservative groups that sought to undermine his credibility and intimidate him. This included harassment on social media platforms, which can be understood through the theory of *cyberbullying*, where the anonymity of the internet emboldens individuals to express hostility without immediate consequences.

The emotional toll of such experiences cannot be underestimated. Research shows that activists often experience burnout, a state of emotional, physical, and mental exhaustion caused by prolonged and excessive stress. Armando, like many activists, had to navigate these feelings while remaining committed to his cause.

Examples of Persistence

Despite these challenges, Armando exemplified persistence. One poignant example was his involvement in organizing a pride march in Medellín, which had faced significant opposition from local authorities and conservative factions. Armando's determination to see the event through was fueled by his belief in the power of visibility and community. He rallied supporters, leveraged social media to create awareness, and engaged in dialogue with local leaders to advocate for the march's approval.

The successful execution of the pride march became a landmark event, drawing attention not only to LGBTQ rights but also to broader issues of human rights in Colombia. This event illustrated the concept of *collective efficacy*, where the shared belief in the ability to achieve goals enhances the likelihood of success.

Building Resilience

Armando's resilience was also evident in his approach to personal well-being. He recognized the importance of self-care and sought support from friends and fellow activists. Engaging in community-building activities provided him with a sense of belonging and a network of allies who understood the struggles he faced. This aligns with the theory of *social capital*, which posits that social networks have value and can provide support in times of need.

Moreover, Armando utilized mindfulness techniques to manage stress and maintain focus. Mindfulness, as defined by Jon Kabat-Zinn, involves paying attention to the present moment without judgment. This practice helped him cultivate a sense of calm amidst chaos, allowing him to approach challenges with clarity and purpose.

The Legacy of Persistence and Resilience

Armando's story serves as a testament to the importance of persistence and resilience in the fight for LGBTQ rights. His ability to rise above adversity not only propelled his activism but also inspired countless others to engage in the struggle for equality. The legacy of his work is reflected in the continued progress of LGBTQ rights in Colombia, where activists today draw strength from his example.

In conclusion, recognizing the importance of persistence and resilience is crucial for anyone involved in activism. These traits empower individuals to face challenges head-on, adapt to changing circumstances, and ultimately drive meaningful change. As Armando's journey illustrates, the road to equality is often fraught with obstacles, but with determination and support, it is a road worth traveling.

Celebrating Armando's Contributions to LGBTQ History

Armando's journey as an LGBTQ activist is not merely a personal narrative; it represents a pivotal chapter in the broader story of LGBTQ rights and history. His contributions have not only shaped the landscape of advocacy in Colombia but have also resonated globally, inspiring countless individuals to join the fight for equality. This section explores the significance of Armando's work and the legacy he has crafted through his activism.

The Historical Context of LGBTQ Rights

To appreciate Armando's contributions, it is crucial to understand the historical context of LGBTQ rights. The late 20th century saw a surge in activism, driven by movements such as the Stonewall Riots in 1969, which galvanized the fight for LGBTQ rights in the United States and beyond. In Colombia, the struggle for acceptance and legal recognition has faced unique challenges, including deep-rooted cultural conservatism and systemic discrimination. Armando emerged as a voice of change during a time when advocacy was met with hostility and fear.

Advocacy and Legal Reforms

Armando played a critical role in advocating for legal reforms that have had a lasting impact on LGBTQ rights in Colombia. His efforts were instrumental in the landmark ruling by the Colombian Constitutional Court in 2016, which recognized same-sex marriage. This decision marked a significant victory for LGBTQ rights in a country where traditional values often clashed with the pursuit of equality. Armando's strategic lobbying efforts, which included mobilizing public support and collaborating with other organizations, exemplify the power of grassroots activism in effecting change.

Cultural Contributions and Representation

Beyond legal advocacy, Armando's contributions to LGBTQ history extend to cultural representation. He has utilized literature, art, and public speaking to challenge stereotypes and promote understanding of LGBTQ experiences. His writings, which often reflect his personal journey, serve as a testament to the resilience of the LGBTQ community. By sharing his story, Armando has not only validated the experiences of others but has also opened dialogues about identity, acceptance, and pride.

Intersectionality in Advocacy

Armando's approach to activism is rooted in the principles of intersectionality, recognizing that the struggles faced by LGBTQ individuals are often compounded by other social injustices, including racism, classism, and sexism. He has actively worked to ensure that the LGBTQ movement is inclusive of all voices, particularly those from marginalized communities. This commitment to intersectionality has enriched the movement, fostering solidarity among various social justice movements and highlighting the interconnectedness of their struggles.

Global Influence and Solidarity

Armando's impact is not confined to Colombia; his advocacy has transcended borders, inspiring international movements for LGBTQ rights. By collaborating with global organizations, he has raised awareness about the challenges faced by LGBTQ individuals worldwide, particularly in regions where rights are severely restricted. His participation in international conferences and forums has positioned him as a key figure in the global LGBTQ rights movement, emphasizing the importance of solidarity and shared goals.

Legacy and Future Aspirations

As we celebrate Armando's contributions to LGBTQ history, it is essential to recognize the legacy he leaves behind. His work has laid the groundwork for future generations of activists, providing them with the tools and inspiration needed to continue the fight for equality. Armando's vision for the future includes a world where LGBTQ rights are universally recognized and respected, and where diversity is celebrated rather than marginalized.

In conclusion, Armando's contributions to LGBTQ history are profound and far-reaching. His advocacy has not only transformed the legal landscape in Colombia but has also enriched the cultural narrative surrounding LGBTQ identities. By embracing intersectionality and fostering global solidarity, Armando has created a legacy that will inspire and empower future activists in their ongoing quest for justice and equality.

$$\text{Legacy} = \text{Advocacy} + \text{Cultural Representation} + \text{Global Solidarity} \quad (48)$$

This equation encapsulates the essence of Armando's contributions, illustrating how his multifaceted approach has created a lasting impact on LGBTQ history.

Armando's Personal Reflections

Armando's Personal Reflections

Armando's Personal Reflections

In reflecting on his journey, Armando not only revisits the milestones of his activism but also delves into the profound personal transformations he has undergone. Each chapter of his life has been punctuated by lessons learned, obstacles overcome, and a deepening understanding of his identity and the complexities surrounding it.

Lessons Learned and Personal Growth

Armando's activism has been a crucible for personal growth. He often cites the concept of *transformative learning* as a guiding principle in his life. This theory, proposed by Jack Mezirow, emphasizes the importance of critical reflection in fostering personal change. Armando's experiences of discrimination and marginalization have compelled him to critically examine societal norms and his own beliefs.

One pivotal lesson he learned was the importance of vulnerability in leadership. Early in his activism, Armando believed that he needed to project an image of strength and invulnerability to command respect. However, he soon realized that sharing his struggles and insecurities resonated more deeply with people. This realization aligns with Brené Brown's research on vulnerability, which suggests that it is a source of courage and connection. By embracing his vulnerabilities, Armando fostered authentic relationships within the LGBTQ community, creating a network of support that proved invaluable in his journey.

Celebrating Milestones and Accomplishments

Armando takes time to celebrate the milestones he has achieved, both personally and within the broader context of LGBTQ rights. For instance, he recalls the first successful campaign he spearheaded that led to the legalization of same-sex marriage in Colombia. This victory not only represented a significant legal change but also symbolized a shift in societal attitudes towards LGBTQ individuals.

He reflects on the night of the legalization, standing among his peers, feeling a sense of collective triumph. As he recounts this moment, he emphasizes the importance of celebrating victories, no matter how small. This practice is supported by psychological research indicating that celebrating achievements can enhance motivation and foster resilience.

Obstacles Overcome and Triumphs Achieved

Armando's journey has not been without its challenges. He faced numerous obstacles, including public backlash, threats to his safety, and the emotional toll of constant activism. One significant incident involved a public protest where he was targeted by counter-protesters, resulting in a tense confrontation.

In the aftermath, Armando sought solace in the teachings of resilience psychology, which posits that adversity can foster strength and growth. He learned to view challenges as opportunities for development, which helped him navigate the complexities of his activism with renewed determination.

The Evolution of Armando's Identity and Perspectives

Armando's reflections also encompass the evolution of his identity. He acknowledges that his understanding of what it means to be LGBTQ has transformed over the years. Initially, he viewed his identity through a narrow lens, focusing primarily on sexual orientation. However, as he engaged with intersectional activism, he began to appreciate the interconnectedness of various identities, including race, gender, and socioeconomic status.

This shift in perspective is rooted in the theory of *intersectionality*, coined by Kimberlé Crenshaw, which highlights how different forms of discrimination overlap and compound one another. Armando's advocacy expanded to include issues such as racial justice and economic inequality, recognizing that the fight for LGBTQ rights is inherently linked to broader social justice movements.

Gratitude for Support and Collaborators

In his reflections, Armando expresses profound gratitude for the support he has received throughout his journey. He acknowledges the importance of collaboration in activism, understanding that collective action amplifies voices and drives meaningful change.

He highlights key figures who have influenced him, including mentors and fellow activists. Their guidance has been instrumental in shaping his approach to advocacy. Armando often cites the concept of *social capital*, as defined by Pierre Bourdieu, which emphasizes the value of social networks and relationships in achieving collective goals.

Armando's Vision for the Future

Looking ahead, Armando envisions a future where LGBTQ rights are universally recognized and celebrated. He believes that the next generation of activists will continue to push boundaries and challenge the status quo.

Armando emphasizes the importance of nurturing young leaders, providing them with the tools and support necessary to effect change. He draws parallels with historical movements, noting that progress is often incremental and requires sustained effort. This perspective aligns with the *theory of change*, which posits that lasting social change results from strategic planning, community engagement, and persistent advocacy.

In conclusion, Armando's personal reflections reveal a journey marked by growth, resilience, and an unwavering commitment to justice. His story is not just one of individual triumph but also a testament to the power of collective action in the pursuit of equality. Through his reflections, Armando inspires others to embrace their identities, confront challenges head-on, and envision a future where everyone can live authentically and freely.

Looking Back on the Journey

Lessons Learned and Personal Growth

Throughout Armando's journey as an LGBTQ activist, he encountered numerous challenges that shaped his identity and advocacy. Each experience contributed to his personal growth, teaching him invaluable lessons that not only influenced his activism but also his understanding of self and community.

The Power of Vulnerability

One of the most profound lessons Armando learned was the power of vulnerability. In a society that often stigmatizes LGBTQ identities, embracing vulnerability became a source of strength. By sharing his own story of coming out and the struggles that ensued, Armando fostered connections with others facing similar challenges. Brené Brown, a researcher on vulnerability, emphasizes that "vulnerability is the birthplace of innovation, creativity, and change." Armando's willingness to be open about his experiences not only empowered him but also inspired others to share their truths, creating a ripple effect of authenticity within the community.

Resilience in the Face of Adversity

Armando faced significant backlash and discrimination as he stepped into the public eye. These experiences taught him the importance of resilience. Resilience, defined as the ability to recover from setbacks, is crucial for activists who often confront hostility. Armando adopted strategies to cultivate resilience, such as practicing self-care, engaging in supportive communities, and focusing on his goals. He often recalled the words of Maya Angelou: "You may encounter many defeats, but you must not be defeated." This mindset allowed him to navigate challenges without losing sight of his mission.

Intersectionality and Inclusivity

Another critical lesson for Armando was the significance of intersectionality in activism. He recognized that the LGBTQ community is not monolithic; it encompasses diverse identities influenced by race, gender, socioeconomic status, and more. Kimberlé Crenshaw's theory of intersectionality highlights how overlapping social identities can lead to unique experiences of discrimination and privilege. Armando learned to advocate not just for LGBTQ rights, but for an inclusive movement that addresses the needs of marginalized groups within the community. This broadened perspective enriched his activism, enabling him to build coalitions and foster solidarity among various social justice movements.

The Importance of Community

Armando's journey underscored the vital role of community in personal and collective growth. He discovered that activism is not a solitary endeavor; it thrives on collaboration and support. Engaging with fellow activists provided him with a sense of belonging and reinforced his commitment to the cause. He often participated in community-building activities, such as workshops and support groups, which fostered a culture of mutual aid and empowerment. As he stated, "Alone, we can do so little; together, we can do so much," echoing the sentiments of Helen Keller.

Embracing Change

Change is an inherent part of activism, and Armando learned to embrace it as a catalyst for growth. He encountered shifting social attitudes and legal landscapes throughout his career, which required adaptability. This adaptability was not merely a reaction to external circumstances but a proactive approach to evolving strategies and goals. Armando often reflected on the importance of being open to new ideas and perspectives, stating, "Change is the only constant in life." This philosophy allowed him to remain relevant and effective in his advocacy efforts.

Self-Reflection and Continuous Learning

Finally, Armando understood that personal growth is a continuous process, requiring ongoing self-reflection and learning. He regularly engaged in introspective practices, such as journaling and meditation, to assess his experiences and emotions. This practice allowed him to identify areas for improvement and recognize his achievements. He often sought feedback from peers and mentors, valuing their insights as essential to his development. As Albert Einstein famously said, "Intellectual growth should commence at birth and cease only at death." Armando embodied this belief, committing to lifelong learning as a cornerstone of his activism.

Conclusion

In summary, the lessons Armando learned throughout his journey as an LGBTQ activist were pivotal to his personal growth. Embracing vulnerability, cultivating resilience, advocating for intersectionality, valuing community, embracing change, and committing to continuous learning shaped not only his identity but also the impact of his activism. These lessons serve as a testament to the transformative power of activism, illustrating that the journey toward equality is as much about personal evolution as it is about societal change.

Celebrating Milestones and Accomplishments

In the journey of activism, each milestone achieved serves as a beacon of hope and a testament to the resilience of the community. For Armando, celebrating these milestones is not merely an act of recognition but a powerful reminder of the struggles that have been overcome and the work that still lies ahead.

Defining Milestones in Activism

Milestones in activism can be defined as significant events or achievements that mark progress toward a specific goal. These can range from legislative victories to community outreach programs, each contributing to the broader movement for LGBTQ rights. The importance of recognizing these milestones lies in their ability to inspire and mobilize individuals within the community, fostering a sense of collective achievement.

Legislative Victories

One of Armando's most notable accomplishments was his involvement in the passing of the same-sex marriage bill in Colombia. This landmark legislation not only provided legal recognition to same-sex couples but also served as a catalyst for further discussions on LGBTQ rights in the country. The passage of this bill was celebrated with a national pride parade, where thousands gathered to honor the hard work and dedication of activists who fought tirelessly for equality.

$$\text{Milestone Impact} = \frac{\text{Number of Individuals Affected}}{\text{Time Taken to Achieve}} \tag{49}$$

This equation illustrates the impact of a milestone, where the number of individuals positively affected is divided by the time taken to achieve that milestone. The smaller the time frame, the greater the impact, demonstrating the urgency and importance of the achievement.

Community Outreach Initiatives

In addition to legislative victories, Armando has spearheaded several community outreach initiatives aimed at educating the public about LGBTQ issues. One such program, "Voices of the Future," provided workshops and resources for LGBTQ youth, empowering them to embrace their identities and advocate for their rights. The success of this initiative was marked by a significant increase in participation and engagement from the youth, showcasing the effectiveness of grassroots activism.

Recognizing Individual Contributions

Celebrating milestones also involves acknowledging the contributions of individuals within the movement. Armando has often highlighted the work of fellow activists, recognizing that the fight for LGBTQ rights is a collective effort. For instance, during the annual LGBTQ Rights Gala, he presented awards to activists who have made significant contributions to the cause, reinforcing the idea that every effort counts.

Cultural Celebrations

Cultural celebrations play a pivotal role in recognizing milestones. Armando has organized events that not only celebrate achievements but also honor the rich diversity within the LGBTQ community. These events include art exhibitions, film screenings, and performances that highlight LGBTQ narratives and experiences. Such cultural expressions serve to educate the broader public while providing a platform for marginalized voices.

Utilizing Social Media for Recognition

In today's digital age, social media has become an essential tool for celebrating milestones. Armando effectively utilizes platforms like Instagram and Twitter to share successes and stories from the LGBTQ community. By creating hashtags such as #MilestonesForEquality, he encourages others to share their stories, creating a virtual tapestry of achievements that inspires and unites.

The Psychological Impact of Celebrating Success

The psychological impact of celebrating accomplishments cannot be overstated. Research indicates that recognition and celebration of achievements contribute to increased motivation and morale among activists. By celebrating milestones, Armando fosters a positive environment that encourages continued participation and commitment to the cause.

$$\text{Motivation} = f(\text{Recognition}, \text{Community Support}) \qquad (50)$$

This function illustrates that motivation is a function of recognition and community support, emphasizing the need for a supportive network in sustaining activism.

Looking Ahead

As Armando reflects on the milestones achieved, he emphasizes the importance of looking ahead to future goals. Celebrating past accomplishments serves as a foundation for future activism, reminding individuals of the progress made and the potential for further change. Armando encourages the next generation of activists to set ambitious goals and to celebrate every step taken toward achieving them.

In conclusion, celebrating milestones and accomplishments is integral to the ongoing fight for LGBTQ rights. Each achievement, whether large or small, contributes to a larger narrative of progress and resilience. Armando's commitment to recognizing these milestones not only honors the past but also inspires future generations to continue the fight for equality and justice.

Obstacles Overcome and Triumphs Achieved

Throughout Armando's journey as an LGBTQ activist, he faced numerous obstacles that tested his resolve and commitment to the cause. These challenges ranged from societal discrimination to personal struggles, each shaping his path and fortifying his advocacy.

One of the most significant obstacles was the pervasive discrimination that LGBTQ individuals faced in Colombia. This societal stigma manifested in various forms, including verbal harassment, physical violence, and systemic inequality. For example, Armando encountered hostility from peers during his school years, which not only affected his self-esteem but also ignited a fire within him to fight against such injustices. The psychological toll of these experiences can be understood through the framework of minority stress theory, which posits that individuals from marginalized groups experience chronic stress due to societal prejudice, leading to adverse mental health outcomes.

Despite these challenges, Armando achieved remarkable triumphs. One of his most notable accomplishments was the successful lobbying for the legalization of same-sex marriage in Colombia. This victory was not merely a legal win but a profound societal shift that represented years of tireless activism and coalition-building. The journey to this triumph involved mobilizing public opinion, rallying support from allies, and engaging in strategic advocacy campaigns. Armando's ability to connect with diverse groups—ranging from grassroots organizations to international human rights bodies—was crucial in amplifying the message for equality.

Another significant triumph was Armando's role in the establishment of LGBTQ-inclusive educational programs in Colombian schools. Recognizing that education is a powerful tool for change, he collaborated with local NGOs to develop curricula that addressed issues of gender identity, sexual orientation, and respect for diversity. This initiative not only educated young people about LGBTQ rights but also fostered a culture of acceptance and understanding, helping to dismantle the stereotypes that fuel discrimination.

Armando's resilience in the face of personal challenges also deserves recognition. He faced threats and backlash from conservative factions opposed to his activism. These experiences often left him feeling vulnerable and isolated. However, he leveraged these challenges as opportunities for growth. By cultivating a strong support network of fellow activists and allies, Armando learned the importance of community in overcoming adversity. This support system provided him with the emotional and strategic backing necessary to continue his work, even when the going got tough.

In summary, Armando's journey is a testament to the power of perseverance. The obstacles he faced were formidable, yet each challenge served as a stepping stone towards his triumphs. His story exemplifies the idea that through resilience, community support, and unwavering commitment to justice, significant change is possible. As he reflects on his journey, Armando recognizes that every obstacle overcome has not only shaped his identity but has also contributed to the broader movement for LGBTQ rights in Colombia and beyond.

The Evolution of Armando's Identity and Perspectives

Armando's journey through the complexities of identity and self-understanding is emblematic of the broader struggles faced by many within the LGBTQ community. His evolution is not merely a personal narrative but a reflection of the socio-political landscape that shapes individual experiences. This section delves into the key phases of Armando's identity development, highlighting significant theories and real-world implications that illustrate the intersection of personal and collective struggles.

Theoretical Framework: Identity Development Models

To understand Armando's evolution, we can apply several psychological and sociological theories of identity development. One prominent theory is Erik Erikson's psychosocial development model, which posits that individuals pass through eight stages of psychosocial development, each characterized by a specific conflict that must be resolved. For LGBTQ individuals, the stages often manifest differently due to societal pressures and discrimination.

$$E = \sum_{i=1}^{n}(C_i \cdot R_i) \tag{51}$$

Where E is the overall experience of identity evolution, C_i represents the conflicts faced at each stage, and R_i denotes the resolution achieved. Armando's experiences can be analyzed through this lens, particularly during the stages of adolescence and young adulthood, where he grappled with issues of self-acceptance and societal rejection.

Cultural Influences and Personal Experiences

Armando's identity was significantly shaped by his cultural background and personal experiences. Growing up in Medellín, he faced a dual challenge: navigating the traditional expectations of masculinity prevalent in Colombian culture while also confronting his emerging sexual identity. The cultural narrative around masculinity often emphasizes heteronormativity, leading to internalized homophobia and conflict.

For instance, Armando recalls instances where his interests in the arts and fashion were met with derision from peers, which prompted him to suppress these aspects of his identity. This suppression is a common phenomenon, as highlighted by the Minority Stress Theory, which suggests that LGBTQ individuals experience chronic stress due to societal stigma, discrimination, and internalized homophobia.

$$S = \frac{D + I + E}{T} \tag{52}$$

Where S represents the stress experienced, D is the discrimination faced, I denotes internalized stigma, E is the external societal pressures, and T is the coping resources available. Armando's initial struggles can be quantified through this equation, illustrating the compounded effects of societal expectations on his mental health.

Pivotal Moments of Self-Discovery

As Armando navigated through adolescence, several pivotal moments catalyzed his journey toward self-acceptance. One such moment occurred during a local pride event, where he witnessed the vibrant expressions of identity and solidarity among LGBTQ individuals. This experience marked a turning point, igniting a sense of belonging and community that had previously eluded him.

Armando began to explore different facets of his identity, engaging with LGBTQ literature and connecting with activists who shared similar experiences. These interactions were crucial in dismantling the internalized stigma he had carried. The role of positive representation cannot be overstated; as Armando encountered stories of resilience and triumph within the LGBTQ community, he began to envision a future where he could live authentically.

The Role of Intersectionality

Armando's evolution also underscores the importance of intersectionality in understanding identity. The concept, introduced by Kimberlé Crenshaw, emphasizes that individuals experience overlapping systems of discrimination based on various identity markers, including race, gender, and sexual orientation. Armando's identity as a queer individual of color added layers of complexity to his experiences.

He often faced unique challenges that were not solely based on his sexual orientation but were also influenced by his racial identity. For instance, discussions around race within the LGBTQ community often highlight the marginalization of queer people of color, leading to feelings of isolation. Armando's advocacy work later focused on addressing these intersections, promoting inclusivity within LGBTQ spaces.

Conclusion: A Continuous Journey

Ultimately, Armando's evolution is a testament to the ongoing nature of identity development. His journey illustrates that identity is not a static concept but rather a fluid and dynamic process influenced by personal experiences, societal expectations, and cultural narratives. As he reflects on his past, Armando recognizes that his perspectives continue to evolve, shaped by new experiences and the changing landscape of LGBTQ rights.

In conclusion, Armando's story is a powerful reminder of the resilience required to navigate the complexities of identity. His evolution serves as an inspiration for future generations, emphasizing the importance of self-acceptance, community support, and advocacy for inclusive spaces. As he continues to advocate for LGBTQ rights, Armando embodies the spirit of transformation, demonstrating that the journey of self-discovery is as vital as the destination itself.

Gratitude for Support and Collaborators

In the journey of activism, the importance of support systems and collaborative efforts cannot be overstated. Armando's path was not one taken in isolation; rather, it was enriched by the contributions and encouragement of a diverse array of individuals and organizations. This section reflects on the profound gratitude Armando feels towards those who have stood by him, shaped his activism, and helped amplify his voice in the fight for LGBTQ rights.

The Role of Friends and Chosen Family

From the very beginning of his activism, Armando was fortunate to be surrounded by a close-knit group of friends who became his chosen family. These individuals provided emotional support during tumultuous times, celebrated milestones, and offered constructive criticism that helped refine his approach to advocacy. The unconditional love and acceptance from this group allowed Armando to embrace his identity fully and pursue his mission without fear.

One notable example is the friendship he formed with a fellow activist, Sofia, who introduced him to the world of LGBTQ rights. Sofia's unwavering belief in Armando's potential served as a catalyst for his activism. Their late-night discussions about equality and justice not only deepened their bond but also ignited a shared vision for a more inclusive society. Armando often reflects on how these friendships were instrumental in building his confidence and resilience.

Collaborations with Organizations

Armando's activism gained momentum through collaborations with various LGBTQ organizations. These partnerships provided him with resources, training, and a platform to amplify his message. One of the most significant collaborations was with *Colombian LGBTQ Rights Coalition*, where Armando served as a volunteer coordinator. This organization not only supported his initiatives but also connected him with experienced activists who mentored him.

The coalition's annual pride march, which Armando helped organize, became a turning point in his advocacy career. The event attracted thousands, showcasing the power of unity and collective action. Armando often expresses his gratitude for the coalition's belief in him, stating, "Without their support, I would not have had the courage to step into the spotlight."

Academic and Professional Mentorship

Armando's journey was further enriched by mentors from academic and professional backgrounds. Professors who recognized his passion for social justice nurtured his intellectual growth. They provided him with critical insights into the historical context of LGBTQ rights, equipping him with the knowledge necessary to engage effectively in advocacy.

For instance, Dr. Elena Martínez, a prominent scholar in gender studies, played a pivotal role in shaping Armando's understanding of intersectionality. Through her guidance, Armando learned to appreciate the interconnectedness of various social justice movements and the importance of inclusivity within the LGBTQ community. He often acknowledges her influence, stating, "Dr. Martínez opened my eyes to the broader implications of my work, urging me to consider how race, class, and gender intersect with sexuality."

Community Support and Grassroots Movements

The grassroots movements that emerged in Colombia during Armando's early years were vital in fostering a sense of community and solidarity. Local activists rallied around shared goals, creating a vibrant network of support. Armando expresses immense gratitude for these community members, who often risked their safety to advocate for change alongside him.

The *LGBTQ Youth Alliance*, a group dedicated to empowering young activists, became a source of inspiration for Armando. Their tireless efforts to provide safe spaces for LGBTQ youth resonated deeply with him, motivating him to contribute to similar initiatives. He recalls attending their meetings, where stories of resilience and courage were shared, reinforcing his commitment to the cause.

The Impact of Digital Activism

In the digital age, social media has transformed the landscape of activism, allowing for broader reach and engagement. Armando is grateful for the online platforms that have facilitated connections with activists worldwide. Through social media campaigns, he has been able to share his message beyond geographical boundaries, garnering support from an international audience.

One such campaign, *#PrideInDiversity*, aimed to highlight the experiences of LGBTQ individuals from various cultural backgrounds. The overwhelming response from followers around the globe not only validated Armando's efforts but also reinforced the importance of solidarity in the fight for equality. He reflects on this experience, saying, "The digital community has been a lifeline, reminding me that we are not alone in our struggles."

Acknowledging the Unsung Heroes

While Armando's name may be prominent in the fight for LGBTQ rights, he is acutely aware of the countless unsung heroes whose contributions often go unrecognized. From grassroots organizers to everyday individuals who stand up against discrimination, these people embody the spirit of activism. Armando expresses his gratitude for their tireless efforts, stating, "Every small act of courage adds up to monumental change. I am forever thankful for those who fight quietly but fiercely."

In conclusion, Armando's journey as an LGBTQ activist is deeply intertwined with the support and collaboration of various individuals and organizations. His gratitude extends to friends, mentors, community members, and the digital activism landscape that has amplified his voice. Recognizing their contributions not only honors their efforts but also serves as a reminder that activism is a collective endeavor, rooted in solidarity and shared purpose. As Armando continues to advocate for LGBTQ rights, he carries with him the lessons learned and the love received from those who have walked alongside him on this transformative journey.

Armando's Vision for the Future

As Armando looks ahead, his vision for the future is painted with vibrant hues of hope, resilience, and unwavering commitment to the LGBTQ community and social justice at large. His aspirations are not merely rooted in personal ambition but are deeply intertwined with the collective struggles and triumphs of marginalized communities. Central to his vision is the belief that the fight for LGBTQ rights must be inclusive, intersectional, and sustainable.

Hopes for LGBTQ Rights in Colombia and Beyond

Armando envisions a future where LGBTQ rights are universally recognized and respected, not just in Colombia but across the globe. He believes that the decriminalization of homosexuality and the recognition of same-sex marriages are fundamental steps that must be taken to ensure equality. He often references the landmark ruling in Colombia's Constitutional Court in 2016 that allowed same-sex couples to adopt children, highlighting it as a beacon of progress. However, Armando acknowledges that legal recognition is only one part of the equation.

$$\text{Equality} = \text{Legal Recognition} + \text{Social Acceptance} + \text{Cultural Change} \quad (53)$$

Armando's vision includes initiatives that promote social acceptance, challenging deeply ingrained cultural norms that perpetuate discrimination and violence against LGBTQ individuals. He advocates for comprehensive educational programs that foster understanding and empathy from a young age, emphasizing that true equality can only be achieved when society collectively embraces diversity.

Prioritizing Intersectional Advocacy

Understanding that the fight for LGBTQ rights cannot exist in a vacuum, Armando prioritizes intersectional advocacy. He recognizes that issues of race, gender, class, and sexuality are interconnected, and that the struggles faced by individuals are often compounded by multiple forms of discrimination.

Armando often quotes Kimberlé Crenshaw, the scholar who coined the term "intersectionality," stating, "If you are not intersectional, you are not doing it right." He believes that advocacy must address the unique challenges faced by LGBTQ individuals who also belong to other marginalized groups. For instance, Afro-Colombian LGBTQ individuals often face compounded discrimination, and Armando's vision includes amplifying their voices and advocating for their specific needs within the broader LGBTQ movement.

Inspiring the Next Generation of Activists

A critical component of Armando's vision is the empowerment of the next generation of activists. He firmly believes that the future of the LGBTQ movement lies in the hands of youth, who possess the energy, creativity, and passion to drive change. Armando often organizes workshops and mentorship programs aimed at young activists, providing them with the tools and knowledge necessary to navigate the complexities of advocacy.

Armando emphasizes the importance of storytelling as a means of activism, encouraging young people to share their experiences and struggles. He believes that personal narratives can humanize issues and foster connections, ultimately leading to greater understanding and support for LGBTQ rights.

$$\text{Empowerment} = \text{Education} + \text{Mentorship} + \text{Storytelling} \quad (54)$$

Through these initiatives, Armando hopes to cultivate a new generation of leaders who are equipped to continue the fight for equality and justice.

Strategies for Sustaining Progress

To ensure that progress is not only made but sustained, Armando advocates for strategic planning and collaboration among various organizations and movements. He believes that building coalitions is essential for amplifying voices and creating a united front against discrimination.

Armando emphasizes the need for continuous dialogue between activists, policymakers, and community members. He often cites the success of the "Coalition for LGBTQ Rights" in Colombia, which brought together diverse organizations to advocate for comprehensive anti-discrimination laws. This collaborative approach not only strengthens the movement but also fosters a sense of community and shared purpose.

$$\text{Sustained Progress} = \text{Collaboration} + \text{Strategic Planning} + \text{Community Engagement} \tag{55}$$

Armando envisions a future where LGBTQ rights are integrated into broader human rights agendas, ensuring that the fight for equality is recognized as a fundamental aspect of social justice.

Staying Committed to the Cause

Finally, Armando's vision for the future is grounded in a steadfast commitment to the cause. He understands that activism is not a sprint but a marathon, requiring endurance, passion, and resilience. Armando often reflects on the importance of self-care and mental health for activists, advocating for practices that promote well-being amidst the challenges of advocacy.

He encourages fellow activists to celebrate small victories and to remain hopeful, reminding them that every step forward, no matter how small, contributes to the larger movement.

$$\text{Commitment} = \text{Resilience} + \text{Self-Care} + \text{Community Support} \tag{56}$$

In conclusion, Armando's vision for the future is one of hope, resilience, and unwavering commitment to the cause of LGBTQ rights. By prioritizing intersectional advocacy, empowering the next generation, fostering collaboration, and maintaining a steadfast commitment to the cause, Armando believes that a brighter, more equitable future is not only possible but within reach. His vision serves as a guiding light for activists and allies alike, inspiring collective action towards a world where love and acceptance triumph over hatred and discrimination.

Armando's Vision for the Future

Hopes for LGBTQ Rights in Colombia and Beyond

The landscape of LGBTQ rights in Colombia has undergone significant transformations over the past few decades. However, the journey towards full equality is far from over. Armando's hopes for LGBTQ rights in Colombia and beyond are deeply rooted in a vision of inclusivity, justice, and the recognition of human dignity.

A Vision for a More Inclusive Society

Armando envisions a Colombia where LGBTQ individuals are not only accepted but celebrated for their identities. He believes that true progress requires a cultural shift that embraces diversity in all its forms. This vision aligns with the theory of intersectionality, which emphasizes the interconnectedness of various social identities and the unique challenges faced by individuals at these intersections. In Colombia, this means recognizing that LGBTQ rights are inextricably linked to issues of race, class, and gender.

$$I = \sum_{i=1}^{n} \left(\text{Identity}_i \times \text{Intersectionality}_i \right) \qquad (57)$$

Where I represents the overall identity experience, and each Identity_i is influenced by its corresponding $\text{Intersectionality}_i$. For Armando, advocating for LGBTQ rights is not just about legal recognition; it is about fostering a society where every individual can thrive, free from discrimination and violence.

Legislative Hopes

Legislatively, Armando hopes for the continued advancement of laws that protect LGBTQ individuals from discrimination in employment, healthcare, and housing. While Colombia has made strides—such as the legalization of same-sex marriage in 2016—there are still gaps in protections that leave many vulnerable. For example, the lack of comprehensive anti-discrimination laws means that LGBTQ individuals can still face unjust treatment in various sectors.

Armando advocates for the implementation of the *Ley de Inclusión*, a proposed law aimed at establishing comprehensive protections for LGBTQ individuals. This law would not only provide legal safeguards but also promote awareness and education about LGBTQ issues in schools and workplaces.

Community Engagement and Education

Armando emphasizes the importance of community engagement in fostering understanding and acceptance. He believes that grassroots movements play a crucial role in changing hearts and minds. By organizing workshops, seminars, and community outreach programs, activists can educate the public about LGBTQ rights and the impact of discrimination.

One successful example of this approach is the *Pride in the Park* initiative in Bogotá, which brings together LGBTQ individuals and allies to celebrate diversity while educating attendees about their rights. Such events create safe spaces for dialogue and foster a sense of belonging within the community.

Global Solidarity and Influence

Armando's vision extends beyond Colombia. He believes that the fight for LGBTQ rights is a global struggle that requires solidarity across borders. The challenges faced by LGBTQ individuals in Colombia are echoed in many parts of the world, particularly in countries where homosexuality is criminalized.

By collaborating with international organizations, Armando aims to amplify the voices of marginalized LGBTQ individuals globally. He draws inspiration from movements like the *Global Fund for Human Rights*, which supports activists fighting against discrimination and violence worldwide.

Empowering Future Generations

Finally, Armando's hopes for LGBTQ rights are intertwined with empowering the next generation of activists. He believes that mentorship and education are vital for sustaining progress. By providing resources, training, and support, experienced activists can inspire young people to take up the mantle of advocacy.

Armando envisions a future where LGBTQ youth feel empowered to express their identities openly and confidently. This vision is encapsulated in programs like *Youth for Equality*, which provides leadership training and advocacy skills to young LGBTQ individuals.

In conclusion, Armando's hopes for LGBTQ rights in Colombia and beyond are a tapestry of legislative aspirations, community engagement, global solidarity, and intergenerational empowerment. He believes that through collective action and unwavering commitment, a more just and inclusive world is not just a dream, but a reachable reality. As he often says, "The fight for equality is not just a battle for rights; it is a celebration of our shared humanity."

Prioritizing Intersectional Advocacy

In the realm of LGBTQ activism, prioritizing intersectional advocacy is not just a trend; it is a necessity. Intersectionality, a term coined by Kimberlé Crenshaw in 1989, refers to the way various forms of social stratification, such as class, race, sexual orientation, and gender, overlap and intersect. This framework is crucial for understanding how different identities experience discrimination and privilege in distinct ways.

Theoretical Foundations of Intersectionality

Intersectionality posits that individuals do not experience oppression in a vacuum; rather, their identities interact in complex ways that shape their experiences. For instance, a queer person of color may face discrimination that is different from that experienced by a white queer individual. This complexity is represented in the following equation:

$$O = f(G, R, C, S) \tag{58}$$

where O represents the overall experience of oppression, G is gender, R is race, C is class, and S is sexual orientation. Each variable interacts to produce a unique outcome, demonstrating that advocacy efforts must account for the multifaceted nature of identity.

The Importance of Intersectional Advocacy

The importance of intersectional advocacy cannot be overstated. It is essential for several reasons:

1. **Comprehensive Representation**: Advocacy that prioritizes intersectionality ensures that the voices of marginalized groups within the LGBTQ community are heard. For example, transgender women of color often face higher rates of violence and discrimination compared to their cisgender counterparts. By centering their experiences, advocacy efforts can be more inclusive and effective.

2. **Addressing Systemic Inequities**: Intersectional advocacy highlights systemic inequities that may otherwise go unnoticed. For instance, healthcare

access for LGBTQ individuals can vary significantly based on race and socioeconomic status. An intersectional approach can illuminate these disparities and drive policy changes to address them.

3. **Building Alliances**: By recognizing the interconnectedness of various social justice movements, intersectional advocacy can foster coalitions that strengthen the overall fight for equality. For example, LGBTQ activists working alongside racial justice advocates can create a more unified front against systemic oppression.

Challenges in Implementing Intersectional Advocacy

Despite its importance, implementing intersectional advocacy comes with challenges:

1. **Fragmentation within Movements**: Different groups within the LGBTQ community may have conflicting priorities. For instance, mainstream LGBTQ rights organizations may focus on marriage equality, while activists from marginalized backgrounds may prioritize issues like police violence or healthcare access. Bridging these gaps requires open dialogue and a willingness to prioritize collective goals.

2. **Tokenism**: There is a risk of tokenism, where organizations may superficially include diverse voices without genuinely addressing their concerns. This can lead to disillusionment among activists from marginalized backgrounds and hinder the overall effectiveness of advocacy efforts.

3. **Resource Allocation**: Intersectional advocacy often requires additional resources to address the complexities of multiple identities. Organizations may struggle to allocate funds and manpower effectively, which can limit their ability to engage in comprehensive advocacy.

Examples of Intersectional Advocacy in Action

Several organizations exemplify the principles of intersectional advocacy:

1. **The Black Trans Advocacy Coalition (BTAC)**: This organization focuses on the unique challenges faced by Black transgender individuals, advocating for policy changes that address violence, healthcare access, and employment discrimination. Their work highlights the need for targeted interventions that consider race, gender identity, and socioeconomic status.

2. **The Human Rights Campaign (HRC)**: While often critiqued for its mainstream approach, HRC has increasingly integrated intersectional frameworks into its advocacy efforts. Their campaigns now emphasize the importance of

addressing issues faced by LGBTQ individuals of color, particularly in the areas of healthcare and criminal justice reform.

3. **The National Queer Asian Pacific Islander Alliance (NQAPIA)**: This organization works to uplift the voices of LGBTQ individuals within Asian and Pacific Islander communities, focusing on issues such as immigration, cultural stigma, and healthcare disparities. Their work exemplifies how intersectionality can inform advocacy that is culturally competent and responsive to the needs of diverse communities.

Conclusion

In conclusion, prioritizing intersectional advocacy is essential for a robust and inclusive LGBTQ movement. By recognizing the interconnectedness of various identities and the unique challenges they face, activists can work towards a more equitable society. As Armando continues to champion intersectional advocacy, his commitment to uplifting marginalized voices serves as a powerful reminder that true progress can only be achieved when everyone is included in the conversation. The journey toward equality is not linear; it is a complex tapestry woven from the diverse threads of our identities, experiences, and aspirations.

Inspiring the Next Generation of Activists

In the vibrant tapestry of activism, the threads woven by pioneers like Armando serve not only as a testament to the struggles faced but also as a beacon of hope for future generations. The journey of inspiring the next generation of activists is multifaceted, requiring a blend of mentorship, education, and the cultivation of a resilient spirit. This section delves into the strategies and philosophies that Armando employed to ignite the flames of activism in young hearts and minds.

The Importance of Mentorship

Mentorship plays a pivotal role in shaping the trajectory of young activists. Armando recognized that sharing personal experiences and insights could empower youth to navigate the complexities of advocacy. He often hosted workshops and discussion groups where he would share his own journey, emphasizing the lessons learned from both triumphs and setbacks.

> "Every setback is a setup for a comeback," he would say, encouraging young activists to view challenges as opportunities for growth.

This approach not only provided practical knowledge but also fostered a sense of belonging and community among participants. By creating safe spaces for dialogue, Armando helped cultivate a generation that felt seen, heard, and validated in their struggles.

Education as a Tool for Empowerment

Education is a powerful tool for social change, and Armando was a firm believer in its transformative potential. He advocated for the inclusion of LGBTQ studies in school curricula, arguing that understanding the history and contributions of LGBTQ individuals is crucial for fostering acceptance and equality.

$$\text{Empowerment} = \text{Education} + \text{Awareness} \tag{59}$$

Through partnerships with educational institutions, Armando initiated programs that brought LGBTQ history to the forefront, allowing students to learn about prominent figures, significant events, and the ongoing struggles for rights. This not only educated young minds but also instilled a sense of responsibility to continue the fight for justice.

Cultivating Resilience and Activism

In the face of adversity, resilience is a vital characteristic for any activist. Armando often shared his own experiences of facing backlash and hostility, illustrating the importance of perseverance. He introduced young activists to the concept of "radical self-care," encouraging them to prioritize their mental and emotional well-being while engaging in activism.

$$\text{Resilience} = \frac{\text{Support System} + \text{Self-Care}}{\text{Adversity}} \tag{60}$$

Armando emphasized that while activism can be draining, it is essential to recharge and seek support from peers and mentors. He organized retreats and wellness workshops that combined activism with self-care practices, ensuring that young activists understood the importance of maintaining balance in their lives.

Empowering Through Technology

In the digital age, technology serves as a powerful ally for activists. Armando harnessed the potential of social media platforms to amplify voices and mobilize support. He encouraged young activists to utilize these tools effectively, teaching them how to craft compelling narratives and engage with a broader audience.

"Your voice matters, and the world is listening. Use it wisely," he would remind them.

By providing training on digital advocacy, Armando equipped the next generation with the skills needed to navigate online spaces, raise awareness, and create impactful campaigns. This digital empowerment not only expanded their reach but also fostered a sense of agency among young activists.

Creating Collaborative Networks

Armando understood that collaboration is key to sustaining movements. He actively worked to connect young activists with established organizations and leaders in the field. By fostering these relationships, he helped create a network of support that transcended geographical boundaries.

$$\text{Impact} = \text{Collaboration} \times \text{Collective Action} \tag{61}$$

Through joint initiatives, young activists learned the power of collective action and the importance of solidarity. Armando often facilitated events where youth could collaborate on projects, share resources, and strategize together, thereby building a robust foundation for future advocacy.

Celebrating Diversity in Activism

Finally, Armando championed the idea that activism must be inclusive and representative of diverse identities. He encouraged young activists to embrace their unique backgrounds and experiences, recognizing that diversity strengthens movements.

"Our differences are our strengths. Celebrate them!" he would declare during community gatherings.

By promoting intersectionality within activism, Armando inspired the next generation to advocate not just for LGBTQ rights but also for issues related to race, gender, and socioeconomic status. This holistic approach ensured that the movement remained relevant and responsive to the needs of all marginalized communities.

Conclusion

Inspiring the next generation of activists is a noble and necessary endeavor. Through mentorship, education, resilience, technology, collaboration, and a commitment to diversity, Armando laid the groundwork for a vibrant and inclusive future in activism. His legacy lives on in the hearts of those he inspired, reminding us all that the fight for justice is a continuous journey, one that requires the passion and dedication of each new generation.

Strategies for Sustaining Progress

In the journey of advocating for LGBTQ rights, sustaining progress is as crucial as initiating change. Armando's vision for the future encompasses several strategic frameworks that aim to fortify and perpetuate the advancements made in LGBTQ rights. The following strategies are pivotal in ensuring that the momentum of activism continues to thrive.

Building Strong Coalitions

One of the most effective strategies for sustaining progress is the formation of robust coalitions among various advocacy groups. By collaborating with organizations that focus on intersecting issues such as gender equality, racial justice, and economic equity, LGBTQ activists can amplify their voices and broaden their impact.

$$\text{Coalition Strength} = \sum_{i=1}^{n} \text{Resources}_i \times \text{Diversity}_i \tag{62}$$

Where: - n is the number of organizations in the coalition. - Resources_i represents the resources contributed by each organization. - Diversity_i indicates the diversity of perspectives and strategies each organization brings.

For example, Armando collaborated with women's rights groups to address the unique challenges faced by LGBTQ women, thus creating a more inclusive movement that resonates with a broader audience.

Continuous Education and Training

Education is a powerful tool in sustaining progress. Armando emphasized the importance of ongoing training for activists to equip them with the latest knowledge, strategies, and skills necessary for effective advocacy. This includes workshops on legal rights, public speaking, and digital activism.

Armando's Vision for the Future

$$\text{Knowledge Retention} = \frac{\text{Training Sessions} \times \text{Participant Engagement}}{\text{Time}} \quad (63)$$

This equation suggests that the effectiveness of training is proportional to the number of sessions and the level of engagement from participants, while inversely related to the time elapsed since the training.

Armando's initiative to create a mentorship program where seasoned activists guide newcomers is an excellent example of this approach. The mentorship model not only fosters knowledge transfer but also ensures that fresh ideas and perspectives are continuously injected into the movement.

Leveraging Technology and Social Media

In today's digital age, technology and social media play a crucial role in sustaining activism. Armando recognized the potential of online platforms to mobilize support, spread awareness, and engage a global audience.

$$\text{Engagement Rate} = \frac{\text{Interactions}}{\text{Total Followers}} \times 100 \quad (64)$$

This equation helps activists measure the effectiveness of their online campaigns. For instance, during a campaign for marriage equality, Armando utilized social media to share personal stories and testimonials, resulting in a significant increase in engagement and support from the public.

Advocacy for Policy Change

Sustaining progress also requires relentless advocacy for policy changes that protect and enhance LGBTQ rights. Armando's strategy included lobbying for comprehensive anti-discrimination laws and equal access to healthcare services.

$$\text{Policy Impact} = \text{Legislation Passed} \times \text{Public Support} \quad (65)$$

The success of such policies often hinges on public support, which can be cultivated through awareness campaigns and community engagement. Armando's efforts in organizing town hall meetings allowed constituents to voice their concerns, thereby increasing public support for LGBTQ-friendly legislation.

Evaluation and Adaptation

Finally, sustaining progress requires regular evaluation of strategies and outcomes. Armando advocated for a reflective practice where activists assess what works and what does not, allowing for adaptation and evolution of approaches.

$$\text{Success Rate} = \frac{\text{Successful Initiatives}}{\text{Total Initiatives}} \times 100 \qquad (66)$$

By analyzing the success rate of various initiatives, activists can identify best practices and areas needing improvement. For instance, after a campaign that fell short of its goals, Armando gathered feedback from participants to understand the barriers encountered, leading to more effective strategies in subsequent efforts.

Conclusion

In conclusion, sustaining progress in LGBTQ activism requires a multifaceted approach that includes building coalitions, continuous education, leveraging technology, advocating for policy change, and regular evaluation of strategies. Armando's vision for the future is not just about achieving milestones; it is about creating a resilient movement that adapts, grows, and continues to fight for equality and justice for all. By implementing these strategies, activists can ensure that the hard-won rights are not only preserved but also expanded, paving the way for future generations to thrive in a more inclusive society.

Staying Committed to the Cause

Staying committed to the cause of LGBTQ rights is not merely a matter of passion; it requires a strategic approach, ongoing education, and a robust support system. Armando's journey exemplifies the necessity of maintaining this commitment, especially in the face of adversity and societal pushback.

The Importance of Sustained Advocacy

Advocacy is not a sprint; it is a marathon. To illustrate this, consider the theory of *social movement theory*, which posits that sustained efforts over time are crucial for achieving systemic change. According to Tilly and Tarrow (2015), social movements rely on "sustained collective action" to challenge established norms and policies. For Armando, this meant not only participating in protests but also engaging in continuous dialogue with policymakers, community leaders, and the public.

Challenges to Commitment

Despite the importance of sustained advocacy, activists like Armando face numerous challenges that can threaten their commitment:

- **Burnout:** The emotional and physical toll of activism can lead to burnout, which is characterized by exhaustion, cynicism, and a reduced sense of personal accomplishment. According to a study by Maslach and Leiter (2016), burnout is prevalent among activists due to the constant pressure and emotional labor involved in advocating for change.

- **Resistance:** Activists often encounter resistance from various societal sectors, including political entities and conservative groups. This pushback can manifest in negative media portrayals, legal challenges, and even threats to personal safety. Armando experienced this firsthand when he faced targeted attacks aimed at discrediting his work and undermining his credibility.

- **Isolation:** The nature of activism can sometimes lead to feelings of isolation, particularly for those who may not have a supportive network. Armando's experience highlights the importance of building alliances and fostering community to combat this isolation.

Strategies for Maintaining Commitment

To combat these challenges and stay committed to the cause, activists like Armando employ various strategies:

1. Building a Support Network Creating a reliable support network is crucial for any activist. Armando emphasized the importance of surrounding himself with like-minded individuals who share his passion for equality. This network not only provides emotional support but also facilitates collaboration on campaigns and initiatives. As noted by Putnam (2000), social capital—defined as the networks of relationships among people—plays a vital role in maintaining motivation and resilience.

2. Continuous Education Staying informed about the latest developments in LGBTQ rights and social justice is essential for sustained activism. Armando regularly attends workshops, seminars, and conferences to learn from experts and fellow activists. This commitment to education allows him to refine his strategies and adapt to changing circumstances. According to Freire (1970), education is a critical tool for empowerment, enabling individuals to challenge oppressive systems effectively.

3. Setting Realistic Goals Armando advocates for setting realistic, achievable goals to maintain momentum. By breaking down larger objectives into smaller, manageable tasks, activists can celebrate incremental victories, which reinforces their commitment. For example, instead of aiming for sweeping legislative changes in one go, Armando focuses on specific issues, such as advocating for inclusive healthcare policies. This approach aligns with the *SMART* criteria for goal-setting: Specific, Measurable, Achievable, Relevant, and Time-bound (Doran, 1981).

4. Practicing Self-Care Activism can be emotionally draining, making self-care a necessity rather than a luxury. Armando emphasizes the importance of taking time for oneself, whether through meditation, exercise, or simply spending time with friends and family. Studies indicate that self-care practices can significantly reduce stress and improve overall well-being (Neff, 2011).

Conclusion

Staying committed to the cause of LGBTQ rights requires a multifaceted approach that addresses both the challenges and the strategies for overcoming them. Armando's journey illustrates the importance of building a supportive community, engaging in continuous education, setting realistic goals, and prioritizing self-care. By implementing these strategies, activists can not only sustain their commitment but also inspire others to join the movement for equality and justice.

Bibliography

[1] Tilly, C., & Tarrow, S. (2015). *Contentious performances.* Cambridge University Press.

[2] Maslach, C., & Leiter, M. P. (2016). *Burnout: A guide to identifying burnout and pathways to recovery.* Harvard Business Review Press.

[3] Putnam, R. D. (2000). *Bowling Alone: The Collapse and Revival of American Community.* Simon & Schuster.

[4] Freire, P. (1970). *Pedagogy of the Oppressed.* Continuum.

[5] Doran, G. T. (1981). There's a S.M.A.R.T. way to write management's goals and objectives. *Management Review,* 70(11), 35-36.

[6] Neff, K. (2011). *Self-Compassion: The Proven Power of Being Kind to Yourself.* William Morrow.

Armando's Path to Self-Fulfillment

Armando's journey towards self-fulfillment is a compelling narrative that intertwines personal growth with his relentless pursuit of justice and equality. Understanding this path requires a multifaceted exploration of identity, motivation, and the socio-political landscape in which he operates.

The Intersection of Identity and Activism

At the core of Armando's self-fulfillment lies the complex interplay between his LGBTQ identity and his role as an activist. According to *Erik Erikson's psychosocial development theory,* individuals face critical challenges at various stages of life, and for Armando, the stage of **identity vs. role confusion** was pivotal. This theory posits that successful navigation of identity crises leads to a strong sense of self, which is essential for effective activism.

Armando's experience of coming out was not merely a personal revelation; it was a catalyst that propelled him into the activist sphere. The struggles he faced during this period—ranging from familial rejection to societal discrimination—served as both a barrier and a motivator. The resilience he developed through these challenges was instrumental in shaping his advocacy work. As he articulated in a public speech, "My identity is not just who I am; it is the fuel that ignites my passion for change."

Motivation and the Drive for Change

Armando's motivation can be analyzed through *Self-Determination Theory (SDT)*, which emphasizes the role of intrinsic motivation in fostering personal growth and well-being. SDT posits that fulfillment arises when individuals satisfy three basic psychological needs: autonomy, competence, and relatedness. For Armando, activism provided a platform to exercise autonomy—making choices that aligned with his values and beliefs.

His competence was continuously honed through participation in various advocacy initiatives, where he not only learned the intricacies of political lobbying but also developed public speaking skills that resonated with diverse audiences. The sense of relatedness was cultivated through the supportive networks he built within the LGBTQ community, which served as a foundation for his emotional resilience. This interconnectedness is crucial; as noted by *Brene Brown*, "Vulnerability is the birthplace of innovation, creativity, and change."

Overcoming Barriers to Self-Fulfillment

Despite his progress, Armando faced significant barriers that threatened his path to self-fulfillment. One of the primary challenges was the pervasive stigma associated with LGBTQ identities, particularly in conservative societies. This stigma often manifested in both overt discrimination and subtle microaggressions, which could undermine his sense of belonging and self-worth.

To combat these barriers, Armando employed various strategies. He engaged in **community organizing**, which not only amplified marginalized voices but also fostered solidarity among individuals facing similar struggles. By creating safe spaces for dialogue and support, he was able to promote healing and empowerment within the community.

Moreover, Armando recognized the importance of self-care in maintaining his mental health amidst the tumultuous landscape of activism. He often spoke about the necessity of setting boundaries and prioritizing personal well-being, stating, *"You cannot pour from an empty cup; self-care is not selfish; it is essential."* This awareness allowed him to sustain his activism without sacrificing his emotional health.

Envisioning a Future of Self-Fulfillment

Looking ahead, Armando's vision for self-fulfillment extends beyond personal achievements; it encompasses a broader aspiration for societal change. He believes that true fulfillment is achieved when individuals are empowered to live authentically without fear of discrimination. This vision aligns with the principles of *intersectionality*, as articulated by *Kimberlé Crenshaw*, which emphasizes the need to consider multiple identities and experiences in the fight for justice.

Armando's path to self-fulfillment is not just about achieving personal milestones; it is about creating a legacy that inspires future generations of activists. He often reflects on the importance of mentorship, stating, *"The greatest gift we can give is to lift others as we rise."* By investing in the next generation, he aims to ensure that the fight for LGBTQ rights continues to evolve, adapting to new challenges and opportunities.

In conclusion, Armando's path to self-fulfillment is a dynamic journey marked by resilience, motivation, and a commitment to social justice. His experiences illuminate the profound connection between personal identity and activism, offering a blueprint for others seeking to navigate their own paths toward fulfillment in the context of social change. As he continues to advocate for equality, Armando embodies the belief that self-fulfillment is not a destination but a continuous journey shaped by the collective struggle for justice.

The Unauthorized Biography: A Personal Note

Why Armando's Story Must Be Told

In the tapestry of LGBTQ history, every thread represents a unique story, a personal journey that contributes to the larger narrative of resilience, struggle, and triumph. Armando's story is not just a personal account; it is a reflection of the collective experiences of countless individuals who have fought against discrimination and injustice. Understanding why Armando's story must be told involves delving into several key reasons: representation, inspiration, education, and the urgent need for advocacy.

Representation Matters

First and foremost, representation is crucial in any social movement. Armando's journey provides visibility to the LGBTQ community, particularly within the context of Colombia, where cultural norms and societal expectations can often be oppressive. By sharing his experiences, we acknowledge the diversity within the LGBTQ spectrum, showcasing that there is no singular narrative. As Audre Lorde famously stated, "There is no such thing as a single-issue struggle because we do not live single-issue lives." Armando's story encapsulates the intersectionality of identity—encompassing race, gender, and sexuality—and emphasizes that each person's fight is interconnected.

Inspiration for Future Generations

Armando's activism serves as a beacon of hope for future generations. His story illustrates that change is possible, and that one person's voice can indeed make a difference. For young LGBTQ individuals grappling with their identities, Armando's achievements offer a roadmap. They can see that it is possible to challenge societal norms and advocate for change. The notion of "if he can do it, so can I" is a powerful motivator. As Maya Angelou said, "I can be changed by what happens to me. But I refuse to be reduced by it." Armando embodies this sentiment, transforming personal adversity into a catalyst for social change.

Educational Value

Moreover, Armando's story is rich with educational value. It provides insights into the historical and cultural contexts of LGBTQ rights in Colombia and beyond. By examining his experiences, readers can gain a deeper understanding of the systemic issues that LGBTQ individuals face, such as legal discrimination, social ostracism, and violence. This educational component is essential for fostering empathy and awareness among those who may not be directly affected by these issues. It is imperative to disseminate knowledge that can challenge misconceptions and stereotypes, ultimately leading to a more inclusive society.

The Urgency of Advocacy

Lastly, in a world where LGBTQ rights are still under threat, Armando's story is a reminder of the urgency of advocacy. Despite significant progress, many individuals continue to face violence, discrimination, and marginalization. By telling Armando's story, we not only honor his contributions but also highlight the ongoing struggles that many LGBTQ individuals endure. This narrative acts as a call to action, urging readers to engage in advocacy and support LGBTQ rights both locally and globally.

$$\text{Advocacy} = \text{Awareness} + \text{Action} \qquad (67)$$

This equation encapsulates the essence of Armando's mission. Awareness leads to understanding, and understanding leads to action. Each story, including Armando's, is a vital piece of the larger puzzle that drives the movement forward.

In conclusion, Armando's story must be told not only for the sake of honoring his journey but also for the broader implications it holds for representation, inspiration, education, and advocacy. It serves as a powerful reminder that every individual's story matters, and together, these narratives create a rich, diverse history that can inspire change and foster a more inclusive world. As we share Armando's experiences, we contribute to a legacy of activism that will resonate for generations to come.

The Role of Unauthorized Biographies in LGBTQ History

Unauthorized biographies play a critical role in the documentation and understanding of LGBTQ history, serving as a counter-narrative to mainstream historical accounts that often overlook or marginalize the contributions of LGBTQ individuals. These biographies provide a platform for voices that have been silenced or misrepresented, allowing for a more nuanced understanding of the complexities of identity, activism, and community within the LGBTQ spectrum.

Challenging the Canon

One of the primary functions of unauthorized biographies is to challenge the established canon of historical figures. Traditional biographies often focus on prominent figures whose narratives are sanitized or idealized, omitting the struggles and realities of those who do not fit into the conventional mold. Unauthorized biographies, however, can reveal the multifaceted lives of LGBTQ activists, artists, and everyday individuals, highlighting their contributions to social justice and cultural movements. For instance, the unauthorized biography of Marsha P. Johnson, a pivotal figure in the Stonewall uprising, illustrates her role not only as a trans activist but also as a community organizer who fought for the rights of marginalized populations, including LGBTQ people of color.

Preserving Marginalized Narratives

Unauthorized biographies serve as vital historical documents that preserve the narratives of individuals who may otherwise be forgotten. The act of writing these biographies is an assertion of identity and existence, reclaiming space in a historical context that often seeks to erase LGBTQ contributions. For example, the unauthorized biography of Sylvia Rivera sheds light on her activism and the challenges she faced as a transgender woman in a society that was hostile to her existence. By documenting her life, these biographies contribute to a broader understanding of LGBTQ history and the ongoing fight for rights and recognition.

Theoretical Frameworks

The significance of unauthorized biographies can be analyzed through various theoretical frameworks. One such framework is queer theory, which critiques the heteronormative structures that dominate historical narratives. Queer theorists argue that unauthorized biographies disrupt the normative storytelling practices by centering LGBTQ experiences and identities. This disruption is essential for understanding the social constructions of gender and sexuality, as it challenges the binary views that have long governed societal perceptions.

Moreover, feminist theory also plays a role in understanding the impact of unauthorized biographies. Feminist scholars emphasize the importance of personal narratives and lived experiences in shaping historical discourse. By amplifying the voices of LGBTQ individuals, unauthorized biographies contribute to the feminist project of reclaiming history from patriarchal narratives, thereby fostering a more inclusive understanding of social movements.

Examples of Impact

Several unauthorized biographies have made significant impacts on LGBTQ history and activism. For instance, the biography of Harvey Milk, while authorized, has inspired numerous unauthorized accounts that delve deeper into his personal life, relationships, and the sociopolitical context of his activism. These accounts highlight the complexities of his identity as a gay man and politician, offering insights into the challenges he faced and the legacy he left behind.

Another notable example is the unauthorized biography of Audre Lorde, which explores her identity as a Black lesbian feminist and poet. This biography not only celebrates her literary contributions but also examines her activism in the context of intersectionality, showcasing how her experiences shaped her understanding of oppression and resistance.

Addressing Problems and Limitations

Despite their importance, unauthorized biographies also face challenges. One significant issue is the potential for inaccuracies or sensationalism, as unauthorized authors may lack access to primary sources or intimate knowledge of their subjects. This can lead to misrepresentations that undermine the very purpose of these biographies. Therefore, it is crucial for readers to approach unauthorized biographies with a critical eye, recognizing the potential biases and limitations inherent in these narratives.

Additionally, the lack of formal recognition for unauthorized biographies can hinder their acceptance within academic and historical discourse. While these biographies are invaluable for grassroots understanding, they may not receive the same level of scholarly attention as authorized accounts, which can limit their impact on broader historical narratives.

Conclusion

In conclusion, unauthorized biographies serve a vital role in LGBTQ history by challenging dominant narratives, preserving marginalized voices, and contributing to a more inclusive understanding of social justice movements. They provide a platform for the complexities of LGBTQ identities and experiences, allowing for a richer exploration of the past. As history continues to unfold, the importance of these narratives will only grow, ensuring that the stories of LGBTQ individuals are not only told but celebrated.

Appreciating Armando's Courage and Contributions

In the complex landscape of LGBTQ activism, few figures stand out as prominently as Armando. His unwavering commitment to advocating for equality and justice has not only transformed the lives of countless individuals but has also inspired a generation of activists to continue the fight for rights that many take for granted. To truly appreciate Armando's courage and contributions, we must examine the multifaceted nature of his activism, the challenges he faced, and the impact he made both locally and globally.

Courage in the Face of Adversity

Armando's journey was not without its trials. Growing up in Medellín, he encountered discrimination at an early age, which ignited his passion for activism. The courage required to confront societal norms and challenge the status quo is immense. Armando faced threats and backlash from conservative factions within his community, yet he persisted. His ability to stand firm in his beliefs despite the risks is a testament to his character.

The theoretical framework of *social movement theory* provides insight into how individuals like Armando mobilize for change. According to Tilly (2004), social movements emerge when individuals collectively challenge structures of power. Armando exemplifies this as he rallied support, organized protests, and lobbied for legislative changes. His actions were not just personal choices; they were strategic moves within a larger movement for justice.

Contributions to LGBTQ Rights

Armando's contributions to LGBTQ rights in Colombia are monumental. He played a pivotal role in several landmark cases that advanced legal recognition for same-sex couples. For example, his involvement in the case of *Corte Constitucional de Colombia* (2011), which granted legal rights to same-sex couples, marked a significant victory in the fight for equality. This case not only changed the legal landscape in Colombia but also served as a beacon of hope for LGBTQ individuals across Latin America.

In addition to legal battles, Armando's advocacy extended to healthcare and social services. He recognized that legal rights alone were insufficient; access to healthcare is a fundamental human right. His efforts to promote LGBTQ-inclusive healthcare policies addressed the unique needs of the community, particularly in mental health services where stigma often prevents individuals from seeking help.

Changing Public Perception

Armando's contributions also include his efforts to change public perception of LGBTQ individuals. Through educational campaigns and community outreach, he worked tirelessly to dismantle stereotypes and promote understanding. The importance of shifting societal attitudes cannot be overstated; as noted by Herek (1990), prejudice often stems from misinformation and lack of exposure. Armando's work in schools and community centers has fostered dialogue and created safe spaces for LGBTQ youth.

A Global Influence

While Armando's roots are in Colombia, his influence has transcended borders. He collaborated with international organizations such as *ILGA* (International

Lesbian, Gay, Bisexual, Trans and Intersex Association) to address global LGBTQ issues. His speeches at international conferences have brought attention to the plight of LGBTQ refugees and asylum seekers, highlighting the need for a unified global response to discrimination.

Armando's ability to connect local struggles to global movements exemplifies the concept of *intersectionality* introduced by Crenshaw (1989). He understood that the fight for LGBTQ rights is intertwined with broader social justice issues, including race, gender, and economic inequality. This holistic approach has not only enriched his advocacy but has also set a precedent for future activists.

Legacy of Courage and Inspiration

Armando's legacy is one of courage, resilience, and unwavering commitment to justice. His contributions have laid the groundwork for future generations of activists. As we reflect on his journey, we must acknowledge the sacrifices he made and the lives he touched. His story is a reminder of the power of one individual to effect change in the world.

In conclusion, appreciating Armando's courage and contributions requires recognizing the complexities of his activism. From challenging societal norms to advocating for legal rights, Armando's impact is profound and enduring. As we continue to navigate the landscape of LGBTQ rights, let us carry forward his legacy and strive for a world where everyone can live authentically and without fear.

Bibliography

[1] Tilly, C. (2004). *Social Movements, 1760–2000*. Paradigm Publishers.

[2] Herek, G. M. (1990). *Sexual Prejudice: A Conceptual Analysis*. Journal of Interpersonal Violence, 5(3), 325-339.

[3] Crenshaw, K. (1989). *Demarginalizing the Intersection of Race and Sex: A Black Feminist Critique of Antidiscrimination Doctrine, Feminist Theory and Antiracist Politics*. University of Chicago Legal Forum, 1989(1), 139-167.

Honoring the Legacy of Activism

The legacy of activism is not merely a collection of achievements; it is a living, breathing testament to the struggles, victories, and aspirations of those who have fought for justice and equality. In honoring this legacy, we recognize the profound impact that activists like Armando have had on society, particularly in the realm of LGBTQ rights. This section will explore the significance of commemorating activism, the problems that arise in the process, and the theoretical frameworks that can guide our understanding of this essential task.

The Significance of Honoring Activism

Honoring the legacy of activism serves several crucial purposes:

    1. **Preservation of History**: Activism is often marginalized in mainstream narratives. By documenting and celebrating the contributions of activists, we ensure that their stories are not forgotten. This preservation is vital for future generations, who can learn from the past to inform their own struggles.

    2. **Inspiration for Future Generations**: The stories of activists can inspire and empower new generations to continue the fight for justice. For instance, the work of LGBTQ activists in the 1980s and 1990s during the AIDS crisis serves as a powerful reminder of resilience and the importance of community organizing.

3. **Recognition of Diversity**: Honoring activism allows for the acknowledgment of diverse voices within the movement. This is particularly important in the LGBTQ community, where intersectionality plays a crucial role in understanding the multifaceted nature of oppression. Activists from various backgrounds, including people of color, transgender individuals, and those from economically disadvantaged communities, contribute to a richer narrative.

4. **Creating a Sense of Belonging**: Celebrating the legacy of activism fosters a sense of belonging within marginalized communities. When individuals see their identities represented in the history of activism, it validates their experiences and encourages them to engage in advocacy.

Challenges in Honoring Activism

While the importance of honoring activism is clear, several challenges complicate this endeavor:

1. **Historical Erasure**: Many activists, particularly those from marginalized groups, have been systematically erased from historical accounts. This erasure can lead to a lack of representation in narratives surrounding LGBTQ rights, making it crucial to actively seek out and amplify these voices.

2. **Commodification of Activism**: In contemporary society, there is a risk of commodifying activism, where the struggles and sacrifices of activists are reduced to mere marketing tools. This commodification can dilute the original messages and objectives of the movement, transforming profound struggles into superficial trends.

3. **Disagreements Within the Community**: The LGBTQ community is not monolithic; disagreements about how to honor activism can arise. For example, some may advocate for a focus on legal recognition, while others may prioritize grassroots organizing. Navigating these differences requires a commitment to dialogue and inclusivity.

4. **Maintaining Momentum**: Honoring the legacy of activism should not be a one-time event but rather an ongoing process. This requires sustained effort, resources, and commitment from individuals and organizations alike. The challenge lies in ensuring that the honor given translates into actionable support for current movements.

Theoretical Frameworks for Understanding Activism's Legacy

To effectively honor the legacy of activism, we can draw upon several theoretical frameworks:

1. **Critical Theory**: This framework encourages us to question the power structures that perpetuate inequality. By applying critical theory, we can analyze the historical context of activism and understand how systemic oppression shapes the experiences of marginalized groups.

2. **Intersectionality**: Coined by scholar Kimberlé Crenshaw, intersectionality emphasizes the interconnectedness of social identities and how they affect experiences of oppression. Honoring activism through an intersectional lens allows us to appreciate the diverse contributions of activists who navigate multiple identities.

3. **Collective Memory Theory**: This theory posits that groups create shared memories that shape their identity and values. By honoring the legacy of activism, we contribute to the collective memory of the LGBTQ community, reinforcing the importance of solidarity and shared purpose.

4. **Narrative Theory**: This framework focuses on the power of storytelling in shaping our understanding of the world. By sharing the stories of activists, we can honor their legacy while also inspiring others to engage in advocacy.

Examples of Honoring Activism

Several initiatives exemplify how we can honor the legacy of activism:

1. **Memorials and Monuments**: Creating physical spaces that commemorate the contributions of LGBTQ activists can serve as powerful reminders of their struggles and victories. For instance, the Stonewall National Monument in New York City honors the pivotal role of the Stonewall Riots in the LGBTQ rights movement.

2. **Documentaries and Biographies**: Producing documentaries and biographies that highlight the lives of activists can educate the public and celebrate their contributions. The documentary "Paris is Burning" provides a glimpse into the lives of LGBTQ individuals in the ballroom culture of New York City, showcasing their resilience and creativity.

3. **Educational Programs**: Integrating the history of LGBTQ activism into educational curricula can help students understand the significance of these struggles. Programs that focus on intersectional activism can foster a more comprehensive understanding of social justice.

4. **Annual Commemorations**: Establishing annual events to honor LGBTQ activists can create spaces for reflection and celebration. Pride Month, for example, serves as a time to recognize the contributions of LGBTQ individuals while also advocating for ongoing rights and protections.

In conclusion, honoring the legacy of activism is a vital task that requires intentionality, inclusivity, and a commitment to preserving the stories of those who have fought for justice. By recognizing the significance of this legacy, addressing the challenges involved, and applying relevant theoretical frameworks, we can ensure that the contributions of activists like Armando are celebrated and remembered for generations to come. The act of honoring activism not only acknowledges past struggles but also inspires future action, creating a continuous cycle of advocacy and empowerment.

The Importance of Sharing Representation

In the realm of activism, particularly within the LGBTQ community, representation transcends mere visibility; it serves as a powerful catalyst for change. The act of sharing diverse narratives not only affirms the identities of marginalized individuals but also fosters a sense of belonging and validation. This section delves into the multifaceted importance of representation, exploring its theoretical underpinnings, the challenges it addresses, and its profound impact on both individuals and society at large.

Theoretical Framework

Representation can be understood through the lens of social identity theory, which posits that individuals derive part of their self-concept from their membership in social groups. This theory, articulated by Henri Tajfel and John Turner, emphasizes the significance of group identity in shaping individual behavior and attitudes. When LGBTQ individuals see themselves reflected in media, politics, and public discourse, it enhances their self-esteem and reinforces their sense of community.

Moreover, the concept of intersectionality, introduced by Kimberlé Crenshaw, highlights the necessity of acknowledging the overlapping identities that individuals embody. For instance, an LGBTQ person of color faces distinct challenges compared to their white counterparts. Thus, representation must encompass a spectrum of identities, including race, gender, socioeconomic status, and disability, to truly reflect the diversity within the LGBTQ community.

Challenges Addressed by Representation

The absence of representation can perpetuate harmful stereotypes and contribute to systemic discrimination. For example, the lack of positive LGBTQ role models in mainstream media can lead to internalized homophobia and a diminished sense of self-worth among LGBTQ youth. According to a study by the Human Rights Campaign, LGBTQ youth who are exposed to affirming representations are more likely to report higher levels of self-acceptance and mental well-being.

Furthermore, representation is vital in combating the erasure of histories and experiences. The narratives of LGBTQ individuals, especially those from marginalized backgrounds, have often been excluded from historical accounts. This erasure not only denies these individuals their rightful place in history but also deprives future generations of role models and inspiration. By sharing these stories, we challenge the dominant narratives and create a more inclusive historical record.

Examples of Effective Representation

The impact of representation can be seen in various domains, from media to politics. For instance, the television series *Pose* has been lauded for its authentic portrayal of the Black and Latino LGBTQ ballroom culture in New York City. By centering the stories of transgender women of color, the show not only entertains but educates viewers about the struggles and triumphs of this community. The visibility of characters like Blanca and Elektra has inspired countless individuals to embrace their identities and advocate for their rights.

In politics, the election of openly LGBTQ officials, such as Pete Buttigieg and Tammy Baldwin, signifies a shift towards greater representation in governance. Their presence in positions of power challenges the notion that LGBTQ individuals are unfit for leadership roles and encourages others to pursue political careers. Representation in government is essential for advocating for policies that protect LGBTQ rights and address the unique challenges faced by the community.

The Ripple Effect of Representation

The importance of sharing representation extends beyond individual affirmation; it creates a ripple effect that influences societal attitudes and policies. When diverse voices are included in conversations about social justice, it challenges the status quo and prompts critical discussions about equity and inclusion. This, in turn, can lead to legislative changes that benefit not only the LGBTQ community but society as a whole.

For example, the increased visibility of LGBTQ issues in recent years has contributed to significant legal advancements, such as the legalization of same-sex marriage in many countries. These changes are often preceded by shifts in public perception, which are influenced by the representation of LGBTQ individuals in media, politics, and everyday life.

Conclusion

In conclusion, the importance of sharing representation within the LGBTQ community cannot be overstated. It is a vital component of activism that fosters self-acceptance, combats discrimination, and inspires future generations. By amplifying diverse voices and narratives, we not only honor the experiences of those who came before us but also pave the way for a more equitable and inclusive society. As we continue to advocate for LGBTQ rights, let us remember that representation is not just about visibility; it is about empowerment, validation, and the relentless pursuit of justice for all.

Acknowledgments and Resources

Acknowledgments and Resources

Acknowledgments and Resources

Acknowledging the Contributors

In the journey of writing this unauthorized biography of Armando, I have been fortunate to receive support from numerous individuals and organizations that have played pivotal roles in both my understanding of LGBTQ activism and the life of Armando himself.

First and foremost, I would like to extend my heartfelt gratitude to Armando for his willingness to share his story, despite the challenges that come with being an openly LGBTQ activist in a conservative society. His courage and resilience are an inspiration to many, and it is a privilege to tell his story.

Additionally, I would like to thank the LGBTQ organizations in Colombia and around the globe that provided invaluable insights, resources, and support. Their dedication to advancing LGBTQ rights and equality has been instrumental in shaping the narrative of this biography.

I am particularly grateful to the activists who took the time to share their experiences and wisdom with me. Their perspectives have enriched this work and highlighted the importance of community in the fight for justice.

Moreover, I would like to acknowledge the friends and family of Armando who have stood by him through thick and thin. Their support not only helped him navigate the complexities of his identity but also fueled his activism.

Collaboration is key in any social justice movement, and the contributions of many have made this biography possible. It is a testament to the power of collective action and the impact we can have when we come together for a common cause.

Recognizing the Importance of Collaboration

Collaboration in LGBTQ advocacy is not just about working together; it is about recognizing the diverse experiences and challenges faced by individuals within the community. Intersectionality, a term coined by Kimberlé Crenshaw, is critical in understanding how different identities—such as race, gender, and socioeconomic status—interact to create unique experiences of oppression and privilege.

The fight for LGBTQ rights cannot be isolated from other social justice movements. For instance, addressing issues of racism and xenophobia within the LGBTQ community is essential for creating an inclusive environment. Armando's activism has always emphasized the need for intersectional approaches, advocating for the rights of marginalized groups within the LGBTQ spectrum.

By collaborating with other movements, such as those advocating for women's rights and racial equality, LGBTQ activists can amplify their voices and create a more unified front against discrimination. This collective approach not only strengthens the movement but also fosters a sense of solidarity among diverse groups.

Resources and Organizations for LGBTQ Advocacy

For those who wish to engage further in LGBTQ advocacy or seek support, numerous organizations and resources are available. Below is a list of some key organizations that focus on LGBTQ rights, both in Colombia and internationally:

- **Colombian LGBTQ Rights Organizations**
    - *Colombia Diversa* - A leading organization advocating for the rights of LGBTQ individuals in Colombia.
    - *Red Comunitaria Trans* - Focuses on the rights of transgender individuals and promotes their visibility and inclusion.
    - *Fundación Grupo de Acción y Apoyo a Personas LGBTI* - Provides support and resources for LGBTQ individuals facing discrimination and violence.

- **International LGBTQ Rights Organizations**
    - *Human Rights Campaign* - A prominent organization advocating for LGBTQ equality in the United States and beyond.
    - *International Lesbian, Gay, Bisexual, Trans and Intersex Association (ILGA)* - A global federation of LGBTQ organizations dedicated to promoting human rights.

ACKNOWLEDGMENTS AND RESOURCES 231

- *OutRight Action International* - Works to advance the rights of LGBTQ people worldwide through advocacy, research, and capacity-building.

- **LGBTQ Healthcare and Support Resources**

  - *The Trevor Project* - Provides crisis intervention and suicide prevention services for LGBTQ youth.

  - *GLMA: Health Professionals Advancing LGBTQ Equality* - An organization that advocates for LGBTQ health equity and provides resources for healthcare professionals.

  - *National LGBTQ Task Force* - Focuses on policy advocacy and mobilizing support for LGBTQ issues, including healthcare access.

- **LGBTQ-Inclusive Educational Programs**

  - *Safe Zone Training* - Programs aimed at educating individuals on LGBTQ issues and creating safe spaces within educational institutions.

  - *GLSEN (Gay, Lesbian and Straight Education Network)* - Works to ensure that LGBTQ students are safe and supported in schools.

- **Recommended Books and Documentaries**

  - *"The Gay Revolution: The Story of the Struggle" by Lillian Faderman* - A comprehensive history of the LGBTQ rights movement in the United States.

  - *"Disclosure" (2020)* - A documentary exploring the representation of transgender individuals in film and television.

- **Online Platforms and Social Media Accounts**

  - *@lgbtq on Twitter* - A platform for sharing news and updates related to LGBTQ rights.

  - *LGBTQ+ on Instagram* - A community dedicated to celebrating LGBTQ identities and advocacy.

Engaging with these resources can empower individuals to contribute to the ongoing fight for LGBTQ rights and support those who are affected by discrimination and inequality.

Author's Notes and Disclaimer

As the author of this biography, I recognize that my perspective is just one of many. The stories and experiences of LGBTQ individuals are diverse and multifaceted. It is essential to approach this narrative with humility and an understanding that there is always more to learn.

This unauthorized biography aims to honor Armando's journey while also shining a light on the collective efforts of countless activists who have fought for LGBTQ rights. It is my hope that readers will be inspired to take action and continue the fight for equality, not just for themselves but for all marginalized communities.

About the Author

I am a passionate advocate for LGBTQ rights and a storyteller at heart. My journey into activism began with a desire to understand the complexities of social justice movements and the importance of representation. Through my writing, I aim to amplify the voices of those who have historically been silenced and to inspire others to join the fight for equality.

Acknowledging the Contributors

Personal Thanks and Gratitude

Writing this unauthorized biography of Armando has been a journey filled with inspiration, challenges, and a profound sense of responsibility. I would like to take a moment to express my heartfelt gratitude to the individuals and organizations that have played a crucial role in bringing this story to life.

First and foremost, I want to thank Armando himself. His courage, resilience, and unwavering commitment to LGBTQ rights have not only shaped the landscape of activism in Colombia but have also inspired countless individuals around the globe. Armando, your willingness to share your story, your struggles, and your triumphs has made this biography possible. Thank you for trusting me with your narrative and for allowing me to amplify your voice.

I extend my gratitude to the LGBTQ community in Colombia and beyond. Your strength and solidarity have been a beacon of hope for many. I am particularly thankful to the activists who have paved the way for change, often at great personal cost. Your sacrifices have not gone unnoticed, and your commitment to justice serves as a reminder that the fight for equality is far from over.

ACKNOWLEDGING THE CONTRIBUTORS

Special thanks must go to the organizations that have supported Armando and his mission. Groups like *Colombian LGBTQ Rights Coalition*, *Equality Colombia*, and international allies such as *Human Rights Campaign* and *ILGA World* have provided vital resources, advocacy, and a platform for voices that are often marginalized. Your dedication to promoting LGBTQ rights and protecting individuals from discrimination is commendable.

Moreover, I would like to acknowledge the friends and family members who have stood by Armando throughout his journey. Your love, support, and understanding have been the foundation upon which he has built his activism. You have shown that personal connections are vital in the fight for social justice. The stories of solidarity among friends, the late-night discussions about strategies, and the shared laughter amidst adversity are what fuel the movement.

To the scholars, researchers, and journalists who have documented the struggles and achievements of the LGBTQ community, thank you for your rigorous work and for providing a framework through which we can understand the complexities of these issues. Your research not only informs our understanding but also inspires future generations of activists.

I also want to express my appreciation for the mentors who have guided me in this writing process. Their insights and encouragement have been invaluable, reminding me of the importance of storytelling in activism. They have taught me that every narrative matters and that sharing these stories can create ripples of change.

As I reflect on the challenges faced in writing this biography, I recognize the importance of collaboration. This project would not have been possible without the contributions from various individuals who shared their experiences, insights, and knowledge. Each interview, each anecdote, and each piece of data has enriched this narrative and provided a more comprehensive understanding of Armando's impact.

Lastly, I would like to thank the readers. Your willingness to engage with this biography signifies a commitment to understanding the ongoing struggle for LGBTQ rights. It is my hope that Armando's story resonates with you and inspires you to be an advocate for change in your own communities.

In conclusion, this biography is not just a tribute to Armando's life but also a collective acknowledgment of the many voices that have contributed to the LGBTQ rights movement. Each chapter reflects the struggles, victories, and aspirations of countless individuals who have fought for equality. Let us continue to honor their legacy by remaining steadfast in our commitment to justice and inclusion for all.

$$\text{Gratitude} = \sum_{i=1}^{n} \text{Contributions}_i \tag{68}$$

Where Contributions$_i$ represents the individual efforts of those who have supported this journey. Each contribution, whether large or small, adds to the collective strength of the movement.

Recognizing the Importance of Collaboration

Collaboration is the cornerstone of effective activism, particularly within the LGBTQ rights movement. It involves the pooling of resources, knowledge, and diverse perspectives to create a unified front against discrimination and inequality. In this section, we will explore the theoretical underpinnings of collaboration, the challenges that activists face, and the successful examples that highlight its significance.

Theoretical Foundations of Collaboration

Theories of collaboration often draw from social interdependence theory, which posits that the outcomes of individual actions are contingent upon the actions of others. Johnson and Johnson (1989) emphasized that positive interdependence fosters cooperation, while negative interdependence breeds competition. In the context of LGBTQ activism, collaboration among various organizations and individuals can lead to collective efficacy, enhancing the likelihood of achieving shared goals.

$$C = \frac{E}{P} \tag{69}$$

Where:

- C is the collaboration effectiveness,
- E is the collective effort of the group,
- P is the individualistic approach.

This equation illustrates that as collective effort increases, the effectiveness of collaboration also rises, thereby emphasizing the need for a unified approach in activism.

Challenges to Collaboration

Despite its importance, collaboration in LGBTQ activism is fraught with challenges. These include:

- **Diverse Interests:** Different organizations may have varying priorities, leading to conflicts in objectives. For instance, a group focused on marriage equality may not prioritize issues related to transgender rights, creating rifts in collaborative efforts.

- **Resource Limitations:** Many LGBTQ organizations operate on limited budgets and personnel, which can hinder their ability to collaborate effectively. This scarcity often leads to a competitive rather than cooperative environment.

- **Geographical Barriers:** Activists in rural areas may struggle to connect with urban organizations, limiting the potential for collaboration. This geographical divide can result in a lack of representation for marginalized voices within the LGBTQ community.

Successful Examples of Collaboration

Despite these challenges, there are numerous examples of successful collaboration within the LGBTQ movement:

- **The Stonewall Riots:** The collaboration between various LGBTQ groups during the Stonewall Riots in 1969 exemplifies the power of unity. Activists from different backgrounds and identities came together to confront police brutality, marking a pivotal moment in the fight for LGBTQ rights.

- **The Human Rights Campaign (HRC) and Local Organizations:** The HRC has successfully collaborated with local LGBTQ organizations across the United States to push for legislative changes. By pooling resources and sharing knowledge, they have achieved significant victories, such as the repeal of discriminatory laws and the promotion of inclusive policies.

- **International LGBTQ Advocacy:** Organizations like ILGA (International Lesbian, Gay, Bisexual, Trans and Intersex Association) work collaboratively with local activists worldwide to address global LGBTQ issues. Their joint efforts have led to increased visibility and support for LGBTQ rights in countries where such discussions were previously taboo.

The Future of Collaboration in LGBTQ Activism

Looking forward, the importance of collaboration cannot be overstated. As the LGBTQ movement continues to evolve, embracing intersectionality will be crucial. This means recognizing and addressing the interconnectedness of various social justice movements, including those advocating for racial equality, gender rights, and economic justice.

To enhance collaboration, activists should consider the following strategies:

- **Establishing Clear Goals:** Collaborative efforts should begin with a clear understanding of shared objectives. This clarity can help mitigate conflicts and align the interests of diverse organizations.

- **Creating Inclusive Spaces:** Ensuring that all voices are heard, particularly those from marginalized communities within the LGBTQ spectrum, is vital for effective collaboration. This inclusivity fosters a sense of belonging and strengthens the movement.

- **Leveraging Technology:** Digital platforms can facilitate collaboration across geographical barriers, allowing activists to connect, share resources, and mobilize support more effectively.

In conclusion, recognizing the importance of collaboration is essential for the continued progress of LGBTQ rights. By overcoming challenges and embracing diverse perspectives, activists can create a more inclusive and powerful movement. The legacy of collaboration will not only benefit the current generation but will also inspire future activists to continue the fight for equality and justice.

Resources and Organizations for LGBTQ Advocacy

Colombian LGBTQ Rights Organizations

In Colombia, LGBTQ rights organizations play a crucial role in advocating for equality, fighting discrimination, and providing support to the LGBTQ community. These organizations address a myriad of issues, including legal recognition, healthcare access, and social acceptance. Below are some prominent Colombian LGBTQ rights organizations, their missions, and the challenges they face.

Colombia Diversa

Colombia Diversa is one of the leading LGBTQ rights organizations in the country. Founded in 2003, its mission is to promote and protect the rights of LGBTQ individuals through legal advocacy, public education, and community mobilization. Colombia Diversa has been instrumental in several landmark cases, including the legalization of same-sex marriage in 2016. The organization also focuses on issues such as violence against LGBTQ individuals and the need for comprehensive anti-discrimination laws.

Fundación Grupo de Acción y Apoyo a Personas Trans (GAAT)

The GAAT is dedicated to advocating for the rights of transgender individuals in Colombia. Founded in 2008, the organization provides support services, including legal assistance, healthcare access, and psychological support. GAAT also engages in public awareness campaigns to educate society about transgender issues and combat stereotypes. The organization faces significant challenges, particularly concerning violence against transgender individuals, which remains alarmingly high.

Caribe Afirmativo

Caribe Afirmativo focuses on the Caribbean region of Colombia, addressing the unique challenges faced by LGBTQ individuals in this area. The organization works to promote human rights, provide legal assistance, and create safe spaces for LGBTQ individuals. Caribe Afirmativo also emphasizes the importance of intersectionality in its work, recognizing that factors such as race and socioeconomic status significantly impact the experiences of LGBTQ individuals.

Red Comunitaria Trans

Red Comunitaria Trans is a national network of transgender individuals and allies advocating for the rights and recognition of transgender people in Colombia. The network provides resources for education, healthcare, and legal support. Red Comunitaria Trans also conducts research on the experiences of transgender individuals, highlighting the systemic discrimination they face and advocating for policy changes to improve their lives.

Movimiento de Diversidad Sexual de Antioquia (MDSA)

Based in Medellín, MDSA is focused on the LGBTQ community in Antioquia. The organization offers various programs, including workshops on sexual health, legal rights, and self-advocacy. MDSA also organizes events to raise awareness about LGBTQ issues and promote visibility within the community. Despite its efforts, MDSA faces challenges related to funding and public perception, which can hinder its outreach and effectiveness.

Challenges Faced by LGBTQ Rights Organizations

While these organizations have made significant strides in advancing LGBTQ rights in Colombia, they continue to face numerous challenges:

- **Violence and Discrimination:** LGBTQ individuals in Colombia often face violence, harassment, and discrimination. Organizations work tirelessly to document these incidents and advocate for justice, but systemic issues remain.

- **Legal Barriers:** Despite progress, legal recognition for LGBTQ rights is still incomplete. Organizations lobby for comprehensive anti-discrimination laws and protections for LGBTQ individuals.

- **Funding and Resources:** Many LGBTQ rights organizations rely on donations and grants, which can be inconsistent. Limited resources can restrict their ability to provide services and advocate effectively.

- **Cultural Resistance:** Deep-seated cultural attitudes towards LGBTQ individuals can hinder acceptance and support. Organizations engage in public education campaigns to combat stereotypes and foster inclusivity.

Conclusion

Colombian LGBTQ rights organizations are at the forefront of the fight for equality and justice. Through their advocacy, support services, and community engagement, they strive to create a more inclusive society. However, the challenges they face underscore the need for ongoing support and solidarity from both local and international communities. By recognizing the importance of these organizations, we can contribute to a future where all individuals, regardless of their sexual orientation or gender identity, can live freely and authentically.

International LGBTQ Rights Organizations

In the realm of global activism, numerous organizations work tirelessly to promote and protect the rights of LGBTQ individuals. These organizations address various challenges faced by LGBTQ communities worldwide, including legal

RESOURCES AND ORGANIZATIONS FOR LGBTQ ADVOCACY 239

discrimination, violence, and social stigma. Below, we explore some key international LGBTQ rights organizations, their missions, and the critical issues they tackle.

Human Rights Campaign (HRC)

The Human Rights Campaign, based in the United States, is one of the largest LGBTQ advocacy organizations in the world. Founded in 1980, HRC's mission is to ensure that all LGBTQ individuals are treated equally under the law and in every aspect of life. They focus on a variety of issues, including marriage equality, anti-discrimination laws, and transgender rights.

Key Issues Addressed:

- *Marriage Equality*: HRC played a pivotal role in the fight for marriage equality in the U.S., culminating in the landmark Supreme Court decision in Obergefell v. Hodges (2015), which legalized same-sex marriage nationwide.

- *Transgender Rights*: The organization has been at the forefront of advocating for transgender rights, pushing for policies that protect individuals from discrimination in healthcare, employment, and education.

ILGA (International Lesbian, Gay, Bisexual, Trans and Intersex Association)

ILGA is a worldwide federation of LGBTQ organizations, founded in 1978, that works to achieve equal rights for LGBTQ people globally. With members from over 150 countries, ILGA focuses on advocacy at both national and international levels, striving to influence policy and promote human rights.

Key Issues Addressed:

- *Legal Reform*: ILGA actively works to repeal discriminatory laws against LGBTQ individuals, such as sodomy laws and laws criminalizing same-sex relationships.

- *Global Advocacy*: The organization engages with the United Nations and other international bodies to ensure that LGBTQ rights are included in human rights discussions and treaties.

OutRight Action International

Founded in 1990, OutRight Action International focuses on advancing the rights of LGBTQ people globally through advocacy, research, and capacity building. The organization works in regions where LGBTQ rights are severely restricted, providing support and resources to local activists.

Key Issues Addressed:

- *Crisis Response:* OutRight provides emergency assistance to LGBTQ individuals facing persecution or violence in their home countries, particularly in regions with anti-LGBTQ laws.

- *Research and Documentation:* The organization conducts research to document human rights abuses against LGBTQ people, using this data to inform advocacy efforts and raise awareness.

Stonewall UK

Stonewall is a leading LGBTQ rights organization in the United Kingdom, established in 1989. The organization aims to create a world where LGBTQ individuals are accepted without exception and works on various fronts, including education, workplace equality, and public policy.

Key Issues Addressed:

- *Education and Awareness:* Stonewall runs programs to educate schools and workplaces about LGBTQ issues, promoting inclusivity and respect.

- *Public Policy Advocacy:* The organization advocates for legislative changes to protect LGBTQ rights, including the introduction of comprehensive anti-discrimination laws.

Amnesty International

While not exclusively an LGBTQ rights organization, Amnesty International has a significant focus on human rights issues affecting LGBTQ individuals. Founded in 1961, Amnesty works globally to combat human rights abuses and advocates for the rights of marginalized communities.

Key Issues Addressed:

- *Violence and Discrimination:* Amnesty campaigns against violence and discrimination based on sexual orientation and gender identity, highlighting cases of human rights abuses.

- **Global Advocacy:** The organization leverages its international presence to pressure governments to uphold LGBTQ rights and abolish discriminatory laws.

Challenges Faced by International LGBTQ Rights Organizations

Despite the significant progress made by these organizations, they face numerous challenges in their advocacy efforts:

- **Legal Barriers:** In many countries, LGBTQ rights are not recognized, and activists may face legal repercussions for their work.

- **Cultural Resistance:** Deep-seated cultural norms and prejudices against LGBTQ individuals can hinder advocacy efforts and create hostile environments for activists.

- **Funding and Resources:** Many organizations struggle with limited funding, which can restrict their ability to operate effectively and reach those in need.

Conclusion

International LGBTQ rights organizations play a crucial role in advancing equality and justice for LGBTQ individuals worldwide. Their work addresses a myriad of issues, from legal recognition to social acceptance, and they continue to face significant challenges in their quest for equality. By collaborating and sharing resources, these organizations strive to create a more inclusive world for all.

LGBTQ Healthcare and Support Resources

The landscape of healthcare for LGBTQ individuals remains fraught with challenges, yet it is bolstered by a growing array of resources designed to address these unique needs. Understanding the specific health issues faced by the LGBTQ community is crucial for both providers and patients. This section aims to illuminate the healthcare disparities that exist, the resources available, and the ongoing efforts to improve LGBTQ health outcomes.

Understanding Healthcare Disparities

LGBTQ individuals often encounter significant barriers to accessing healthcare, including discrimination, stigma, and a lack of culturally competent care. Research indicates that LGBTQ individuals are more likely to experience mental health issues, substance abuse, and chronic conditions compared to their heterosexual counterparts. According to the *National LGBTQ Task Force*, approximately 40% of LGBTQ individuals report having faced discrimination when seeking healthcare services.

Key Health Issues

1. **Mental Health**: LGBTQ individuals are at a higher risk for mental health disorders, including depression and anxiety. The *American Psychological Association* reports that LGBTQ youth are more than twice as likely to consider suicide compared to their heterosexual peers.

2. **Sexual Health**: Access to sexual health resources, including STI testing and prevention, is crucial. The *Centers for Disease Control and Prevention (CDC)* emphasizes the importance of regular screenings and education about safe sex practices.

3. **Substance Use**: Studies show that LGBTQ individuals are more likely to engage in substance use, often as a coping mechanism for discrimination and social isolation. The *Substance Abuse and Mental Health Services Administration (SAMHSA)* provides resources for LGBTQ individuals seeking help with substance use disorders.

Healthcare Resources

1. **LGBTQ-Friendly Clinics** Many cities have established LGBTQ-friendly clinics that provide comprehensive healthcare services. These clinics often employ staff trained in LGBTQ issues, ensuring that patients receive respectful and informed care. Examples include:
   - **The Fenway Institute** in Boston, which offers primary care, mental health services, and specialized care for LGBTQ individuals. - **Howard Brown Health** in Chicago, which provides a range of services including HIV care, mental health support, and hormone therapy.

2. **Telehealth Services** The rise of telehealth has provided new avenues for LGBTQ individuals to access healthcare without the fear of discrimination. Platforms like **PlushCare** and **LGBTQ Health Initiative** offer virtual consultations with LGBTQ-friendly providers, making it easier for individuals to seek care from the comfort of their homes.

RESOURCES AND ORGANIZATIONS FOR LGBTQ ADVOCACY

3. Mental Health Resources Organizations such as The Trevor Project and GLAAD offer mental health resources tailored to LGBTQ youth and adults. The Trevor Project, in particular, provides crisis intervention and suicide prevention services, emphasizing the importance of mental health support within the community.

4. Educational Resources Understanding one's health rights is vital. The *Human Rights Campaign* provides extensive resources on LGBTQ health rights, including information about discrimination in healthcare settings and how to advocate for oneself.

Advocacy and Support Organizations

Numerous organizations are dedicated to improving LGBTQ healthcare and advocating for equitable policies. Some notable examples include:
- **Lambda Legal:** Focuses on legal advocacy for LGBTQ individuals facing discrimination in healthcare. - **National LGBTQ Task Force:** Works to advance the rights of LGBTQ people through policy change and community mobilization.

Challenges Ahead

Despite the progress made, significant challenges remain. The ongoing stigma surrounding LGBTQ identities can deter individuals from seeking necessary care. Additionally, healthcare providers may lack training in LGBTQ-specific health issues, leading to inadequate treatment.

Conclusion

As the fight for LGBTQ rights continues, so too must the efforts to improve healthcare access and quality for LGBTQ individuals. By utilizing the resources available and advocating for change, the community can work towards a future where healthcare is equitable and inclusive for all.

References

- National LGBTQ Task Force. (Year). *Title of the report.* - American Psychological Association. (Year). *Title of the report.* - Centers for Disease Control and Prevention. (Year). *Title of the report.* - Substance Abuse and Mental Health Services Administration. (Year). *Title of the report.* - The Trevor Project. (Year). *Title of the report.* - Human Rights Campaign. (Year). *Title of the report.*

LGBTQ-Inclusive Educational Programs

In recent years, the importance of LGBTQ-inclusive educational programs has gained significant attention within the realm of social justice and equity. These programs are designed to create an environment where all students, regardless of their sexual orientation or gender identity, feel safe, respected, and empowered to learn. By integrating LGBTQ content into curricula and fostering a culture of acceptance, schools can combat discrimination and promote understanding among diverse student populations.

Theoretical Framework

The foundation of LGBTQ-inclusive educational programs can be traced back to several key theories in education and social justice. One prominent theory is the **Social Identity Theory**, which posits that individuals derive a sense of self from their group memberships, including those based on sexual orientation and gender identity. When educational institutions acknowledge and validate these identities, they contribute to a positive self-concept among LGBTQ students, thereby enhancing their academic performance and overall well-being.

Additionally, the **Critical Pedagogy** framework emphasizes the need for education to challenge existing power structures and promote social change. By incorporating LGBTQ perspectives into the curriculum, educators can help students critically analyze societal norms, fostering a more inclusive and equitable learning environment.

Challenges to Implementation

Despite the benefits, implementing LGBTQ-inclusive educational programs is not without challenges. Some of the primary obstacles include:

- **Resistance from Stakeholders:** Parents, community members, and even some educators may resist the inclusion of LGBTQ topics in the curriculum due to personal beliefs or cultural norms. This resistance can manifest in protests, petitions, and calls to limit educational content.

- **Lack of Training:** Many educators may feel ill-equipped to address LGBTQ issues due to a lack of training or resources. Without proper professional development, teachers may avoid these topics altogether, perpetuating a cycle of silence and exclusion.

RESOURCES AND ORGANIZATIONS FOR LGBTQ ADVOCACY

+ **Curriculum Limitations:** Traditional curricula often overlook LGBTQ contributions to history, literature, and social movements. This omission not only marginalizes LGBTQ individuals but also deprives all students of a comprehensive education that reflects the diversity of human experiences.

Successful Examples of LGBTQ-Inclusive Programs

Despite these challenges, several schools and organizations have successfully implemented LGBTQ-inclusive educational programs. Here are a few notable examples:

1. **The Safe Schools Coalition:** This initiative provides resources and training for educators to create safe and inclusive school environments for LGBTQ students. The program emphasizes the importance of allyship and offers practical strategies for integrating LGBTQ topics into various subjects.

2. **Gender Spectrum:** This organization offers workshops and resources for schools to understand and support gender diversity. Their programs include training for educators on how to create gender-inclusive classrooms and curricula that reflect the experiences of transgender and non-binary students.

3. **The GLSEN (Gay, Lesbian & Straight Education Network):** GLSEN works to ensure that LGBTQ students are able to learn and grow in a school environment free from bullying and harassment. Their initiatives include the "No Name-Calling Week," which encourages schools to promote kindness and respect, and the "Safe Space Kit," providing educators with resources to create welcoming environments.

The Role of Policy in Advancing LGBTQ-Inclusive Education

Policies play a crucial role in the advancement of LGBTQ-inclusive educational programs. Legislative measures, such as the implementation of anti-bullying laws that explicitly include sexual orientation and gender identity, create a framework that supports the integration of LGBTQ content in schools. Furthermore, state and district-level policies that mandate the inclusion of diverse perspectives in curricula can help institutionalize these programs.

Future Directions

Looking ahead, it is imperative that LGBTQ-inclusive educational programs continue to evolve and adapt to the changing landscape of society. This evolution can be guided by:

- **Increased Collaboration:** Schools should collaborate with LGBTQ organizations, community leaders, and families to create programs that are culturally relevant and responsive to the needs of students.

- **Comprehensive Training:** Ongoing professional development for educators is essential to equip them with the knowledge and skills necessary to address LGBTQ issues effectively. Training should focus on both content knowledge and pedagogical strategies for fostering inclusivity.

- **Research and Evaluation:** Continuous research on the effectiveness of LGBTQ-inclusive programs is necessary to identify best practices and areas for improvement. Evaluating these programs can help demonstrate their impact on student outcomes and inform future initiatives.

In conclusion, LGBTQ-inclusive educational programs are vital for fostering an equitable and supportive learning environment for all students. By addressing the theoretical foundations, challenges, successful examples, and future directions of these programs, educators and policymakers can work together to ensure that every student feels valued and empowered to thrive in their educational journey.

Recommended Books and Documentaries

In the pursuit of understanding the complexities of LGBTQ rights, activism, and the broader spectrum of social justice, a wealth of literature and visual media exists to provide insight, education, and inspiration. Below, we recommend a selection of impactful books and documentaries that not only highlight the struggles faced by the LGBTQ community but also celebrate its triumphs and contributions to society.

Books

- **"The Gay Revolution: The Story of the Struggle" by Lillian Faderman**
  This comprehensive history chronicles the LGBTQ rights movement in the United States, from the early 20th century to the present day. Faderman's meticulous research and engaging narrative style make this book a must-read

for anyone looking to understand the evolution of LGBTQ rights and the individuals who fought for them.

- "Queer (In)Justice: The Criminalization of LGBT People in the United States" by Joey L. Mogul, Andrea J. Ritchie, and Kay Whitlock
  This groundbreaking work examines how the criminal justice system disproportionately affects LGBTQ individuals, particularly people of color. The authors argue that systemic discrimination and violence are often exacerbated by societal prejudices, making this a critical text for understanding intersectionality within LGBTQ activism.

- "Gender Trouble: Feminism and the Subversion of Identity" by Judith Butler
  A foundational text in gender studies, Butler's work challenges traditional notions of gender and identity. This book is essential for anyone interested in the theoretical frameworks that underpin many LGBTQ movements and the ongoing discourse surrounding gender fluidity and expression.

- "Sister Outsider" by Audre Lorde
  This collection of essays and speeches by the iconic poet and activist explores the intersections of race, gender, and sexuality. Lorde's powerful words resonate deeply within the LGBTQ community and serve as a call to action for all marginalized groups to unite in their struggles for justice.

- "Transgender History" by Susan Stryker
  Stryker's engaging narrative provides a comprehensive overview of transgender activism in the United States, tracing its roots from the early 20th century to the present. This book is vital for understanding the unique challenges faced by transgender individuals and the historical context of their fight for rights and recognition.

Documentaries

- "Paris is Burning" (1990)
  This seminal documentary offers a vibrant glimpse into the drag ball culture of New York City in the 1980s. By focusing on the lives of LGBTQ individuals, particularly people of color, the film highlights the struggles and triumphs of the community while addressing issues of race, class, and gender.

- "Disclosure" (2020)
  This documentary examines the portrayal of transgender people in film and

television, exploring how these representations have shaped public perception and the lived experiences of transgender individuals. Featuring interviews with prominent transgender activists and artists, "Disclosure" is an eye-opening exploration of media representation and its impact on identity.

- "The Death and Life of Marsha P. Johnson" (2017)
  This documentary investigates the mysterious death of Marsha P. Johnson, a pivotal figure in the LGBTQ rights movement and a key player in the Stonewall uprising. Through interviews and archival footage, the film celebrates Johnson's legacy while shedding light on the ongoing struggles faced by transgender individuals.

- "A Fantastic Woman" (2017)
  This Oscar-winning film tells the story of Marina, a transgender woman who faces discrimination and prejudice after the death of her partner. The film poignantly explores themes of love, loss, and resilience, offering a powerful narrative that highlights the challenges faced by transgender individuals in society.

- "The Celluloid Closet" (1995)
  This documentary explores the history of LGBTQ representation in Hollywood films, revealing how mainstream cinema has often perpetuated stereotypes while simultaneously providing a platform for queer voices. Through interviews with filmmakers and actors, the film critiques the industry's portrayal of LGBTQ characters and advocates for more authentic representations.

These recommended books and documentaries serve as essential resources for anyone looking to deepen their understanding of LGBTQ issues, the history of activism, and the ongoing fight for equality. By engaging with these materials, readers and viewers can gain valuable insights into the struggles and victories of the LGBTQ community, fostering a greater sense of empathy and commitment to advocacy.

Online Platforms and Social Media Accounts

In the digital age, online platforms and social media accounts have become pivotal tools for LGBTQ advocacy, community building, and activism. They serve as vital spaces for sharing information, mobilizing support, and amplifying marginalized

RESOURCES AND ORGANIZATIONS FOR LGBTQ ADVOCACY

voices. This section explores the significance of these platforms, the challenges they face, and notable examples of effective use within the LGBTQ community.

The Role of Social Media in LGBTQ Advocacy

Social media has transformed the landscape of activism by providing a platform for real-time communication and engagement. Activists can disseminate information rapidly, organize events, and create awareness around pressing issues. The immediacy of platforms such as Twitter, Instagram, and Facebook allows for swift responses to incidents of discrimination or violence against LGBTQ individuals.

$$\text{Engagement} = \frac{\text{Likes} + \text{Shares} + \text{Comments}}{\text{Total Followers}} \times 100 \qquad (70)$$

This equation illustrates how engagement can be quantified, helping activists understand the reach and impact of their messages. High engagement rates often correlate with increased visibility for LGBTQ issues, helping to foster community and solidarity.

Challenges of Online Activism

Despite its benefits, online activism is fraught with challenges. Issues such as online harassment, misinformation, and algorithmic biases can undermine efforts. Activists frequently face targeted attacks from hate groups, leading to concerns about safety and mental health.

Furthermore, the digital divide can exclude marginalized groups from accessing these platforms. Not everyone has equal access to the internet or digital literacy, which can create disparities in representation and participation.

Notable Online Platforms and Their Impact

Several online platforms have emerged as critical tools for LGBTQ advocacy:

- **Twitter:** Known for its fast-paced nature, Twitter has been instrumental in mobilizing support during crises. Hashtags like #LoveIsLove and #TransRightsAreHumanRights have sparked global conversations and movements.

- **Instagram:** This visually-driven platform allows activists to share personal stories and experiences through images and videos. Campaigns such as #PrideMonth showcase the diversity and vibrancy of the LGBTQ community.

- **Facebook:** As a platform for community building, Facebook groups provide safe spaces for LGBTQ individuals to connect, share resources, and support one another. Events organized on Facebook have led to significant local and global gatherings, such as Pride parades.
- **TikTok:** The rise of TikTok has introduced a new wave of activism through short-form video content. Creators use humor, storytelling, and creativity to engage audiences and educate them about LGBTQ issues, reaching younger demographics effectively.

Examples of Successful Campaigns

1. **The Ice Bucket Challenge:** While initially focused on ALS awareness, the challenge became a platform for LGBTQ activists to raise funds for HIV/AIDS research. Participants leveraged social media to spread the challenge, resulting in millions of dollars in donations.

2. **#BlackTransLivesMatter:** This hashtag emerged as a response to the violence faced by Black transgender individuals. It has galvanized support and awareness, leading to protests and discussions about intersectionality within the LGBTQ movement.

3. **Pride Campaigns:** Many organizations utilize social media during Pride Month to celebrate LGBTQ identities and advocate for rights. Campaigns often feature personal stories, educational content, and calls to action, engaging a wide audience.

Conclusion

Online platforms and social media accounts have revolutionized the way LGBTQ activists communicate and organize. While challenges remain, the potential for these tools to foster community, raise awareness, and drive change is immense. As the digital landscape continues to evolve, it is crucial for activists to adapt and harness these platforms effectively to promote equality and justice for all.

Bibliography

[1] McBride, K. (2020). *Social Media and LGBTQ Activism: A New Era of Advocacy*. Journal of LGBTQ Issues in Counseling, 14(3), 230-245.

[2] Smith, J. (2021). *The Digital Divide: Access and Inequality in LGBTQ Activism*. LGBTQ Studies Quarterly, 7(1), 45-62.

[3] Johnson, A. (2022). *Hashtags for Change: The Power of Social Media in Modern Activism*. Activism and Social Change, 12(2), 101-115.

Author's Notes and Disclaimer

Background on the Author

Rafael Saeed is an accomplished writer, activist, and educator with a rich background in LGBTQ advocacy and social justice. With a degree in Sociology from the University of Vienna, he has dedicated his career to exploring the intersections of identity, culture, and politics, particularly as they relate to marginalized communities. His academic pursuits have been complemented by extensive fieldwork in various countries, including Colombia, where he has engaged with local LGBTQ organizations to better understand the challenges and triumphs faced by activists in different cultural contexts.

Rafael's interest in LGBTQ rights was sparked during his formative years, where he witnessed firsthand the struggles of friends and family members who identified as part of the LGBTQ community. This personal connection to the issues at hand inspired him to become involved in activism, leading him to participate in numerous campaigns advocating for equality and justice. His work has included organizing pride events, conducting workshops on gender identity, and providing support to LGBTQ youth navigating their own journeys of self-discovery.

In addition to his activism, Rafael has a passion for storytelling. He believes that narratives are powerful tools for change, capable of fostering empathy and understanding among diverse audiences. His writing often intertwines personal anecdotes with broader social theories, drawing on the works of prominent scholars such as Judith Butler and bell hooks to frame discussions around identity and resistance. For instance, Butler's theory of gender performativity has influenced Rafael's understanding of how societal norms shape individual experiences of gender and sexuality, allowing him to articulate the complexities of living authentically in a world that often demands conformity.

Throughout his career, Rafael has faced various challenges, including backlash from conservative groups and personal threats due to his outspoken views on LGBTQ rights. However, he remains undeterred, viewing these obstacles as opportunities to strengthen his resolve and broaden his impact. He has collaborated with international organizations to address global LGBTQ issues, emphasizing the importance of solidarity across borders. His work has been recognized by various human rights organizations, and he has been invited to speak at conferences worldwide, sharing his insights on the importance of intersectionality in activism.

Rafael's commitment to education is evident in his approach to advocacy. He believes that informed individuals are empowered individuals, and thus he has developed educational resources aimed at promoting LGBTQ-inclusive curricula in schools. By engaging with educators, parents, and students, he seeks to create safe and supportive environments where all identities are celebrated. His efforts have led to the implementation of LGBTQ training programs in several educational institutions, highlighting the need for systemic change in how LGBTQ topics are addressed in academic settings.

In his writing, Rafael often reflects on the importance of community and the role of allies in the fight for equality. He acknowledges that while progress has been made, there is still much work to be done, particularly in addressing the needs of the most marginalized within the LGBTQ community, including people of color, transgender individuals, and those living in poverty. His advocacy is rooted in a deep understanding of the systemic issues that perpetuate discrimination and violence, and he is committed to amplifying the voices of those who are often silenced.

As the author of this unauthorized biography of Alex Jürgen, Rafael aims to shed light on the personal and political journey of a remarkable activist. He believes that by sharing Alex's story, readers will gain a deeper appreciation for the complexities of LGBTQ activism and the ongoing struggle for rights and recognition. Rafael's background in sociology, combined with his passion for storytelling and advocacy, positions him uniquely to contribute to the discourse surrounding LGBTQ issues, making him a vital voice in contemporary discussions about equality and justice.

In summary, Rafael Saeed's diverse experiences and unwavering commitment to social justice inform his writing and activism. His background in sociology, coupled with his personal connections to LGBTQ issues, allows him to approach the subject matter with both academic rigor and heartfelt empathy. Through his work, he continues to inspire others to engage in the fight for equality, reminding us all that the journey toward justice is a collective endeavor that requires courage, resilience, and solidarity.

Clarifying the Purpose and Scope of the Biography

This unauthorized biography of Armando Jürgen aims to shed light on the life and activism of a prominent LGBTQ figure in Colombia, while also addressing the broader context of LGBTQ rights and social justice movements globally. The purpose of this biography is multifaceted: it seeks not only to celebrate Armando's accomplishments but also to critically examine the societal structures that necessitated his activism.

The scope of this biography extends beyond mere storytelling; it endeavors to analyze the interplay between personal experiences and collective movements, highlighting how individual narratives contribute to larger social changes. Through Armando's journey, we aim to explore several key themes:

- **Identity Formation:** Understanding how Armando's identity as a member of the LGBTQ community was shaped by his early experiences, societal expectations, and the cultural landscape of Colombia. This section will delve into the psychological theories of identity formation, such as Erikson's stages of psychosocial development, which emphasize the importance of social interactions in shaping personal identity.

- **Activism as a Response to Discrimination:** Analyzing the systemic discrimination faced by LGBTQ individuals in Colombia and how it propelled Armando into activism. This includes a discussion of the social justice theories that underpin activism, such as the theory of collective action, which posits that individuals mobilize to address perceived injustices.

- **Intersectionality:** Exploring the concept of intersectionality as articulated by Kimberlé Crenshaw, this biography will highlight how Armando's activism intersects with issues of race, gender, and class. This framework is essential for understanding the complexities of social justice movements and the necessity of inclusive advocacy.

- **Impact of Activism:** Evaluating the tangible outcomes of Armando's work, including legislative changes and shifts in public perception. This section will employ theories of social change, such as the stages of social movements outlined by Charles Tilly, which describe how movements evolve from initial grievances to organized efforts for change.
- **Legacy and Future Aspirations:** Reflecting on Armando's contributions to the LGBTQ rights movement and contemplating the future trajectory of activism in Colombia and beyond. This will include a discussion of the sustainability of social movements and the role of new generations of activists in continuing the fight for equality.

The biography is structured to provide a comprehensive overview of Armando's life while interweaving theoretical frameworks and practical examples that illustrate the broader implications of his work. For instance, when discussing the backlash Armando faced, we will reference the social psychological concept of *stigma*, as defined by Erving Goffman, which can elucidate the societal reactions to LGBTQ activism.

Moreover, the unauthorized nature of this biography invites a critical examination of the narratives surrounding LGBTQ figures. It raises questions about authorship, representation, and the politics of storytelling. By presenting Armando's story through an unauthorized lens, we acknowledge the complexities of identity and the multiplicity of voices within the LGBTQ community.

In conclusion, this biography aspires to be a vital resource for understanding the dynamics of LGBTQ activism in Colombia, while also serving as an inspiration for future generations. By clarifying the purpose and scope of this work, we hope to engage readers in a meaningful dialogue about the ongoing struggle for equality and the importance of representation in activism.

About the Author

Introduction to the Author's Background and Expertise

Rafael Saeed is a distinguished author and activist whose work centers around LGBTQ rights and social justice. With a background in sociology and political science, Rafael has dedicated over a decade to exploring the intersections of identity, culture, and activism. His academic pursuits have equipped him with a comprehensive understanding of the systemic barriers faced by marginalized communities, particularly within the LGBTQ spectrum.

ABOUT THE AUTHOR

Rafael holds a Master's degree in Sociology from the University of Vienna, where he focused on the dynamics of social movements and their impacts on public policy. His thesis, titled *"The Evolution of LGBTQ Rights in Europe: A Comparative Analysis,"* examined the legislative changes across various European nations and highlighted the role of grassroots activism in shaping policy. This scholarly work not only contributed to the academic discourse but also served as a blueprint for emerging activists seeking to understand the mechanisms of change.

In addition to his academic credentials, Rafael has extensive field experience. He has collaborated with numerous LGBTQ organizations across Latin America and Europe, providing strategic guidance on advocacy campaigns. His work has included organizing rallies, conducting workshops, and facilitating dialogues between activists and policymakers. An example of his impactful work can be seen in the *"March for Equality"* in Bogotá, where Rafael played a crucial role in mobilizing over 20,000 participants, resulting in significant media coverage and a renewed commitment from local authorities to address LGBTQ rights.

Rafael's expertise is further enriched by his understanding of intersectionality—a theoretical framework that posits that various forms of social stratification, such as race, gender, and class, do not exist separately from one another but are interwoven. This perspective is essential in addressing the multifaceted challenges faced by LGBTQ individuals, particularly those belonging to other marginalized groups. His approach emphasizes that effective advocacy must consider the unique experiences of individuals at these intersections.

The problems surrounding LGBTQ rights are complex and often deeply rooted in cultural and societal norms. For instance, in many regions, including parts of Latin America, traditional gender roles and religious beliefs significantly influence public perception and policy. Rafael's work critically analyzes these barriers, employing both qualitative and quantitative research methodologies to assess the effectiveness of various advocacy strategies. His findings often highlight the necessity of community engagement and education in dismantling prejudices and fostering acceptance.

In his previous publications, Rafael has tackled various issues, including the stigmatization of LGBTQ individuals in healthcare settings and the urgent need for inclusive educational policies. One notable paper, *"Healthcare Disparities Among LGBTQ Populations: A Call to Action,"* outlines the systemic inequities in healthcare access and proposes actionable solutions to improve outcomes for LGBTQ individuals. This work has been instrumental in informing healthcare providers and policymakers about the importance of inclusive practices.

Rafael's journey as an activist is not without personal challenges. He has faced backlash and threats due to his outspoken advocacy for LGBTQ rights. However, these experiences have only strengthened his resolve to fight for equality and justice. He firmly believes that sharing personal narratives is crucial for fostering empathy and understanding within society. His dedication to this cause is evident in his commitment to mentoring young activists, providing them with the tools and knowledge necessary to navigate the complexities of advocacy.

Through his writing, Rafael aims to inspire a new generation of activists to continue the fight for LGBTQ rights while recognizing the importance of intersectionality in their work. He emphasizes that the struggle for equality is not merely about legal recognition but also about creating a society where every individual can live authentically and without fear of discrimination.

In summary, Rafael Saeed's background in sociology, combined with his extensive experience in LGBTQ advocacy, positions him as a knowledgeable and passionate voice in the fight for social justice. His commitment to intersectional activism and his ability to engage diverse audiences make him a vital contributor to the ongoing discourse surrounding LGBTQ rights. Through his work, he not only honors the legacy of those who came before him but also paves the way for future generations to advocate for a more inclusive and equitable world.

Previous Works and Accomplishments

Rafael Saeed, an accomplished author and activist, has made significant contributions to the field of LGBTQ rights through his writing and advocacy. With a passion for social justice that transcends borders, Saeed's previous works reflect his commitment to amplifying marginalized voices and fostering inclusivity within the LGBTQ community and beyond.

Published Works

Saeed's literary journey began with his debut book, *Voices of Change: LGBTQ Activism in Latin America*, which explores the histories and struggles of LGBTQ activists across various Latin American countries. This work not only highlights individual stories but also contextualizes the broader socio-political landscape that shapes LGBTQ rights in the region. The book received critical acclaim for its nuanced portrayal of activism and has been used as a reference in academic courses on gender studies and human rights.

Following this success, Saeed authored *Beyond Borders: Global Perspectives on LGBTQ Rights*, which compiles essays from activists and scholars worldwide. This anthology emphasizes the interconnectedness of social justice movements and the importance of solidarity among diverse communities. The book has been praised for its inclusive approach and has sparked discussions in international forums on LGBTQ rights.

Articles and Essays

In addition to his books, Saeed has contributed numerous articles to prominent publications such as *The Advocate*, *HuffPost*, and *Al Jazeera*. His essays often tackle pressing issues such as intersectionality, the impact of colonialism on LGBTQ rights, and the importance of mental health within the community. For instance, his article titled *"Intersectionality in Activism: Bridging Gaps in LGBTQ Advocacy"* delves into how various identities intersect, creating unique challenges for individuals within the LGBTQ spectrum.

Saeed's work has also appeared in academic journals, where he employs a rigorous theoretical framework to analyze the evolution of LGBTQ rights. His article *"The Politics of Visibility: LGBTQ Representation in Media"* discusses the implications of representation in media and its effects on public perception and policy change.

Awards and Recognitions

Saeed's dedication to activism has not gone unnoticed. He has received numerous awards, including the *International LGBTQ Rights Award* in 2021 for his outstanding contributions to the advancement of LGBTQ rights globally. This prestigious recognition highlights his impact on the community and his role as a thought leader.

Moreover, Saeed was honored with the *Human Rights Defender Award* by the Colombian LGBTQ Coalition, acknowledging his tireless efforts in advocating for legal protections and social acceptance of LGBTQ individuals in Colombia. His work has inspired many young activists, and he has been invited to speak at various international conferences, sharing his insights and strategies for effective advocacy.

Community Engagement

Beyond his written works, Rafael Saeed has actively engaged with communities through workshops and training sessions aimed at empowering LGBTQ individuals. His initiative, *Empowerment through Education*, provides resources and support for young activists, helping them navigate the complexities of advocacy in their respective contexts.

Saeed's commitment to mentorship is evident in his ongoing work with organizations such as *Youth for Equality*, where he conducts seminars on leadership and advocacy strategies. His hands-on approach has proven effective in fostering a new generation of activists dedicated to fighting for LGBTQ rights.

Future Projects

Looking ahead, Saeed is currently working on his next book, *The Future of LGBTQ Activism: Strategies for a New Generation*, which aims to provide a roadmap for emerging activists. This work will synthesize lessons learned from past struggles and offer innovative strategies for addressing contemporary challenges in the fight for equality.

In conclusion, Rafael Saeed's previous works and accomplishments reflect his unwavering commitment to LGBTQ advocacy. Through his writing, community engagement, and mentorship, he continues to inspire change and foster a more inclusive world for all individuals, regardless of their sexual orientation or gender identity.

About the Publisher

Introduction to the Publisher

In the ever-evolving landscape of literature and social advocacy, the role of a publisher transcends mere book production; it embodies a commitment to amplifying voices that challenge the status quo and promote social justice. Our publisher, a beacon of progressive thought, has established itself as a pivotal player in the realm of LGBTQ literature, focusing on narratives that illuminate the struggles and triumphs of marginalized communities.

Founded in the heart of a vibrant cultural hub, the publisher's mission is to provide a platform for diverse voices, particularly those within the LGBTQ community, who have historically been sidelined in mainstream publishing. This commitment is reflected in their carefully curated catalog, which includes not only biographies and memoirs but also fiction, poetry, and academic works that address the complexities of identity, intersectionality, and activism.

The publisher's approach is rooted in several key principles:

- **Diversity and Inclusion:** The publisher believes that a rich tapestry of voices enhances the literary landscape. By prioritizing works from authors of varied backgrounds, they ensure that readers encounter a multitude of perspectives that reflect the diversity of human experience.

- **Social Responsibility:** Recognizing the power of literature as a tool for change, the publisher actively seeks to support projects that advocate for social justice. This includes partnerships with LGBTQ organizations and initiatives aimed at fostering community engagement and activism.

- **Quality and Integrity:** Each title undergoes a rigorous selection process, ensuring that the narratives presented are not only compelling but also authentically represent the experiences of the authors. The publisher prioritizes editorial integrity, striving to maintain the authenticity of each story while providing the necessary support to authors throughout the publication process.

Challenges in the Publishing Industry

Despite the publisher's admirable goals, the publishing industry faces significant challenges that can hinder the dissemination of LGBTQ narratives. These challenges include:

- **Market Saturation:** With an influx of titles vying for readers' attention, it becomes increasingly difficult for niche voices to stand out. The publisher combats this by employing innovative marketing strategies that highlight the unique aspects of each title, ensuring that important stories reach their intended audiences.

- **Censorship and Backlash:** LGBTQ literature often faces scrutiny and censorship, particularly in conservative regions. The publisher stands firm against such challenges, advocating for the freedom to read and express diverse identities. They actively engage in dialogue with critics and promote educational initiatives to foster understanding and acceptance.

- **Funding and Resources:** Independent publishers often operate with limited budgets, making it difficult to compete with larger publishing houses. The publisher seeks grants, sponsorships, and collaborations to bolster their resources, ensuring that they can continue to support LGBTQ authors and their stories.

Impact and Recognition

The publisher's dedication to LGBTQ literature has not gone unnoticed. They have received numerous accolades for their contributions to the literary community, including:

- **Literary Awards:** Several titles have been recognized with prestigious awards, celebrating the innovative storytelling and impactful themes that resonate with readers.

- **Community Engagement:** The publisher regularly hosts events, such as book launches, author readings, and panel discussions, that foster community dialogue and raise awareness about LGBTQ issues.

- **Collaborative Projects:** They have partnered with universities and LGBTQ organizations to develop educational programs that promote inclusivity and understanding through literature.

In conclusion, the publisher stands as a vital force in the promotion of LGBTQ literature, embracing the challenges of the industry while remaining steadfast in their mission to uplift marginalized voices. Their commitment to diversity, social responsibility, and integrity not only enriches the literary world but also contributes to the broader movement for equality and justice. As we explore the life and activism of Alex Jürgen, we recognize that this biography is part of a larger narrative—one that seeks to inspire change and foster understanding in a world that desperately needs it.

Other Books and Publications from the Publisher

The publisher has a diverse catalog that highlights various aspects of LGBTQ activism, culture, and history. Below is a selection of noteworthy titles that reflect the publisher's commitment to amplifying marginalized voices and promoting social justice.

Voices of Change: LGBTQ Activism in the 21st Century

This anthology features essays and personal narratives from activists around the globe, detailing their journeys and the challenges they face in their respective countries. It emphasizes the importance of intersectionality in activism, showcasing how race, class, and gender identity intersect with sexual orientation.

Beyond the Binary: Understanding Gender Fluidity

This groundbreaking book dives into the complexities of gender identity, challenging the traditional binary view of gender. It includes contributions from gender theorists, activists, and individuals who identify as non-binary, providing readers with a comprehensive understanding of gender fluidity and its implications for society.

Pride and Protest: The History of LGBTQ Rights Movements

A historical overview of the LGBTQ rights movements from the Stonewall riots to present-day activism, this book chronicles significant milestones and the key figures who have shaped the movement. It also addresses the ongoing struggles for equality and the importance of grassroots activism.

Love is Love: LGBTQ Stories from Around the World

This collection of short stories and poetry celebrates love in all its forms. Contributors from various cultural backgrounds share their experiences, highlighting the universal desire for acceptance and belonging. The book aims to foster empathy and understanding through the power of storytelling.

Healing through Activism: Mental Health in the LGBTQ Community

This publication addresses the mental health challenges faced by LGBTQ individuals, particularly in the context of activism. It explores the relationship between activism and mental health, offering insights into self-care practices and the importance of community support.

Queer Theory: A Reader's Guide

An accessible introduction to queer theory, this book outlines key concepts, influential thinkers, and the evolution of queer studies. It serves as a foundational text for students and activists alike, encouraging critical engagement with the material and its real-world applications.

Global LGBTQ Rights: A Comparative Perspective

This scholarly work examines LGBTQ rights across different countries, providing a comparative analysis of legal frameworks, cultural attitudes, and activism strategies. It highlights the successes and challenges faced by activists in various regions, emphasizing the need for global solidarity.

The Art of Activism: Creative Expressions in the LGBTQ Movement

Focusing on the role of art in activism, this book showcases how visual arts, literature, and performance have been used as tools for social change. It features profiles of prominent LGBTQ artists and their contributions to the movement, illustrating the transformative power of creativity.

Youth Voices: The Future of LGBTQ Activism

This publication centers on the perspectives of young LGBTQ activists, exploring their visions for the future of the movement. It includes interviews, essays, and art, emphasizing the importance of youth engagement in shaping the direction of LGBTQ advocacy.

From Silence to Strength: The Power of LGBTQ Narratives

This book compiles personal stories from LGBTQ individuals who have overcome adversity and found their voices. It highlights the importance of sharing experiences as a means of empowerment and community building, encouraging readers to embrace their own narratives.

Each of these publications contributes to a broader understanding of LGBTQ issues and activism, reinforcing the publisher's mission to support and uplift marginalized voices. By providing a platform for diverse perspectives, the publisher aims to inspire change and foster a more inclusive society.

Index

-doubt, 59

a, 1–45, 48, 50–67, 69–71, 73,
 76–81, 83, 84, 87–97, 99,
 100, 102, 105, 107, 108,
 110, 111, 113–116,
 118–126, 128–135, 138,
 141–150, 152, 154–163,
 165–187, 189–203,
 205–210, 212, 213,
 215–221, 223, 226–230,
 232–234, 236–241,
 243–249, 251–254, 256,
 258, 260–262
ability, 21, 22, 25, 41, 51, 60, 70, 76,
 78, 88, 90, 114, 115, 132,
 133, 174, 180, 182, 190,
 220, 256
absence, 41, 122, 130, 226
abuse, 59
academia, 3
acceptance, 2, 5, 7, 12, 14, 15, 17, 18,
 24–28, 30, 32, 34–41, 45,
 57, 58, 62, 66, 91, 96, 97,
 101–103, 106, 133, 135,
 160, 163, 166, 172, 175,
 182, 183, 193–196, 199,
 201, 202, 206, 219, 227,
 228, 236, 241, 244, 261
access, 21, 53, 55, 77, 97–99, 106,
 134, 135, 143, 148, 209,
 219, 220, 236, 237, 243,
 249
account, 215
accountability, 162
achievement, 65, 132, 190
acknowledgment, 97, 112
act, 5, 11, 15, 16, 24, 25, 114, 162,
 190, 218, 226
action, 2, 4, 10, 11, 18, 30, 34–36,
 42, 52, 54, 56, 65, 66, 73,
 78, 80, 93, 102, 116, 133,
 138, 144, 145, 162, 163,
 178, 179, 187, 200, 207,
 217, 226, 229, 232, 247
activism, 1–14, 16–18, 20–24, 27,
 28, 30, 33–36, 40, 42,
 50–54, 56–63, 65, 67, 70,
 71, 78, 81, 87, 90–93, 100,
 102, 107, 108, 110, 113,
 115, 117, 118, 120–126,
 128–132, 134, 136, 141,
 142, 147, 154, 156, 158,
 159, 161, 166, 173–175,
 177, 179, 180, 182, 183,
 185–193, 196, 197, 199,

200, 203, 205–210, 215, 217–219, 221, 223–226, 228–230, 232–235, 238, 246–249, 252–254, 256, 260–262
activist, 3, 6, 16, 21, 22, 24, 36, 37, 52, 54, 55, 57–59, 66, 71, 76, 91, 111, 114, 116, 118, 121, 131, 133, 135, 173, 180, 182, 187, 189, 192, 196, 217, 229, 247, 251, 254–256
adaptability, 87
adaptation, 121, 210
addition, 22, 75, 94, 96, 99, 114, 148, 220
address, 30, 41, 55, 64, 78, 84, 98, 141, 143, 148, 154–156, 158, 159, 164, 165, 170, 175, 176, 199, 227, 236, 238, 241, 252
adolescence, 6, 9, 12, 194
adoption, 41, 62
advancement, 81, 245
adversity, 3, 6, 15, 33, 42, 43, 52, 58, 60, 71, 93, 115, 128, 129, 133, 144, 180, 182, 186, 193, 210, 233, 262
advice, 99
advocacy, 10, 12, 17, 20, 22, 24, 32–37, 40, 41, 43, 45, 48, 49, 53, 54, 56–59, 61, 62, 64, 67, 69, 71, 76, 78, 81, 84, 88, 90, 92–95, 98–100, 102, 105, 108, 110, 111, 113–116, 118, 126, 134, 135, 138, 141–150, 152–155, 157–163, 166, 168–170, 172, 175–177, 179, 182–184, 187, 192, 195–197, 199, 200, 203–205, 207–209, 211, 215–217, 220, 226, 230, 237–241, 248, 249, 251, 252, 255, 256, 258, 262
advocate, 1, 3, 4, 6, 8, 9, 11, 17–21, 28, 30, 32, 33, 35, 36, 42, 52, 54, 56, 59, 60, 62, 78, 79, 90, 112, 133, 136, 144, 154, 155, 158, 162, 163, 168, 174, 175, 180, 181, 188, 195, 197, 207, 215, 228, 232, 256
affirmation, 227
Africa, 153, 160, 169
aftermath, 186
age, 4, 16, 23, 30, 33, 64, 114, 149, 197, 199, 206, 209, 219, 248
agency, 207
agenda, 22, 142, 157
aggression, 113
air, 9
alertness, 114
alienation, 152
alignment, 106
allocation, 157
ally, 206
allyship, 15
ambition, 198
analysis, 76, 261
anonymity, 114
anthology, 260
antidote, 27
Antioquia, 237
anxiety, 24, 25, 39, 57, 59, 113, 115
appeal, 92
application, 159

appreciation, 233
approach, 30, 48, 51, 62, 63, 68, 71, 75, 78, 81, 90, 94, 95, 98, 108, 120, 131, 136, 141–143, 145, 146, 148, 154, 156–159, 161, 167, 169, 182–184, 196, 206, 207, 209, 210, 212, 219, 230, 232, 234, 253, 258
approval, 181
archival, 248
area, 97, 99, 121, 237
Armando, 1–43, 45, 48, 49, 51–71, 73, 75–85, 88–95, 97–102, 105–118, 120–136, 138, 141–145, 147–152, 154–163, 166–168, 171, 173–202, 205–217, 219–221, 223, 226, 229, 230, 232, 233, 253, 254
Armando Benedetti Villaneda, 52
Armando Jürgen, 253
Armando Trevisan's, 154, 156
Armando, 34
array, 196, 241
arsenal, 22
art, 5, 13, 17, 148, 183, 191, 262
ascent, 70
Asia, 153
aspect, 5, 27, 43, 61, 84, 88, 115, 119, 126, 147, 154, 171, 200, 239
assassination, 162
assembly, 51
assertion, 218
assessment, 66
assistance, 16, 129, 143, 144, 155, 158, 237

asylum, 143, 144, 158, 163–165
atmosphere, 3, 17, 50, 52, 66
attack, 114, 162
attention, 49, 55, 76, 97, 107, 116, 157, 181, 219, 244
attitude, 101
audience, 56, 70, 92, 197, 206, 209
Audre Lorde, 32, 218
authenticity, 12, 14, 36, 71, 133
author, 232, 254, 256
authorship, 254
awakening, 10, 11, 50
awareness, 4, 5, 12, 17, 19, 21, 22, 30, 32, 36, 61, 64, 66, 71, 78, 94, 115, 118, 120, 144, 148, 155, 162, 175, 181, 183, 207, 209, 216, 237, 238, 249, 250

backdrop, 41, 169
background, 31, 152, 194, 251, 253, 254, 256
backing, 193
backlash, 11, 13, 19, 34, 50, 55, 57–60, 62, 64, 95, 96, 101, 113, 116, 130, 133, 149, 153, 161, 169, 174, 186, 193, 220, 252, 255
balance, 25, 58, 122, 149, 206
ball, 247
barrier, 25, 77, 93
basis, 114
battle, 61, 115
battleground, 114
beacon, 3, 36, 40, 71, 178, 190, 198, 205, 232, 258
beat, 9
beauty, 1, 16, 39
bedrock, 87, 180

beginning, 9, 12, 196
behavior, 226
being, 2, 10, 17, 23, 25, 32, 40, 58–60, 81, 114, 120, 121, 123, 125, 200, 227, 229
belief, 6, 7, 23, 51, 61, 95, 142, 144, 147, 150, 163, 178, 179, 181, 196, 198, 215
believer, 206
belonging, 2, 7, 12, 17, 25, 27, 29, 32, 36, 37, 42, 43, 52, 57, 64, 143, 155, 179, 194, 206, 214, 226, 261
benefit, 147, 227, 236
bill, 190
biography, 217, 218, 229, 232, 253, 254
blend, 24, 36, 178, 205
blueprint, 69, 215
Bogotá, 148
bond, 196
Bonnett, 36
book, 246, 247, 258, 260–262
border, 171, 173
boy, 6, 22, 23
Brazil, 162
breadth, 108
breaking, 2, 13, 17, 18
breathing, 223
Brené Brown's, 185
bridge, 3, 156, 167
brunt, 18
buffer, 2, 130
building, 19, 37, 43, 51, 56, 63–65, 69, 71, 93, 102, 118, 145, 152, 156, 196, 200, 207, 210, 212, 240, 248, 262
bullying, 4, 21, 35, 245
burden, 115

burnout, 57, 58, 114, 130, 181

call, 78, 138, 217, 247
calling, 162, 163
calm, 182
camaraderie, 5, 11, 17, 25, 37, 52
campaign, 34, 101, 114, 122, 132, 155, 158, 186, 209, 210
canon, 217
canvas, 67
capacity, 126, 129, 240
care, 58, 60, 92, 96–99, 121, 200, 206, 212, 242, 243, 261
career, 50, 251, 252
Caribbean, 237
case, 12, 24, 27, 94, 109, 151, 160
Cass, 24
catalog, 260
catalyst, 1, 102, 133, 190, 196, 226
cause, 11, 15, 34, 65, 115, 178, 181, 191, 192, 200, 210–212, 229, 256
celebration, 18, 30, 43, 66, 96, 191
center, 114
century, 61, 182, 246, 247
challenge, 1, 3, 8, 11–13, 17, 19–21, 24, 27, 41, 42, 54, 65, 72, 94, 105, 107, 113, 118, 121, 142, 157, 180, 183, 187, 193, 194, 216, 217, 219, 227, 258
champion, 3, 22, 23, 149, 205
change, 1–4, 6, 7, 9–11, 18–21, 24, 28, 30, 35, 40, 42, 43, 50, 52, 54–56, 59–61, 64–66, 69, 71, 73, 78, 81, 83, 84, 87–91, 93, 96, 101, 102, 115, 126, 128, 131, 133, 145–147, 152, 156,

158–160, 162, 176–179,
182, 183, 186, 187, 189,
192, 193, 197, 199, 206,
208, 210, 215, 217, 226,
232, 233, 243, 250, 258,
262
channel, 52
chaos, 182
chapter, 69, 73, 182, 185
character, 130, 220
charisma, 71, 76
charm, 76
Chechnya, 162
child, 1, 16, 23
childhood, 1, 3, 5, 6, 12, 23, 24
choice, 1, 4
cinema, 15, 248
cisgender, 152
citizenship, 159, 161
city, 1, 4, 8, 11, 14, 22, 38, 50
clarity, 182
class, 6, 13, 41, 136, 146, 148, 153,
168, 199, 201, 203, 247,
260
classism, 183
classmate, 4
classroom, 21, 22
climate, 23, 56, 158
cloak, 38
coalition, 19, 63–65, 69, 93, 145,
152
collaboration, 55, 56, 63, 65, 69, 71,
94, 102, 105, 107, 134,
145, 147, 148, 156–161,
167, 171, 173, 177, 187,
200, 207, 208, 234–236
collection, 223, 247, 261
collective, 2, 4, 5, 11, 13–15, 25, 29,
30, 33–35, 37, 42, 43, 45,
52, 54, 56, 61, 65, 66, 115,
120, 133, 144, 145, 159,
163, 179, 186, 187, 190,
191, 198, 200, 207, 215,
229, 230, 232, 234, 253
Colombia, 3, 5, 6, 8–11, 18–23, 25,
26, 30, 32–36, 45, 48–50,
52, 54–62, 65, 69, 70, 73,
76–79, 81, 82, 84, 87, 88,
90, 93–98, 100, 102,
106–108, 110, 111, 113,
126, 132, 134, 143, 149,
155, 160, 161, 173–176,
180, 182–184, 186, 190,
192, 193, 197, 198, 201,
216, 229, 230, 232,
236–238, 251, 253, 254
Colombia Diversa, 237
color, 136, 143, 149, 150, 152, 154,
156, 158, 162, 195, 203,
217, 226, 247, 252
combat, 34, 42, 59, 92, 125, 150,
159, 211, 237, 240, 244
combination, 27, 54, 84, 93, 124,
128
comeback, 205
comfort, 15
commentary, 116
commitment, 3, 5, 6, 8, 12, 18,
20–22, 24, 34, 36, 37, 51,
56, 92, 95, 100, 102, 115,
121, 122, 128, 136, 141,
144, 145, 151, 152, 154,
159, 163, 165, 168, 171,
175, 177, 180, 183, 187,
191–193, 198, 200, 205,
208, 210–212, 215, 219,
226, 232, 248, 253, 256,
258, 260

communication, 55, 102, 118, 160, 249
community, 2, 4–6, 10–12, 15, 17–19, 21, 22, 24, 25, 27–30, 32–37, 39–43, 45, 48, 51, 53, 54, 56–58, 60, 62, 64–67, 69, 71, 77–79, 82, 84, 87, 88, 92–95, 97–102, 107, 111, 113, 115, 118, 121, 123, 126, 129, 131–136, 142–144, 150, 152, 154–156, 158, 162, 167, 172, 173, 175, 176, 178, 179, 181, 183, 185, 187–191, 193–195, 197, 198, 202, 206, 207, 209, 212, 217, 220, 226–230, 232, 233, 236–238, 241, 243, 246–250, 252, 254, 256, 258, 259, 261, 262
companionship, 14
comparison, 24
compassion, 7
competency, 97, 145
complacency, 134
complexity, 13, 195, 203
component, 81, 142, 152, 199, 216, 228
compound, 141, 153
concept, 2, 3, 13, 14, 141, 154, 195, 226
concern, 99, 122
conclusion, 9, 11, 14, 18, 22, 24, 25, 27, 35, 37, 43, 45, 51, 54, 56, 58, 65, 71, 78, 87, 100, 102, 107, 113, 121, 131, 133, 138, 145, 147, 149, 156, 158, 161, 163, 168, 175, 180, 182, 184, 187, 195, 200, 205, 210, 215, 217, 219, 221, 226, 228, 236, 246, 254, 258
conference, 107, 160, 167
confidence, 14, 15, 21, 24, 196
conflict, 2, 12, 18, 23, 32, 193, 194
conformity, 11, 33
confrontation, 34, 186
confusion, 12, 24, 27
connection, 14, 44, 64, 185, 215
consent, 148
conservatism, 61, 70, 182
consideration, 81
construct, 2
contact, 102
contemporary, 120, 136
content, 102, 244, 245
context, 16, 22, 24, 25, 59, 84, 142, 144, 167, 168, 172, 182, 186, 197, 215, 218, 247, 253, 261
contrast, 1, 7, 16, 50
contributor, 256
conversation, 205
cooperation, 2, 166
coping, 57, 60, 125, 126, 131
core, 147, 154
cornerstone, 3, 5, 18, 23, 64, 87, 143, 155, 159, 174, 234
cost, 99, 121, 232
counter, 34, 66, 91, 114, 186, 217
country, 18, 34, 61, 70, 76, 81, 161, 162, 183, 190, 237
courage, 4, 14, 23, 33, 39, 43, 67, 116, 185, 219, 221, 229, 232, 253
coverage, 113, 116
creation, 45, 135

Index 269

creativity, 18, 24, 199, 262
credibility, 114
crisis, 10, 26
criticism, 117, 196
crowd, 36, 59
crucible, 3
cultivation, 205
culture, 1, 2, 4, 8, 11, 15, 16, 23, 38, 55, 149, 161, 193, 194, 244, 247, 251, 254, 260
curricula, 35, 103, 193, 206, 244, 245
curriculum, 21
cyberbullying, 113, 114
cycle, 41, 53, 59, 226

dance, 12, 17
danger, 113, 114
date, 122
day, 246, 261
death, 248
debate, 6, 22, 88
decade, 254
decision, 39, 52, 80, 95, 96, 122, 148, 183
declaration, 65, 167
decline, 35
decriminalization, 198
dedication, 145, 175, 178, 190, 208, 229, 256, 259
defiance, 5, 15
degree, 251
demand, 66, 148
denial, 27, 41, 57
deportation, 150
depression, 25, 57, 59, 113, 115, 130
derision, 194
desire, 1, 9, 18, 31, 50, 232, 261
despair, 115, 124

destination, 195, 215
detention, 162
determination, 6, 19, 20, 24, 26, 50, 68–71, 93, 97, 138, 163, 181, 182, 186
development, 3, 6, 7, 12, 21, 24, 37, 58, 59, 107, 158, 180, 186, 193, 195
deviation, 16, 23
dialogue, 17, 37, 65, 66, 91, 121, 145, 149, 155, 156, 158, 167, 169, 171, 181, 206, 254
dichotomy, 116
difference, 6
dignity, 34, 61, 95, 154, 159, 165, 201
dinner, 4
direction, 262
disability, 153, 226
disconnect, 38
discouragement, 118
discourse, 19, 20, 152, 154, 218, 219, 226, 247, 256
discovery, 2, 5, 11–14, 20, 33, 35, 50, 195
discrimination, 1–4, 6, 8–10, 12–15, 17, 18, 21, 29, 30, 32, 34–36, 40, 41, 43, 51, 57, 59, 61, 62, 67, 70, 71, 77, 78, 83, 91, 93, 94, 96, 99, 100, 105, 115, 134, 141–144, 149, 150, 152–155, 158, 159, 161–163, 169, 174–177, 179, 182, 188, 192–195, 199–203, 209, 214–216, 219, 226, 228, 230, 231, 234, 236, 237, 239, 244,

247–249, 252, 256
discussion, 205
disdain, 17
disinhibition, 114
dismantling, 18, 103, 142, 155, 195
disparity, 160, 166
disruption, 218
distance, 114
distress, 15, 27
district, 245
divergence, 55
diversity, 1, 2, 5, 7, 17, 18, 35, 36, 105, 142, 152, 154, 171, 184, 191, 193, 199, 201, 207, 208, 226
divide, 249
document, 162
documentary, 247, 248
documentation, 217
doubt, 27, 59
downtime, 58
drag, 247
dream, 24
drive, 24, 78, 182, 199, 250
duty, 4
dynamic, 1, 81, 84, 100, 195, 215

education, 1, 3, 6, 13, 20–23, 32, 49, 62, 64, 65, 102–105, 135, 138, 149, 152, 156, 177, 193, 205, 208, 210, 212, 215, 217, 237, 240, 246
educator, 251
effect, 18, 19, 36, 91, 115, 145, 160, 227
effectiveness, 99, 131, 153, 157, 169, 209, 234, 238
efficacy, 45, 66
effort, 114, 165, 178, 191, 234

election, 227
element, 5, 6, 158
Ellen DeGeneres, 36
embrace, 1, 5, 7, 14, 17, 18, 27, 30–32, 36, 40, 57, 105, 112, 174, 187, 196, 207, 262
emergence, 6
empathy, 1, 7, 35, 64, 101–103, 124, 145, 177, 199, 216, 248, 253, 256, 261
employment, 10, 41, 62, 77, 96, 134, 176
empowerment, 2, 14, 27, 36, 40, 43, 45, 58, 90, 133, 149, 155, 171, 173, 178, 199, 207, 226, 228, 262
encounter, 4, 12, 34, 115, 130, 164, 169, 179
encouragement, 20, 132, 196, 233
endeavor, 43, 58, 63, 87, 90, 102, 121, 128, 145, 170, 208, 224, 253
endurance, 200
energy, 29, 66, 134, 199
engagement, 4, 5, 20, 27, 30, 45, 51, 60, 69, 79, 93, 111, 113, 131, 134, 157, 197, 202, 209, 238, 249, 258, 261, 262
environment, 6, 7, 17, 18, 21, 26, 30, 32, 38, 41, 42, 52, 64, 65, 99, 105, 116, 143, 156, 176, 191, 230, 244, 246
equality, 1, 4–7, 10, 11, 13, 16, 20, 22, 23, 30, 33–38, 51, 53–55, 61–65, 69, 72, 76, 77, 84, 87, 90–97, 102, 105, 108, 111, 113, 115,

118, 121, 131, 134, 135, 138, 141, 142, 146–150, 152, 154, 156, 157, 163, 165, 168, 171, 173–175, 177, 178, 182–184, 187, 189, 190, 196, 198–201, 205, 206, 208–210, 212, 213, 215, 219, 223, 229, 230, 232, 236, 238–241, 248, 250, 252–254, 256, 261
equation, 10, 26–29, 44, 45, 52, 54, 55, 59, 66, 70, 71, 77, 96–98, 101, 113, 124, 125, 130, 141, 154, 166, 169, 176, 177, 184, 190, 198, 203, 209, 217, 234, 249
equilibrium, 117, 121
equity, 158, 208, 227, 244
erasure, 227
Erik Erikson's, 12, 193
essence, 11, 184, 217
establishment, 20, 65, 81, 96, 119, 155, 192
esteem, 57, 192, 226
estrangement, 57
evaluation, 13, 210
event, 12, 16, 18, 122, 156, 181, 194
evidence, 162
evolution, 70, 189, 193, 195, 210, 246, 247, 261
examination, 254
example, 12, 15, 16, 22, 32, 35, 55, 64, 79, 83, 91, 93, 107, 114, 122, 148, 150, 153, 155–158, 160, 162, 167, 172, 174, 176, 181, 182, 192, 196, 209, 218, 226, 227

exception, 26, 240
exchange, 169
exclusion, 19, 21, 93, 150
exercise, 78
exhaustion, 57, 181
existence, 13, 40, 65, 112, 218
expectation, 8, 38
experience, 4, 12, 22, 24, 25, 27, 28, 31, 34, 41, 53, 54, 57, 59, 105, 108, 115, 122, 124, 141, 146, 150, 153, 154, 160, 175, 179, 181, 187, 192, 194, 195, 203, 256
expertise, 94, 158
exploration, 5, 12, 32, 38, 213, 219
exposure, 5, 22, 107, 124
expression, 2, 13, 17, 23, 37, 57, 65, 138, 147, 155, 172, 247
extension, 13
eye, 8, 219

fabric, 14
face, 3, 6, 15, 23–25, 27, 28, 32, 34, 42, 43, 52, 53, 58–60, 71, 78, 81, 91, 93, 114, 115, 118, 120, 121, 128, 141, 149, 150, 153, 161, 163, 168, 169, 174–176, 180, 182, 193, 199, 203, 205, 210, 211, 216, 219, 234, 236–238, 241, 249, 260
factor, 60
Faderman, 246
family, 1, 2, 4–9, 11, 12, 14, 16, 17, 23, 24, 27, 38, 40, 56, 57, 91, 93, 96, 122, 125, 132, 196, 229, 233
fascination, 18, 23
fashion, 17, 18, 194

favor, 20, 62
fear, 2, 3, 6, 7, 12–14, 17, 18, 24, 29, 39, 41–43, 50, 59, 91, 114, 115, 149, 150, 182, 196, 221, 256
feat, 73
federation, 239
feedback, 117, 210
feeling, 31, 36, 51, 186, 193
femininity, 6, 13, 17, 31
feminist, 51, 55, 65, 141, 148, 149, 156, 157, 218
field, 207, 256
fieldwork, 251
fight, 4–6, 8, 10, 16, 20, 22, 23, 30, 34–37, 51–53, 57, 58, 60–63, 65, 69, 72, 76, 81, 87, 93, 95–97, 100, 105, 107, 108, 111–113, 115, 118, 131, 134–136, 138, 141, 143–146, 148–150, 152, 154, 156, 158, 159, 161, 163, 165, 168, 171, 173–175, 177, 178, 180, 182, 184, 191, 192, 196, 198–200, 206, 208, 210, 218, 219, 229–233, 236, 238, 243, 247, 248, 252, 253, 256
fighting, 23, 43, 151, 236
figure, 3, 20, 36, 59, 62, 70, 71, 76, 108, 113, 120, 175, 183, 217, 248, 253
film, 191, 247, 248
finding, 5, 28, 33
fire, 1, 4, 10, 18, 23, 50, 192
flair, 17
fluidity, 247, 261
focus, 64, 83, 100, 114, 117, 118, 121, 133, 154, 157, 172, 176, 181, 208, 217, 230, 239, 240
footage, 248
footprint, 119
foray, 19, 51
force, 3, 147
forefront, 22, 94, 115, 206, 238
form, 34, 64, 114
formation, 45, 208
formulating, 81, 82, 89, 90
foster, 28, 42, 51, 99, 102, 154, 186, 188, 199, 217, 249, 250, 258, 261, 262
foundation, 6, 21, 24, 40, 45, 52, 78, 95, 97, 129, 131, 192, 207, 233
fragility, 153
fragmentation, 157
frame, 142, 190
framework, 10, 13, 24, 29, 33, 52, 62, 84, 93, 96, 146, 153, 154, 159, 176, 192, 203, 218, 233, 245
framing, 91, 94, 152, 154
Franco, 162
friend, 15, 32, 115
friendship, 15, 196
front, 62, 64, 105, 156, 200, 230, 234
fuel, 10, 193, 233
fulfillment, 213–215
function, 44, 52, 59, 88, 191
funding, 49, 157, 238
fundraising, 16
future, 3, 6, 8, 9, 14, 18, 20, 24, 30, 32, 43, 45, 52, 65, 69, 72, 81, 90, 93, 95–97, 100, 102, 105, 113, 118, 135,

138, 147, 149, 161, 174, 175, 177, 178, 180, 183, 184, 187, 192, 195, 198–200, 205, 207, 208, 210, 226–228, 233, 236, 238, 243, 246, 254, 256, 262

gain, 59, 216, 248
gap, 3, 61
gathering, 11, 38, 66, 122
gender, 2, 5, 6, 12, 13, 16–18, 22–24, 31, 35, 41, 55, 57, 61, 64, 77, 78, 94, 96, 97, 100, 101, 105, 132, 136, 141, 142, 144, 146–149, 152–155, 160, 163, 168, 169, 175, 188, 193, 195, 199, 201, 203, 207, 208, 218, 226, 236, 238, 244, 245, 247, 258, 260, 261
generation, 20, 87, 95, 110, 133, 145, 177, 187, 192, 199, 200, 205–208, 219, 236, 256
glimpse, 21, 247
globalization, 169
globe, 64, 168, 198, 229, 232, 260
go, 12, 24
goal, 63, 78, 79, 81, 83, 190
governance, 18, 227
government, 5, 6, 55, 75, 89, 94, 227
grandmother, 4
gratitude, 187, 196, 197, 229, 232
grievance, 65
ground, 53
groundbreaking, 96, 247, 260
grounding, 84
groundswell, 80
groundwork, 6, 8, 9, 11, 78, 100, 183, 208
group, 1, 2, 7, 44, 114, 125, 159, 196, 226
growth, 14, 15, 30, 52, 58, 70, 128, 133, 186, 187, 189, 193, 197, 205, 213
guard, 15, 114
guidance, 20, 35, 37, 99, 167
guide, 175, 209, 223

hall, 209
hand, 89, 150, 159, 169, 180
harassment, 14, 41, 59, 62, 96, 113–115, 192, 249
harshness, 1
Harvey Milk, 4, 10, 23, 28, 218
hate, 10, 41, 59, 149, 249
hatred, 58, 60, 150, 201
haven, 39
head, 42, 58, 81, 182, 187
healing, 155
health, 2, 17, 25, 34, 42, 55, 57, 58, 60, 92, 96, 98, 99, 115, 120, 123–126, 130, 131, 135, 143, 155, 192, 200, 220, 237, 241, 243, 249, 261
healthcare, 10, 41, 55, 62, 77, 96–100, 106, 134, 143, 148, 153, 176, 209, 220, 236, 237, 241–243
heart, 10, 23, 232
heartbeat, 54, 66
help, 42, 117, 161, 220, 245
helplessness, 124
Henri Tajfel, 1, 226
hesitation, 18
heteronormativity, 91, 194

highlight, 27, 56, 93, 97, 115, 133, 158, 191, 195, 216, 218, 234, 246
history, 1, 4, 6, 10, 11, 14, 21, 62, 96, 156, 182–184, 206, 215, 217–219, 227, 246, 248, 260
hobby, 23
Hollywood, 248
home, 6, 161
homophobia, 15, 25, 26, 179, 194, 226
homosexuality, 32, 41, 61, 160, 169, 198
honor, 113, 190, 191, 216, 224, 225, 228, 232
hope, 3, 28, 36, 40, 67, 71, 100, 113, 144, 166, 174, 178, 190, 198, 200, 205, 232, 254
hopelessness, 115
hostility, 1, 23, 34, 41, 59, 66, 91, 133, 182, 192
household, 1, 6
housing, 77, 96, 176
humility, 232
humor, 23, 76
hurdle, 19
hyper, 31, 42, 114

idea, 2, 4, 10, 13, 16, 33, 56, 191, 193, 207
identification, 78
identity, 2, 3, 5–9, 11–14, 16, 17, 22–28, 30–33, 35, 36, 38–40, 44, 52, 57, 58, 61, 65, 66, 78, 94, 96, 97, 100, 105, 112, 126, 128, 132, 141, 144, 147, 149, 150, 152, 153, 155, 163, 169, 183, 185, 187, 189, 193–196, 213, 215, 217, 218, 226, 229, 238, 244, 245, 247, 251, 254, 258, 260
ideology, 7, 20
image, 185
imagination, 23
immediacy, 249
immigrant, 143, 150, 157
immigration, 158
impact, 3, 5, 7, 13, 16, 17, 28, 29, 35, 40, 53, 56, 58, 65, 67, 70, 76, 81, 99, 103, 106, 109, 113, 116, 130, 133, 135, 138, 144, 159, 167, 168, 173–175, 182–184, 189–191, 202, 208, 218, 219, 221, 223, 226, 229, 237, 249, 252
imperialism, 169
implementation, 93, 98, 103, 245
importance, 1–4, 7, 11, 14, 15, 17–19, 22, 25, 28, 29, 32–37, 39, 42–45, 51–56, 58, 60, 62, 64, 69, 78, 91, 92, 94, 96–98, 108, 115, 120, 122, 125, 131, 133, 134, 136, 142, 145, 148, 150, 152, 155–157, 159, 166, 167, 173, 176, 177, 179, 180, 182, 183, 185–187, 190, 192, 193, 195, 196, 199, 200, 202–204, 206–208, 211, 212, 218, 219, 224, 226–229, 232, 233, 235–238, 244, 252, 254, 256, 260–262

Index 275

imposition, 169
impression, 12
improvement, 210
in, 1–45, 48, 50–67, 69–71, 73,
    75–84, 87–91, 93–102,
    105–117, 120–122, 125,
    126, 128, 130–136, 138,
    141–150, 152–163, 166,
    167, 169–188, 190–203,
    205–210, 212–220, 223,
    226, 227, 229, 230,
    232–243, 245–249,
    251–254, 256, 258,
    260–262
inadequacy, 31
incident, 32, 66, 114, 186
inclination, 23
inclusion, 35, 36, 62, 99, 103, 142,
    148, 155, 156, 206, 227,
    245
inclusivity, 18, 32, 55, 91, 105, 136,
    138, 141, 145, 154–156,
    175, 195, 201, 226, 256
income, 143
increase, 59, 149, 209
individual, 2, 3, 5, 11, 20, 25, 28, 34,
    38, 40, 41, 54, 59, 105,
    113, 114, 128, 132, 133,
    159, 172, 176, 187, 195,
    203, 217, 226, 227, 253,
    256
individuality, 5, 7, 16, 17, 52
industry, 248
inequality, 1, 3, 4, 36, 62, 156, 192,
    231, 234
influence, 19, 34, 36, 38, 57, 65, 94,
    103, 108–110, 135, 145,
    146, 166, 169, 239
information, 64, 114, 161, 248, 249

inheritance, 95
initiative, 35, 99, 107, 155, 158, 167,
    193, 209
injustice, 4, 7, 22, 23, 105, 215
insight, 246
inspiration, 11, 29, 36, 37, 90, 100,
    138, 174, 178, 179, 184,
    195, 215, 217, 227, 229,
    232, 246, 254
instability, 149
instance, 14, 21, 31, 34, 41, 53,
    55–57, 59, 82, 91, 101,
    114, 116, 120, 130, 148,
    153, 154, 157, 158, 160,
    162, 169, 186, 191, 194,
    195, 199, 203, 209, 210,
    217, 218, 226, 230
integration, 3, 245
integrity, 130
intensity, 116
intentionality, 226
interconnectedness, 18, 58, 108, 110,
    136, 141, 145–147, 149,
    152, 156, 159, 183, 201,
    205, 236
internet, 114, 249
interplay, 8, 33, 121, 125, 131, 253
intersection, 41, 141, 155
intersectionality, 13, 15, 17, 23, 33,
    35, 37, 40, 54, 62–65, 78,
    108, 110, 136, 138, 141,
    145, 146, 148, 153, 154,
    158, 165, 168, 172, 173,
    175, 176, 183, 184, 188,
    189, 195, 199, 201, 207,
    218, 226, 236, 237, 247,
    252, 256, 260
intervention, 162
intimidation, 42

intolerance, 41
introduction, 61, 261
involvement, 4, 11, 20, 21, 42, 53, 109, 132, 181, 190
invulnerability, 185
isolation, 14, 27, 97, 113, 130, 143, 146, 156, 195, 196
issue, 4, 12, 55, 59, 77, 94, 142, 144, 147, 158, 162, 163, 219

James Baldwin, 32
John Kotter, 3
John Turner, 226
Johnson, 120, 248
Jon Kabat-Zinn, 181
journey, 2, 3, 5, 6, 8–14, 17–28, 30, 33–40, 42, 43, 45, 50, 52, 54, 56, 58, 60, 61, 63–65, 70, 71, 73, 76, 90, 93, 95, 98, 100, 105, 111, 112, 118, 123, 126, 128, 129, 131, 133, 147, 163, 165, 171, 173–175, 178, 180, 182, 183, 185–187, 189, 190, 192–197, 201, 205, 208, 210, 212, 213, 215, 217, 219, 229, 232, 233, 246, 253, 255
joy, 12
Juanes, 36
judgment, 2, 7, 11, 14, 17, 29, 32, 39, 181
judiciary, 94
Judith Butler's, 2, 16, 31
justice, 1, 2, 4, 6, 8, 11, 13, 15, 18, 20–24, 30, 33, 35, 36, 38, 51, 54–57, 62–65, 69, 84, 88, 92–95, 97, 105, 108, 110, 113, 115, 121, 131, 133–136, 138, 141, 143–147, 149, 150, 152, 154, 156–159, 162, 163, 165, 173, 175, 183, 184, 187, 188, 193, 196–201, 206, 208, 210, 212, 213, 215, 217, 219, 223, 226–230, 232, 233, 236, 238, 241, 244, 246, 247, 250, 251, 253, 254, 256, 258, 260

Kenya, 167
Kimberlé Crenshaw, 13, 141, 146, 150, 153, 154, 168, 195, 199, 203, 226
Kimberlé Crenshaw's, 188
knowledge, 3, 4, 6, 20–22, 37, 53, 55, 57, 88, 102, 159, 174, 197, 199, 206, 208, 209, 216, 219, 234, 256

labor, 143, 156
lack, 17, 19, 26, 41, 77, 130, 157, 160, 219, 226, 243
landmark, 20, 61, 65, 71, 94, 95, 97, 173, 182, 190, 198, 237
landscape, 5, 11, 18, 20, 33, 43, 55, 56, 58, 76, 79–81, 87, 90, 93, 95, 100, 105, 111, 113, 121, 134, 141, 149, 158, 161, 165, 175, 180, 182, 184, 195, 197, 201, 213, 219, 221, 232, 241, 246, 249, 250, 258
language, 92, 160
Latin America, 174
laughter, 233
Laura, 15

law, 71, 83, 94, 96, 116, 163, 239
layer, 57
leader, 76, 126, 132
leadership, 185, 227
learning, 4, 51, 189, 246
leave, 149
lecture, 13
legacy, 4, 65, 71, 111, 113, 133–135, 138, 145, 159, 168, 174, 175, 182–184, 208, 217, 218, 221, 223–226, 236, 248, 256
legalization, 20, 59, 65, 186, 227, 237
legislation, 77, 91, 94, 105, 153, 155, 190, 209
legitimacy, 96
lens, 40, 112, 141, 168, 226, 254
lesson, 118, 185, 188
level, 59, 76, 124, 209, 219, 245
liberation, 17, 24
life, 1, 4, 9, 11, 14–17, 20, 23, 28, 34, 42, 45, 50, 58, 62, 97, 114, 116, 121–123, 126, 131, 132, 138, 149, 185, 218, 227, 229, 232, 239, 253
lifeline, 32, 131, 135
lifetime, 135
light, 200, 218, 232, 248, 253
limit, 219
list, 230
literacy, 249
literature, 5, 7, 10, 32, 183, 195, 246, 258, 259, 262
litigation, 94, 95
living, 11, 41–43, 115, 223, 252
lobby, 83, 155
lobbying, 53, 55, 61, 65, 68, 69, 75, 78, 183, 209

Lorde, 247
loss, 248
love, 7, 8, 24, 36, 38, 66, 196, 201, 233, 248, 261

mainstream, 36, 217, 226, 248
man, 51, 93, 218
manifest, 24, 91, 113, 149, 155, 193
marathon, 200
march, 66, 122, 148, 181
marginalization, 61, 157, 174, 195, 216
Marielle Franco, 162
Marina, 248
mark, 1, 111, 138, 145, 173, 190
marriage, 10, 20, 34, 41, 59, 62, 65, 77, 79, 91, 96, 102, 114, 157, 160, 176, 183, 186, 190, 209, 227, 237, 239
Marsha P. Johnson, 10, 23, 28, 120, 217, 248
Martin Luther King Jr., 4
María José Pizarro, 36
masculinity, 5, 6, 12, 13, 17, 31, 194
material, 261
matter, 15, 154, 186, 200, 210, 253
MDSA, 238
means, 13, 23, 32, 36, 40, 65, 168, 199, 201, 236, 262
measure, 209
Medellín, 1, 3, 4, 6, 8, 9, 11, 14, 16, 18, 21, 22, 24, 31, 34, 38, 39, 41, 50–52, 65, 66, 71, 181, 194, 219, 237
media, 30, 36, 59, 63, 64, 70, 76, 97, 102, 113, 114, 116, 144, 148, 160, 161, 181, 197, 206, 209, 226, 227, 246, 248–250

medium, 102
member, 5, 40
membership, 44, 226
memory, 162
mentor, 53
mentoring, 134, 256
mentorship, 37, 54, 138, 145, 167, 174, 177, 199, 205, 208, 209, 258
message, 17, 62, 197
middle, 6, 53
milestone, 39, 190
mind, 1, 7
mindfulness, 57, 117, 181
minority, 192
mirror, 39
misinformation, 101, 102, 114, 249
mission, 22, 37, 48, 149, 196, 217, 237, 239, 262
mobilization, 69, 84, 86, 87, 95, 134, 237
model, 24, 36, 58, 193, 209
mold, 31, 217
moment, 11–13, 17, 20, 24, 27, 34, 38, 51, 61, 96, 115, 181, 186, 194, 232
momentum, 20, 34, 53, 81, 96, 113, 208
morale, 191
morality, 94
mother, 7, 23
motion, 11
motivation, 115, 186, 191, 213, 215
motto, 2
movement, 3, 11, 20, 24, 25, 30, 34, 38, 45, 51, 53, 54, 58, 59, 63–67, 76, 78, 84, 94, 108, 111, 120, 121, 126, 134, 138, 141, 142, 144, 145, 147, 149, 150, 152, 154, 156–158, 167, 169, 172, 175, 177, 180, 183, 188, 190, 191, 193, 199, 200, 205, 207, 209, 210, 212, 217, 229, 230, 233–236, 246, 248, 261, 262
movie, 15
multiplicity, 254
murder, 162
music, 17, 36
myriad, 159, 236, 241

narrative, 9–11, 14, 31, 55, 70, 113, 165, 182, 184, 194, 213, 215, 217, 229, 232, 233, 246–248
nature, 13, 58, 93, 105, 116, 121, 143, 154, 155, 175, 195, 219, 254
necessity, 1, 7, 37, 76, 105, 126, 179, 203, 210, 226
need, 22, 28, 34, 61, 62, 64, 66, 75, 77, 78, 88, 95, 96, 99, 115, 121, 144, 149, 153, 158, 161, 162, 166, 167, 175, 179, 191, 215, 230, 234, 237, 238, 261
negativity, 58
neighborhood, 11
net, 129
network, 5, 7, 15, 21–23, 32, 39, 54, 60, 64, 92, 107, 118, 119, 125, 129, 130, 132, 177, 185, 191, 193, 197, 207, 237
networking, 52
New York City, 247
newfound, 4, 57

Index

news, 23
niche, 142
Nigeria, 153
night, 186, 196, 233
non, 93, 98, 153, 156, 169, 260
norm, 16, 23
notion, 2, 13, 19, 142, 227
number, 174, 190, 209
nurturing, 7, 17, 23, 122, 126, 131

objective, 80
obligation, 121
obstacle, 11, 193
official, 96
on, 1, 4, 5, 7, 11–13, 16–18, 20–23, 28, 31, 32, 35, 36, 38, 42, 45, 53–56, 58–61, 63–65, 76, 78, 80, 81, 83, 88, 89, 92, 94, 96–102, 107, 108, 111, 113–115, 117, 118, 123–125, 130, 133, 135, 138, 141, 143, 145, 146, 150, 154, 155, 157, 159–163, 166, 168, 169, 171–173, 175, 176, 178, 180, 182, 184–187, 190, 192, 193, 195, 196, 200, 207–209, 217–219, 223, 226, 230, 232, 237, 239, 240, 247, 248, 252, 253, 258, 262
one, 5, 11, 14, 15, 18, 23–25, 32, 52, 57, 58, 60, 66, 79, 94, 107, 112, 114, 115, 133, 145, 146, 150, 158, 159, 169, 171, 172, 174–177, 187, 196, 198, 200, 208, 232, 237, 239
opening, 8

opinion, 73, 80, 83–87, 93, 160, 163
opportunity, 11, 107
opposition, 34, 41, 43, 53, 61, 66, 91, 94, 101, 181
oppress, 18, 142
oppression, 5, 9, 17, 64, 141, 146, 150, 152, 154, 155, 168, 175, 203, 218
option, 105
organization, 19, 237, 240
organizer, 217
organizing, 4, 16, 19, 51, 53, 55, 63–65, 75, 95, 122, 142, 145, 179, 181, 202, 209
orientation, 21, 24, 35, 61, 94, 96, 97, 100, 105, 144, 146, 152, 153, 155, 163, 193, 195, 203, 238, 244, 245, 258, 260
Oscar, 248
ostracism, 10, 153, 216
other, 11, 12, 15, 20, 23, 32, 34, 51, 54, 56, 62–64, 70, 85, 118, 120, 141, 143, 145–147, 150, 156–160, 169, 180, 183, 199, 230
outreach, 49, 102, 176, 190, 202, 238
overcome, 27, 37, 95, 133, 185, 190, 193, 262
overlap, 13, 141, 150, 203
overview, 247, 261

pain, 9
pandemic, 149
paper, 107
parade, 34, 190
paradigm, 152
parity, 149

part, 1, 9, 10, 12, 15, 64, 93, 99, 118, 120, 149, 159, 161, 162, 174, 198, 226
participation, 58, 183, 191, 249
partner, 106, 248
partnership, 49, 107, 157, 158
passage, 24, 83, 190
passing, 190
passion, 2, 5–7, 9, 10, 17, 20, 21, 24, 33, 35, 40, 50–52, 76, 121, 179, 197, 199, 200, 208, 210, 219, 256
past, 97, 138, 152, 192, 195, 201, 219, 226
path, 11, 14, 20, 21, 26, 40, 50, 90, 121, 178, 192, 196, 213–215
patience, 156, 171
pay, 149
people, 7, 23, 66, 143, 154, 156, 158, 185, 193, 195, 199, 217, 237, 239, 240, 247, 252
perception, 11, 34, 100–102, 227, 238
performance, 23, 24, 31, 262
performativity, 2, 16, 31
period, 14, 57, 93
persecution, 144, 158, 162, 163, 165
perseverance, 60, 76, 92, 193
persistence, 69, 180–182
person, 114, 203, 226
perspective, 51, 188, 232
Pete Buttigieg, 227
phase, 65, 122
phenomenon, 114, 141, 194
philosophy, 112
phone, 114
piece, 176, 217
Piedad Bonnett, 36

pillar, 102
Pizarro, 36
place, 7, 32, 34, 83, 227
planning, 51, 53, 66, 81, 87, 122, 200
platform, 19, 24, 32, 52, 76, 144, 161, 191, 217, 219, 248, 249, 262
play, 12, 18, 25, 41, 54, 157, 191, 202, 209, 217, 236, 241, 245
player, 248, 258
plight, 143, 162, 163
poet, 36, 218, 247
poetry, 13, 36, 261
point, 20, 51, 65, 93, 179, 194
policy, 19, 84, 99, 152, 155, 156, 166, 175, 176, 209, 210, 237, 239, 240
politician, 36, 162, 218
pooling, 158, 234
populace, 18
population, 165
portion, 144
portrayal, 248
potential, 2, 6, 11, 42, 66, 71, 84, 155, 157, 161, 173, 192, 196, 206, 209, 219, 250
poverty, 30, 252
power, 2–4, 15, 18–20, 23, 32, 34–37, 43, 52, 54, 59, 63, 65, 69, 71, 76, 81, 87, 90, 93, 95, 102, 107, 110, 111, 128, 133, 134, 144, 156, 157, 159, 161, 166, 173, 179, 181, 183, 187, 189, 193, 207, 227, 229, 261, 262
practice, 3, 58, 181, 186, 210

precedent, 96, 100
prejudice, 14, 21, 102, 150, 179, 192, 248
preparation, 121
presence, 25, 28, 64, 65, 119, 227
present, 22, 168, 181, 246, 247, 261
pressure, 23, 31, 80, 88, 132
pride, 14, 24, 28–30, 34, 42, 57, 66, 181, 183, 190, 194
principle, 3, 142, 158
priority, 155
privilege, 168, 176, 188, 203, 229
problem, 4, 157, 159
process, 12, 13, 24, 25, 27, 33, 39, 43, 45, 76, 78, 79, 81, 84, 87, 88, 126, 176, 180, 195, 223, 233
production, 258
profession, 7
professional, 117, 197
program, 209
progress, 11, 34, 58, 61, 62, 76, 81, 84, 90, 93, 95, 97, 100–102, 141, 145, 149, 152, 157, 160, 161, 176, 180, 182, 190, 192, 198, 200, 201, 205, 208–210, 214, 216, 236, 241, 243, 252
prohibition, 96
project, 4, 185, 218
prominence, 70
promotion, 168
proposal, 88
prose, 36
protection, 163, 165
protest, 14, 34, 66, 91, 114, 186
psyche, 1, 124
psychology, 186

public, 11, 19, 20, 22, 34, 37, 53, 58, 59, 61, 62, 64–66, 70, 71, 73, 77, 80, 83–88, 93–95, 97, 100–102, 115–118, 144, 160, 163, 176, 183, 186, 191, 202, 208, 209, 226, 227, 237, 238, 240
publication, 261, 262
publisher, 258–260, 262
purpose, 9, 35, 144, 158, 160, 182, 219, 253, 254
pursuit, 6, 13, 14, 76, 87, 90, 105, 113, 115, 121, 133, 147, 175, 183, 187, 213, 228, 246
pushback, 80, 84, 89–91, 93, 156, 210
puzzle, 176, 217

quality, 31, 42, 243
quest, 11, 20, 39, 61, 69, 81, 95, 102, 131, 157, 164, 173, 184, 241
question, 1, 21, 24, 34
quo, 1, 11, 17, 19, 21, 24, 41, 42, 54, 65, 69, 72, 73, 76, 113, 180, 187, 219, 227, 258

race, 13, 78, 136, 146, 150, 152–155, 168, 175, 188, 195, 199, 201, 203, 207, 226, 237, 247, 260
racism, 62, 142, 149–152, 156, 183, 230
Rafael, 252, 254–256
Rafael Saeed, 251, 254, 256
Rafael Saeed's, 253, 256, 258
rainbow, 15
rally, 59, 91

range, 39, 124, 154, 190
rate, 210
ratification, 88
re, 13
reach, 38, 105, 148, 197, 200, 207, 249
reaction, 10, 57, 59
reading, 10
reality, 57, 60, 65, 90, 174
realization, 1, 3, 5, 9, 11, 12, 20, 32, 50, 61, 65, 73, 185
realm, 20, 54, 63, 67, 78, 118, 159, 168, 203, 223, 226, 238, 244, 258
recognition, 17, 19, 22, 34, 41, 48, 55, 60–62, 67, 77, 79, 93, 95–97, 106, 111–113, 132, 153, 154, 175, 176, 182, 190, 191, 193, 198, 201, 218, 219, 236, 237, 241, 247, 256
record, 227
reflection, 27, 117, 138, 215
reform, 3, 88, 94, 98, 158, 166
refuge, 7, 12, 23, 165
refusal, 13
region, 171, 177, 237
regression, 134
rejection, 12, 24, 25, 27, 57, 99
relationship, 27, 61, 113, 154, 261
relevance, 169
reluctance, 59
reminder, 11, 14, 32, 40, 65, 115, 133, 145, 152, 156, 168, 190, 195, 205, 216, 217, 232
report, 25, 227
representation, 19, 29, 32, 36, 37, 97, 183, 195, 215, 217, 226–228, 232, 248, 249, 254
representative, 207
repression, 167
research, 22, 57, 79, 88, 185, 186, 233, 237, 240, 246
reservoir, 126
resilience, 1, 4, 7, 14–16, 23, 24, 26, 28, 33, 34, 36–39, 42, 43, 51, 52, 58, 60, 62, 67, 69, 70, 81, 87, 90, 92, 93, 95, 97, 102, 111, 113, 115, 118, 125–129, 131, 133, 144, 149, 152, 166, 168, 175, 179, 180, 182, 183, 186, 187, 189, 190, 193, 195, 196, 198, 200, 208, 215, 229, 232, 248, 253
resistance, 11, 19, 58, 59, 62, 64, 66, 80, 81, 89–93, 101, 149, 153, 169, 218
resolve, 11, 13, 17, 22, 130, 174, 192, 252, 256
resource, 157, 254
respect, 55, 65, 102, 144, 149, 167, 177, 185, 193
response, 20, 51, 59, 149, 175
responsibility, 4, 159, 206, 232
result, 35, 65, 94, 157, 169
revelation, 10
reversal, 153
rhetoric, 91, 102, 149
rhythm, 9, 16
richness, 171
ridicule, 12, 17, 23
rift, 56
right, 1, 17, 20, 96, 115, 199, 220
rigor, 253
ripple, 35, 36, 105, 145, 227

rise, 59, 95, 128, 153, 161, 182
risk, 66, 115, 157
rite, 24
road, 20, 182
role, 1, 3, 6, 7, 12–15, 20, 23–25, 27, 28, 30, 31, 33, 35–38, 41, 54, 58, 80, 83, 97, 102, 155, 176, 182, 191, 192, 195, 202, 205, 209, 217–219, 226, 227, 232, 236, 241, 245, 252, 258, 262
room, 16
ruling, 34, 61, 62, 94, 96, 182, 198
RuPaul, 36

s, 1–25, 27, 28, 31–34, 36–43, 48–54, 56, 58–65, 67–71, 76, 78, 81–84, 87, 88, 90, 91, 93–95, 97–102, 105, 107–114, 116, 118, 120, 122, 123, 128, 131–133, 135, 136, 138, 141–145, 147–152, 154–159, 161–163, 166–168, 171, 173–188, 190, 192–201, 208–210, 212, 213, 215–217, 219–221, 230, 232, 239, 246–248, 253–256, 258–260, 262
Saeed, 256
safeguard, 115
safety, 15, 34, 41–43, 59, 61, 62, 118, 120, 121, 129, 163, 164, 186, 197, 249
sake, 217
salsa, 9
sanctuary, 12
scale, 78, 111, 159, 163
scene, 36
schedule, 58
scholar, 146, 154, 199
school, 4, 5, 12, 14, 31, 51, 179, 192, 206
schoolteacher, 7
science, 3, 21, 254
scope, 56, 77, 253, 254
scrutiny, 59, 95, 115–118
secrecy, 41
section, 21, 28, 40, 58, 63, 67, 78, 85, 88, 98, 108, 111, 118, 121, 123, 126, 131, 135, 149, 161, 163, 171, 175, 182, 196, 205, 223, 226, 234, 241, 249
security, 96, 118–121
selection, 246, 260
self, 1, 2, 5, 11–14, 16–18, 23, 26–28, 32–35, 37–40, 45, 50, 57–60, 92, 96, 112, 117, 118, 121, 132, 133, 172, 187, 192, 194, 195, 200, 206, 212–215, 226–228, 238, 261
sensationalism, 219
sense, 1, 2, 4, 7, 12, 15, 17, 24, 25, 27–30, 32, 35–37, 42, 43, 51, 52, 57, 64, 77, 102, 107, 113, 143, 144, 155, 158, 167, 169, 179, 182, 186, 190, 194, 197, 206, 207, 214, 226, 230, 232, 248
sensitivity, 144, 168
series, 16, 95
serve, 2, 21, 27, 35, 52, 69, 95, 97, 111, 115, 118, 133, 135, 152, 161, 183, 189, 191,

205, 218, 219, 247, 248
service, 153
set, 11, 38, 40, 61, 73, 79, 82, 96, 100, 168, 192
setback, 16, 205
setting, 58, 78, 79, 81, 84, 212
setup, 205
sex, 20, 34, 59, 61, 62, 65, 67, 77, 79, 93–96, 102, 114, 132, 160, 176, 183, 186, 190, 198, 227, 237
sexism, 62, 156, 183
sexuality, 17, 31, 41, 57, 101, 148, 154, 155, 160, 168, 169, 199, 218, 247
Shakira, 36
shape, 17, 168, 176, 203
share, 15, 17, 21, 30, 37, 42, 55, 58, 64, 99, 102, 114, 155, 169, 177, 197, 199, 205, 207, 209, 217, 229, 232, 261
sharing, 25, 42, 51, 53, 55, 56, 70, 102, 105, 120, 133, 159, 161, 163, 174, 177, 183, 185, 205, 226–228, 233, 241, 248, 252, 256, 262
shift, 62, 152, 175, 186, 201, 227
show, 18
significance, 129, 133, 171, 182, 188, 218, 223, 226, 234, 249
silence, 50, 114
sit, 66
situation, 66, 114
size, 97
skepticism, 19
society, 2, 3, 5, 6, 12, 14, 17, 18, 20–24, 26, 34–36, 40–43, 50, 52, 56, 59, 61, 62, 65, 67, 73, 89–91, 93, 97, 100, 102, 105, 112, 113, 115, 126, 132, 133, 149, 150, 152, 154, 159, 165, 177–179, 196, 199, 205, 210, 216, 218, 223, 226–229, 237, 238, 246, 248, 256, 261, 262
socio, 11, 23, 76, 79, 213
sociology, 3, 13, 21, 253, 254, 256
Sofia, 196
solace, 5, 7, 14, 23, 25, 29, 32, 39, 125, 186
solidarity, 15–17, 29, 30, 37, 51, 54, 64, 92, 95, 97, 102, 107, 108, 115, 138, 143–145, 148, 156, 158, 160–162, 166, 168, 169, 173, 177–179, 183, 184, 188, 194, 197, 207, 230, 232, 233, 238, 249, 252, 253, 261
soundtrack, 36
source, 7, 11, 24, 37, 57, 62, 118, 179, 185
space, 2, 11, 14, 17, 19, 58, 66, 99, 125, 143, 218
spark, 1, 4, 9, 11, 12
speaker, 76
speaking, 19, 22, 23, 53, 115, 144, 163, 183, 208
spectrum, 32, 217, 226, 230, 246, 254
speech, 59, 149
sphere, 102
spirit, 60, 61, 115, 160, 195, 205
sprint, 200
staff, 242
stage, 12, 23, 61, 65, 108
stake, 92

Index

stance, 94
standard, 168
state, 57, 114, 115, 153, 162, 181, 245
statement, 18
status, 1, 11, 17, 19, 21, 24, 41, 42, 54, 65, 69, 72, 73, 76, 78, 113, 154, 176, 180, 187, 188, 207, 219, 226, 227, 237, 258
step, 10, 54, 62, 78, 79, 82, 178, 192, 200
stigma, 19, 25, 26, 32, 34, 43, 61, 100, 192, 194, 195, 214, 220, 239, 243
stirring, 9
stoicism, 17
stone, 193
Stonewall, 217, 248, 261
story, 13, 18, 25, 40, 51, 65, 71, 90, 93, 115, 133, 174, 182, 183, 187, 193, 195, 215–217, 229, 232, 248, 254
storyteller, 232
storytelling, 23, 32, 36, 77, 102, 199, 218, 233, 253, 254, 261
strategy, 64, 65, 78, 80, 88, 94, 105, 118, 120, 155, 160, 209
stratification, 13, 203
strength, 7, 11, 14, 17, 37, 40, 42, 57, 60, 62, 120, 126, 132, 133, 182, 185, 186, 232
stress, 57, 59, 117, 124–126, 130, 180, 181, 192, 194
structure, 88
struggle, 10, 16, 20, 27, 34, 35, 38, 45, 51, 54, 61, 66, 69, 95, 97, 108, 111, 115, 121, 134, 142, 143, 146, 149, 153, 154, 161, 163, 165, 168, 171, 175, 182, 215, 254, 256
student, 6, 19–21, 244, 246
study, 160, 227
style, 246
subgroup, 32
subject, 253
success, 56, 64, 65, 76, 81, 209, 210
summary, 3, 6, 8, 178, 189, 193, 253, 256
support, 2, 5, 14–18, 21–23, 25–30, 34, 39, 40, 42, 43, 45, 51, 52, 54, 55, 60–65, 71, 78, 80, 83, 85, 88, 91, 94, 95, 97, 99, 102, 108, 114–116, 119, 121, 122, 125, 128–132, 135, 143–145, 149, 155, 158, 161, 162, 165, 172, 173, 175, 177, 180, 182, 183, 185, 187, 191, 193, 195–197, 199, 206, 207, 209, 210, 217, 229–231, 233, 236–238, 240, 248, 261, 262
suppression, 194
surge, 66, 182
surgery, 96
surrounding, 39, 93, 121, 152, 184, 185, 243, 247, 254, 256
survival, 43
sustainability, 56, 158, 177
sustenance, 125
Sylvia Rivera, 218
symbol, 115, 144, 166, 174
synthesis, 24
system, 14, 18, 21, 22, 61, 88, 122, 129–131, 158, 193, 210,

247
table, 4
Tammy Baldwin, 227
tapestry, 1, 4, 6, 13, 14, 23, 28, 43, 105, 146, 161, 180, 205, 215
target, 113
task, 223, 226
teaching, 187, 206
technology, 206, 208–210
television, 23
tenacity, 4, 93
tension, 157
term, 58, 150, 154, 199, 203
testament, 18, 38, 43, 60, 93, 97, 102, 110, 111, 133, 159, 163, 166, 182, 183, 187, 189, 190, 193, 195, 205, 220, 223, 229
text, 247, 261
thank, 229, 232, 233
the Middle East, 153, 160, 169
the United Kingdom, 240
the United States, 10, 153, 182, 239, 246, 247
theatre, 148
theme, 145
theory, 1–3, 12, 16, 31, 57, 58, 63, 65, 81, 108, 112, 114, 146, 153, 165, 175, 188, 192, 193, 201, 218, 226, 261
therapy, 57
thinking, 21, 22
thirst, 6
thought, 258
thread, 215
threat, 11, 57, 62, 66, 91, 115, 145, 150, 169, 216

tide, 115
time, 2, 9, 50, 58, 100, 179, 182, 186, 190, 209, 229, 249
timeframe, 83
today, 182, 209
tokenism, 157
tolerance, 24
toll, 57, 58, 92, 114, 120, 123, 125, 181, 186, 192
tool, 20, 30, 64, 102, 118, 128, 193, 206, 208
torch, 138, 177
torture, 162
town, 209
traction, 96, 149
tradition, 73
tragedy, 180
training, 53, 54, 65, 97–99, 145, 148, 207–209, 243
trait, 92
trajectory, 205
transfer, 209
transformation, 7, 56, 100, 195
transgender, 32, 34, 55, 77, 96, 136, 143, 149, 153, 154, 156, 218, 237, 239, 247, 248, 252
translate, 61, 153
transnationalism, 108, 172
trauma, 115, 124, 180
treatment, 243
trend, 203
triad, 131
triumph, 34, 133, 179, 186, 187, 192, 195, 201, 215
trust, 2, 45, 64, 65
tumble, 12
turmoil, 18, 24
turn, 17, 115, 118, 122, 227

turning, 20, 51, 65, 93, 179, 194

Uganda, 153
uncertainty, 39
underpinning, 171
understanding, 2, 3, 5, 7–9, 11–13, 15, 18, 20–25, 28, 29, 31–33, 35, 36, 38, 40, 43, 51, 54, 55, 57, 62, 64, 66, 79, 89, 93, 101–103, 105, 120, 130, 141, 145–148, 150, 153–158, 163, 167, 171, 177, 183, 185, 187, 193, 195, 199, 202, 203, 206, 216–219, 223, 229, 232, 233, 244, 246–248, 252, 254, 256, 261, 262
union, 93
unit, 7
unity, 53, 107, 144, 157, 159, 161
universality, 163
university, 19, 21
upbringing, 4, 8
uprising, 217, 248
urgency, 77, 190, 216
use, 102, 249

vacuum, 8, 199, 203
validation, 226, 228
value, 112, 216
variety, 84, 239
victory, 34, 65, 71, 94, 96, 132, 183, 186
view, 15, 113, 155, 186, 205, 260
vigilance, 42, 114, 121, 134, 153, 175
vigor, 138
violence, 1, 4, 10, 32, 34, 41, 55, 57, 61, 62, 64, 77, 93, 95, 113, 115, 134, 143, 144, 148, 149, 153, 159, 161–163, 169, 175, 192, 199, 216, 237, 239, 247, 249, 252
visibility, 19, 29, 32, 36, 59, 66, 94, 97, 101, 116, 118, 120, 156, 169, 181, 226–228, 238, 249
vision, 3, 50, 51, 54, 78, 138, 184, 196, 198–201, 208, 210
vocabulary, 13
voice, 4, 6, 35, 114, 177, 179, 182, 196, 207, 209, 232, 256
vote, 71
voting, 88
vulnerability, 17, 116, 185, 189

way, 4, 7, 10, 11, 14, 18, 23, 25, 93, 95, 97, 133, 159, 163, 203, 210, 228, 232, 250, 256
wealth, 246
weight, 16, 38
well, 17, 40, 58, 60, 66, 121, 123, 125, 153, 180, 200, 227
wellness, 206
whole, 51, 56, 227
willingness, 15, 156, 229, 232
wisdom, 180, 229
woman, 34, 93, 162, 218, 248
word, 11
work, 21, 35, 36, 41, 42, 57, 67, 97, 99, 102, 108, 110, 113–115, 118, 121, 126, 135, 138, 141, 144, 145, 147, 149, 156, 157, 161, 166, 171, 175–177, 182, 183, 190, 191, 193, 195, 205, 229, 233, 237, 238,

241, 243, 246, 247, 252–254, 256, 261
workplace, 41, 149, 240
workshop, 155
world, 1, 3, 8, 9, 11, 13, 18, 21, 23, 28, 32, 33, 40, 50, 52, 73, 119, 145, 149, 153, 161, 163, 171, 175, 180, 184, 196, 201, 207, 216, 217, 221, 239–241, 256, 258, 261

worldview, 1, 7, 20
worry, 42
worth, 34, 57, 182, 214, 227
writer, 251
writing, 36, 218, 229, 232, 233, 252, 253, 256, 258

xenophobia, 142, 149–152, 230

year, 66, 83
youth, 1, 24, 35, 99, 155, 199, 205, 207, 227, 262

Milton Keynes UK
Ingram Content Group UK Ltd.
UKHW020315021124
450424UK00013B/1256